Language and Ethnic Relations in Canada

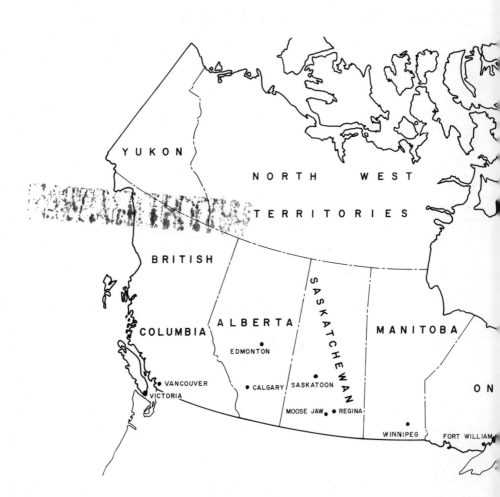

LANGUAGE AND ETHNIC RELATIONS IN CANADA

STANLEY LIEBERSON

Department of Sociology
University of Washington, Seattle

NEWFOUNDLAND

ST. JOHN'S

QUEBEC

RIVIÈRE- du- LOUP

PRINCE
EDWARD
I.

SYDNEY

CHICOUTIMI

NEW
BRUNS-
WICK

QUEBEC

NOVA SCOTIA

TROIS-RIVIÈRES

HALIFAX

GRANBY
MONTREAL

SAINT JOHN

LS

BURY

OTTAWA

MONCTON

SHERBROOKE
PETERBOROUGH

ENER

TORONTO
HAMILTON

DON

JOHN WILEY & SONS, INC.

New York • London • Sydney • Toronto

Abel

To

OTIS DUDLEY DUNCAN

Preface

There is more than one way to write a book on the contact between different language groups. This volume is organized from the perspective of an American sociologist (born in Canada, however, and with a special affection for that nation) who is interested in the ecological facets of race and ethnic relations. The book stems from a curiosity about why groups in contact maintain their distinctive languages over the centuries in some countries but elsewhere give up their native tongues in a few generations. At one and the same time this study deals with Canada, bilingualism, ethnic relations, and human ecology.

The approach taken is very frankly an ecological one, with emphasis on such factors as population composition, residential segregation and isolation, occupational pressures, and age and sex differences in bilingualism. Ecology is only one of many possible approaches that may be used to place linguistic pluralism into a sociological framework; however, I think the dimensions outlined in this study are important considerations in explaining the societal and community outcomes of linguistic contact. They do not explain why two bilingual strangers at a cocktail party choose one language over another, nor does this approach provide any insight into whether stammering is less likely among monolinguals or whether one tongue is a more desirable medium for certain types of message. Rather, whatever the nuances and fascinating subtleties of language contact, there are certain immediate questions about the survival or decline of languages in contact that can be fruitfully explored through an ecological consideration.

Since little emphasis is placed on the influence of norms, cultural tenacity, values, attitudes, and the like, some readers may feel that the kind of variables examined do not get at the heart of ethnic contact, the real questions. There are those whose study of race and ethnic relations places considerable emphasis on the cultural differences between groups. As far as I can tell, "culture" is used by many to incorporate virtually all parts of man's life. Language is surely a part of culture that is of great importance to the remaining elements and to the complex interrelations that exist between them. Recognizing that ethnic groups differ on a plethora of attributes, an all-encompassing cultural approach often becomes—although not necessarily—nothing more than a challenge for the creation of *plausible* explanations rather than valid or testable ones. If groups A and B differ with respect to characteristic X, say, which of the many other characteristics in which the two groups differ can we find to explain the differences in X?

This is perhaps an unfair statement, surely an overstatement, but one must keep in mind that linguistic and other consequences of ethnic contact are phenomena occurring in a specific social context that places limits on the development or expression of certain cultural characteristics. If French Canadians retain their ancestral language, is the high regard held for their culture a sufficient explanation? Would it make any difference whether the French are numerically dominant, as in Montreal, or a handful, figuratively speaking, as in Toronto?

In other words, cultural attributes occur not within a vacuum but within the restrictions imposed by an ecological setting and a social order. We could have a group whose culture places a taboo on all food. Although we *could* have such a culture, the group would promptly disappear. A ridiculous example, perhaps, but the point is that the group's culture operates within certain definite limitations. One critic of the ecological approach objects because it views race relations "as a process or condition operating above and beyond, and perhaps despite, the traits and personalities of the immigrants themselves" (Lennon, 1964, p. 170). This is the very point. The conditions of language maintenance, along with other aspects of contact, are set not merely by the group differences but also reflect inherent social forces that limit the range of possibilities. That the groups differ in culture and the traits and personalities of the participants play a role in influencing the final outcome is true but not central to the perspective taken here. It is not the total, final, absolute explanation that I seek but some understanding of the influence imposed on language maintenance by the social context in which the groups interact.

Whatever the merits of the outcome, I have benefited from the help of a number of graduate students, colleagues, and others. Students working on one phase or another of the project include Patricia G. Thompson, Kathleen Schwartzman, Deborah K. Meyersohn, David L. Sorenson, Elaine F. Green, August P. Guest, Leslie J. Ibach, Leonard R. Berry, Gordon W. Clemans, Edward J. McCabe, James F. O'Connor, and Terrie L. Tsuneta. Without exception, their help and enthusiasm were considerable. The students in my seminar on the ecology of language contributed numerous suggestions and criticisms. A reading of the entire manuscript by one student, Mrs. Lynn K. Hansen, was particularly helpful. On more than one occasion when an obstacle seemed insurmountable a colleague came through with a helpful suggestion or provided a valuable sounding board. David R. Heise and Glenn V. Fuguitt, in particular, spent many a lunchtime chewing over some sticky problem. Norman B. Ryder, Herbert L. Costner, S. Frank Miyamoto, and James F. O'Connor came through with helpful advice at other times. Part of the manuscript was typed at the University of Wisconsin by Miss Janice Deneen, the remainder by Miss Maude H. Allen, Mrs. Terrie L. Tsuneta, and Mrs. Rayma L. Birdsall at the University of Washington. A number of stylistic improvements resulted from their lively interest. The drafting work was done by Mr. Charles B. McVey and Miss Janice A. Jahnke. Diane Wong assisted in the preparation of the index.

Financial support was received from two sources: The National Science Foundation provided the bulk of the funds, but the University of Wisconsin Research Committee also gave necessary support that permitted me to devote more time on this study. I greatly benefited from attending the 10-week faculty workshop on sociolinguistics at Indiana University in the summer of 1964 under the sponsorship of the Social Science Research Council. The seminar and my consequent membership on the S.S.R.C. committee on sociolinguistics have exposed me to the developments occurring among linguists, anthropologists, and other sociologists working on this topic in various American universities. In both cases I greatly benefited from the sharp criticisms and gentle encouragement received from many, but particularly from Charles A. Ferguson of Stanford University.

Finally I want to thank the man who first pointed my sociological curiosity in the direction of language. More than that, as my mentor in graduate school and friend ever since, Otis Dudley Duncan has been a model of scholarship, intellectual integrity, and innovation that has been priceless. If this volume comes close to reaching his own high level of accomplishment, I shall be more than satisfied. Dedication of this book to Dudley Duncan is but a small payment for a large debt.

STANLEY LIEBERSON

King County, Washington
June, 1970

Contents

Language and Ethnic Relations in Canada

I
THE CANADIAN SETTING

1

Language and Ethnic Relations:
A Neglected Problem

Multilingual societies are found in all parts of the world, in older nations as well as the newly created states, in both the present and in man's past. Currently there is more than one viable language spoken in such countries as Belgium, Switzerland, and the Soviet Union in Europe, Canada, Bolivia, and Guatemala in the new world, India, the Philippines, and Cyprus in Asia, and South Africa, Nigeria, and the Congo in Africa. Diverse populations gave up their mother tongues in the course of a few generations in the United States, but ethnic groups in many nations have kept their distinctive languages for centuries. Even in the United States, the Pennsylvania Dutch, the Mexicans, and the French maintain linguistic enclaves which survive to the present day.

The political and social situation created by linguistic diversity ranges from the harmony of Switzerland, a nation created before the days of modern nationalism (Mayer, 1956; McRae, 1964), to India, where the entire political fabric is torn with linguistic conflict. Although both represent extremes, there is usually at least some conflict and dissent within multilingual nations. Linguistic inequality occurs in areas such as Belgium where only two tongues are significant as well as in nations which are so diverse that some tongue must be favored as a *lingua franca* (Kloss, 1966a). Although equality between linguistic groups is sometimes achieved in official political terms, it is rare either socially or economically. Moreover language differences are usually accompanied by racial or ethnic differences, thereby often becoming hopelessly entangled in broader issues.

When peoples with different languages are brought together under a common political entity, whether it be through voluntary migration or by means of conquest and invasion, generally one group is in a more favorable position than others, and likewise one language enjoys a stronger

3

position in schools and the government, in the economy, and socially. Where populations have migrated into a situation of linguistic and ethnic subordination, there normally is much less difficulty since the option of migration back to their home country provides a safety valve. Conflict is often both longer and of greater severity in multilingual societies containing peoples who were overrun by an expanding group, in colonies, and in new nations whose boundaries were carved by European empire builders (Lieberson, 1961). In the latter instance, although the flag of imperialism is down, groups find they are incorporated into a nation where some other group is dominant.

Three broad solutions are possible in a multilingual society for those whose native tongue is subordinate. One is to evolve toward the dominant group, to give up the native language and reduce—if not completely eliminate—the ethnic identity it often symbolizes. Immigrants to Canada after the British conquest are following this path in varying degrees. Another solution is to reduce the handicaps facing speakers of a given language by reforming the societal institutions. This may take place through changes in the educational system, political provisions, substates, economic reform, and the like. After the adoption of Hindi as the language of India's national unity, the central government has repeatedly been forced to acknowledge the demands of other groups for linguistic self-determination, beginning with the creation of a Telegu-speaking state in Madras in 1953 (Bram, 1955, p. 54). The third solution is most explosive of all, namely, abandoning the existing nation through outmigration, revolution, separatism, or expulsion of the dominant language group. The disintegration of the Austro-Hungarian empire was facilitated by the diverse peoples within its boundaries who had maintained their languages despite political conquest (De Carvalho and Delgado, 1962, p. 77). The French in Canada, a conquered people who are subordinate in virtually all respects except their official political status of linguistic equality, are veering in recent years toward institutional reforms if not complete separation.

Recognizing the wide range of sociological problems involved in the contact between racial and ethnic groups with different mother tongues, this volume develops a set of ecological propositions about the nature of linguistic pluralism, the forces which maintain such societies, and those which work toward unilingualism. The framework is then applied to the Canadian setting, focusing on two related but conceptually distinct events: first, the forces which determine how groups will adapt to the presence of others who speak different tongues; second, the long-run factors which determine whether pluralism will be maintained or evolve into a unilingual society.

LANGUAGE, RACE, AND ETHNIC RELATIONS

Much bad anthropology has been made by thus carelessly taking language and race as though they went always and exactly together. Yet they do go together to a great extent. Although what a man's language really proves is not his parentage but his bringing-up, yet most children are in fact brought up by their own parents, and inherit their language as well as their features.

Sir Edward B. Tylor, 1881

An association does exist in the world between ethnic groups and languages, although some scholars have gone too far by suggesting that speakers of language are members of a common race (see the discussion by Thompson, 1961, p. 228). Very likely the forces of isolation in the period prior to widespread literacy and mass communication helped to create the conditions necessary for both new peoples and new tongues. As Znaniecki (1952, pp. 7–8) observes, the maintenance of a cultural complex such as a language requires prolonged direct contacts among those who use it. In many instances, the word for an ethnic group is either identical to or has the same root as the word for their language, for example, French, German, Polish. Thus the Germanic tongue once used by Jews in many parts of Europe is sometimes popularly referred to as "Jewish" rather than "Yiddish."

This tendency in an earlier period to associate language and pronunciation with specific ethnic and racial groups led to some extreme positions such as the assumption that Jews were incapable of acquiring the spoken language of any European country because of physical differences in the anatomy of their speech and hearing organs (Fishberg, 1911, pp. 388–390). The German word "mauscheln" referred to both the peculiar pronunciation of Jews as well as vulgar speech. Fishberg himself advances the more plausible position that these differences in pronunciation were due to the isolation of Jews after the development of ghettoes and the perpetuation of these differences by the absence of non-Jewish teachers.

Since so many instances come to mind where ethnic groups in contact are linguistically distinct and, likewise, where a common tongue is shared by different ethnic groups, debate over this issue is foolhardy. The solution is very simple, but most important: while ethnic differences are sometimes not accompanied by linguistic differences, it is rare to find two or more mutually unintelligible languages used in a society without the speakers belonging to different ethnic groups. "In a great majority of contacts between groups speaking different mother tongues, the groups constitute, at the same time, distinct ethnic or cultural communities" (Weinreich, 1953, p. 91). Indeed the overlap between ethnic and linguistic boundaries, viewed more realistically as a dynamic relationship, is often only partial but never random. In societies where a population has begun its shift to another group's mother tongue, an ethnic group may not be fully distinguishable on the basis of mother tongue. English was the mother tongue of nearly half the second-generation Norwegians in the United States in 1940, for example, but the use of Norwegian as a first language was still far more common in this ethnic group than in any other second-generation subpopulation.

Although linguists pay considerable attention to language contact as a major factor in altering languages through *interference* and *borrowing* (Mackey, 1965, p. 239), the sociological setting in which language contact and bilingual behavior occurs has not received sufficient study. There are some important exceptions, such as the contributions of Weinreich, Haugen, and Deutsch (curiously, all were published in 1953), and, more recently, the work of Fishman and associates (1966), but the processes affecting racial and ethnic maintenance of language are far from fully understood. Language is of importance for a wide array of problems, ranging from its significance in assimilation to the potential for nationalism and separatism inherent in any country where groups maintain distinctive languages. Perhaps because of the remarkable speed and relative ease with which ethnic groups in the United States shifted to English, the linguistic dimension to race and ethnic relations has not received the attention from American sociologists which it merits.

The surrender of distinctive mother tongues is a necessary step in the assimilation of ethnic groups in contact. Although it is true that groups may retain their identity without a unique tongue, it is difficult to visualize complete assimilation in other areas if their native languages are maintained. In this sense language provides an important shield against assimilation. Provision for adequate education in the group's language as well as the opportunity to use their native tongue in the government are two of the special rights which groups tend to seek in order to prevent their assimilation (United Nations Commission on Human Rights, 1950, pp. 2–3). Some immigrant groups in the United States, to no avail, sought to maintain their tongues by establishing voluntary schools for their children. Understandably, from the perspective of the politically dominant ethnic group, linguistic change has been viewed as one of the prime targets for breaking down old loyalties and inducing ethnic assimilation.

Linguistic assimilation is normally an irreversible process since it is unlikely that a dead language will later be revised to the point of actually replacing its successor unless there is large-scale migration of new speakers or selective emigration. The restoration of Gaelic has been a basic part of the national policy in the Irish Free State since the nation was formed, yet the percentage speaking the tongue has "remained more or less constant since 1936 despite intensive efforts during the past quarter century" (O'Brien, 1964, p. 4). Israel provides an exception in that Hebrew was revived from an almost exclusively religious function into a national language (Bachi, 1956, p. 184).

Linguistic similarities can support both in-group unity and out-group distance since language serves both as a symbol of other differences as well as a restriction on the communication possible between ethnic groups. Populations which differ in their native tongues often see themselves as distinctive in other respects. The symbolic element to language has carried over even into major subclasses of language families. Taking cues from German writers who argued that the various dialects of Prussia, Bavaria, Hanover, and Austria all formed one nation and one language, the Pan-Slavic movement "proclaimed the affinity of various peoples, in spite of differences of political citizenship and historical background, of civilization and religion, solely on the strength of an affinity of language" (Kohn, 1960, p. ix).

The means by which communication channels are restricted by linguistic differences is readily seen. If the ethnic groups possess distinctive languages, then clearly monolinguals will have their communication restricted within ethnic groups. Even bilinguals will usually find communication more comfortable in the tongue learned earliest, particularly to express and understand subtleties of thought. Since communication cannot flow as freely across ethnic boundaries as within, ethnic origin will be partially coterminous with communication channels (Deutsch, 1953). However, ethnic and communication boundaries cannot be completely coterminous if the polyethnic society is to exist, since, by definition, there is some interdependence between the groups.

The importance of language for race and ethnic relations is also implicit in the view of language as a collection of symbols which influence social behavior. This position, which has been developed in social psychology (symbolic interaction) and anthropology, places great emphasis on the influence language has on perception and the thought process. If language influences cognition, then ethnic groups with distinctive tongues may respond differently in the same social situations. Ervin (1964) and others have provided some empirical evidence in support of this approach.

All of this suggests that some joint interaction will exist between the maintenance of an ethnic group and its distinctive language, with each reinforcing the other. Linguistic differences, by reducing interethnic contacts, will lower the chances of other forms of assimilation. On the other hand, an ethnic group which maintains its identity will be more likely to retain its language. We should not lose sight of the fact that ethnic and racial groups can perpetuate themselves without distinctive languages —witness current race relations in the United States. But it appears safe to conclude that linguistic differences form a major obstacle to assimilation and merger.

Nationalism

> As an independent nation, our honor requires us to have a system of our own, in language as well as in government. Great Britain whose children we are, and whose language we speak, should no longer be our standard; for the taste of her writers is already corrupted and her language on the decline.
> *Noah Webster, 1789; cited by Bram, 1955, p. 56*

The connection between nationalism, ethnic origin, and language is complex and merits full exploration in its own right (see Deutsch, 1953). At the risk of oversimplification, modern nationalism is usually based on a group's actual or mythological common ethnic past and a perceived unity of purpose and need. In countries that are homogeneous in ethnic terms interest in developing and maintaining loyalties to a political entity led to programs for a national language to be used by the entire population. A commonly shared tongue, ideally one which is different from that held by neighboring nations, is seen as a vehicle for the maintenance of the nation and as a bulwark against outside influences. In Eire it was thought that a "country without its own language was only half a nation and that Ireland could not long survive as a separate independent state if English remained the only language of the people" (O'Brien, 1964, p. 4). Both Hertzler (1965, p. 238) and De Carvalho and Delgado (1962, pp. 84–85) observed that language was not usually an object of political or cultural struggle before the age of nationalism.

Given this general connection between nationalism and linguistic uniformity, the problems become far more complex when ethnic diversity is found in new nation-states. Under these circumstances, linguistic diversity is more of a threat to the broader political order and the urgency of a standard language is greater, but, on the other hand, efforts to create a unilingual society may run into the barrier of ethnic as well as linguistic loyalties. The nationalistic campaign to spread Hindi as India's national language ran into severe obstacles and internal conflict not only because of the attachment that other languages hold but because language was confounded with ethnic loyalties.

The dominant ethnic population may well fear other groups who maintain distinctive and "disruptive" cultural elements such as their own mother tongues. Emphasis on language has been observed in a number of nationalistic settings; Park (1922, p. 33) found that linguistic revivals inevitably precluded every European nationalistic movement beginning with Wales in the eighteenth century. Assimilation policies have varied greatly in multiethnic nations, ranging from coercion to tolerance, but no clear-cut path toward developing loyalties to the existent political order has been found (Royal Institute of International Affairs, 1939, Chapter 16). Subordinate indigenous ethnic groups that maintain their unity, and a distinctive language would be one of the most powerful instruments for doing so, are in fact potential dangers to the maintenance of the ongoing political order since they may demand their own separate nation-state in which to fully realize mastery of their own destiny. Witness the development of a series of independent nations in eastern and central Europe after World War I. That these new nations in turn often contained "minorities" who themselves wished to achieve national independence is reminiscent of the current dilemmas which face many of the newly independent nations of Africa and Asia.

Distinctive languages among ethnic groups will in themselves intensify the difficulties of maintaining loyalties to the larger political body since one form of friction is commonly the position of each group's language in the schools, courts, documents, legislature, and other arms of the government. French Canadians have complained of the inferior status of their language in Canada outside of Quebec (Royal Commission on Bilingualism and Biculturalism, 1965, Ch. 4). As Chapter 3 of this volume makes clear, there is no question that French occupies a minor position in the political system of most of the provinces. The point is that distinctive groups which maintain strong ties, such as that afforded by their own language, are always a *potential* threat to the national order. Not only will groups with their languages intact maintain a degree of cohesiveness, which makes it more likely and more possible for them to reject the national concept imposed on them by some other group, but the existence of distinctive tongues itself provides a breeding ground for potential conflict.

PERSPECTIVE

Competition is inherent between languages in contact because the optimal conditions for their native speakers are normally incompatible. In the simplest setting in which there are two mother tongues in a population each speaker would like to use his tongue as widely and as frequently as possible. For those whose native tongue is A, this would occur if the entire population had A as its mother tongue or if native speakers of B all become bilingual. The same set of optimal conditions, however, hold for those with B as their mother tongue, except that the languages are reversed. Hence each increment in the number of native B speakers is unfavorable to the optimal conditions for A's and vice versa. Moreover bilingualism among the entire population is a solution not normally encountered. As bilingualism among A's rises, the need is reduced for B's to learn A, since it is increasingly possible for monolingual B's to use their mother tongue in communicating with native A speakers. Bilingualism among some A's, by decreasing the chances of B's learning A, ill increase the need for bilingualism among their A compatriots who hav remained monolingual.

Details about the influence of bilingualism and population size on linguistic maintenance need not concern us here since they are developed in later chapters. The important point is to recognize an inherent competition between languages in contact, based on the fact that the optimal linguistic conditions for the speakers of each tongue are incompatible. Since the gains that one language makes are to the detriment of the other, there is competition. Kelley (1966, p. 5) reports that the establishment of Hindi as the official language of India is opposed by those intellectuals with other native tongues who fear that this will place them at a disadvantage in competing for government positions.

Nationalism in a society dominated by A's requires not only that B's learn A, but that A replace B as their native tongue. The role of language in the maintenance of ethnic boundaries is too important, from the perspective of groups seeking to maintain their boundaries, for such a loss to be readily accepted, but a group will maintain its mother tongue only with a loss in potential communication accompanied by disadvantages in the economic, social, political, and educational spheres. The economist Albert Breton (1964) has advanced the intriguing thesis that nationality or ethnic origin may be viewed as investment which, in the absence of confiscation, is at a cost to the group.

Language also enters into other forms of competition as a potential asset in the market place, the political order, or the social realm. In the same way that trading stamps are used by merchants to obtain a competitive edge, so too will language play a role in these normal forms of competition in multilingual communities. If many of the workers who deal with both mother-tongue populations are bilingual, this will be seen as a "natural" outcome in a community such as Montreal in which there are sizable numbers of monoglots in both tongues. What is crucial is the existence of linguistic competition. What forces A speakers to acquire B is not only a population who prefer B, but the existence of B-speaking competition. In normal economic competition this will be sufficient cause; once there is competition between sellers and a sizable B-speaking market it will become advantageous to learn B even if all competitors are initially A monoglots.

In turn, this means that the degree of bilingualism will reflect some sort of interaction among those who create the market and those who seek to meet it. If, for example, only A's require a given service, but it is provided by both A's and B's, then the B speakers will become bilingual unless they monopolize a specialty within the service. The linguistic demands of the population will become less influential in determining the linguistic abilities of those in a monopolistic institution. Hence, governments may be unresponsive to the demands of a linguistic group if the group is so small that the gain for politicians by learning their language or supporting policies advancing the group's interest will be outweighed by the loss in votes from the dominant linguistic group. This latter consideration is by no means trivial in the case of a monopoly such as a government since its policies may be viewed as an instrument affecting language competition; for example, decisions with respect to education can improve or weaken a mother tongue's position. By strengthening a tongue through the provision of good educational facilities and programs a government also weakens another tongue, since, as we have observed, the languages are in competition, whether overtly or not. Governments, we may hypothesize, will do this only when the composition of their constituency is such as to force this or where the group whose needs are not met is able to threaten the maintenance of the society and its functions. From this perspective, national governments of multiethnic societies must weigh their policies in terms of the possibility, actual or potential, of either a revolution or a separatist movement.

Equilibriums

Languages may be thought of as expanding or contracting over space and among peoples within a given area. If all the factors influencing the size of each mother-tongue group and the degree of bilingualism among native speakers of each language were to remain constant, then some form of equilibrium would result such that the position of each language would become stabilized over time. This is unlikely in any society and virtually impossible in most societies because of the constant flux and shift in such relevant conditions as the birth rate, immigration and emigration, the economy, the areal distribution and concentration of the populations, technology, changes in the needs of the labor force, and levels of educational achievement. However, each societal change may be viewed as directing a new influence on the state of the languages in contact that would lead to a new lingustic equilibrium if no further changes occurred. Each change alters, to some degree, what had been the path of linguistic balance in the society. It may accelerate the decline of one of the tongues or it may reverse the trend; it almost surely will help one language more than the other. Moreover each shift that is unfavorable to a language will require counterbalancing changes if the tongue is to maintain its initial position.

The equilibrium of a population aggregate must be distinguished from that of the individuals who constitute the aggregate. The entire population is the essential concern here, namely, the number of native speakers of each tongue and the extent of bilingualism among each mother-tongue component. In point of fact, these may remain rather steady over a long span of time although individuals fluctuate in the course of their lives. An individual may add one or more additional languages to his mother-tongue skills as he reaches certain ages and, as is the case in Canada, also later forget or lose some of his acquired tongues. Yet the analysis of individual fluctuations in linguistic ability will provide important clues to the importance of various social forces in influencing the linguistic status of the aggregate. Shifts in the linguistic abilities of cohorts, individuals of a given age traced through a span of time, can provide useful insights into the relative importance of educational institutions, labor force requirements, preschool experiences, and the like (Lieberson, 1965a).

Bilingualism

Mutual intelligibility must develop between racial or ethnic groups with different native tongues because of the economic, political, and social interdependencies found in any society. Bilingualism, either in the form of learning another group's tongue or some pidgin, is therefore a necessary product of language contact. The *actual* frequency of bilingualism and the degree it is concentrated among one of the mother-tongue groups may vary greatly, however. In a dual economy, in which groups living side-by-side are involved in essentially different economic systems (see Boeke, 1955), the possibility exists of very little bilingualism since there may be very minimal intergroup contact. When a nation's linguistic groups are highly specialized in the niches they fill, then a much greater frequency of bilingualism in one or both populations may be expected if there is considerable interdependency between the groups. Basically, the behavior of bilinguals determines whether a multilingual society will become unilingual or remain pluralistic for generations or even centuries. In working out the forces that maintain linguistic diversity and those that support a one-language society, bilingualism will occupy a good part of our attention, both as a dependent and an independent variable.

Bilingualism in the United States was an intermediate step between the arrival of non-English-speaking immigrants and the establishment of a nation in which nearly all speak the same tongue. The immigrants or their children acquired English as a second language; then somewhere in the interchange between generations only English was passed on to their children. Elsewhere bilingualism has not lead to unilingualism; that is, sufficient numbers of children have been brought up speaking the mother tongue of their bilingual parents to allow the languages to persist over long periods of time. In the Union of South Africa more than 70 percent of Europeans 7 years of age and older can speak both English and Afrikaans (based on 1951 Census), yet both languages have maintained themselves over a number of generations; for example, between 1936 and 1951 neither language changed by more than 1 percent as the tongue used in the homes of Europeans.

The point is that bilingualism can be an end product of linguistic contact or an intermediate stage in the transition from linguistic pluralism to unilingualism. The existence of a large number of bilinguals among an ethnic group is a necessary prerequisite to the shift to another tongue, yet second-language learning by itself does not always mean that the group's mother tongue is about to fade away. It is important to recognize that a high "exposure to risk," i.e., a high degree of bilingualism, cannot be equated with the actual *rate of intergenerational language switching*. Indeed, it is possible for the mother tongue with less bilingualism to actually have a greater loss in the next generation than the more vulnerable tongue (Lieberson, 1965a).

The forces influencing language maintenance in a pluralistic situation are known or at least an arrray of factors has been drawn up by several investigators. Kloss (1966b, p. 206) lists six factors in describing the United States situation: religiosocietal insulation; time of immigration; existence of language islands; parochial schools; preimmigration experience with language maintenance; and former use of the language as an official tongue before the Anglo-American period. He then goes on to list nine additional factors which "are apt to work both ways, in some instances *for* and in others *against* language maintenance" (p. 210). After describing some quantitative relations between language maintenance and societal changes, Deutsch (1953, Ch. 7) discusses a series of additional factors. Bachi (1956, p. 202) is able to explain a fair proportion of the variance in the use of Hebrew in Israel among both immigrants and the native population by means of such factors as sex, age, occupation, country of birth, length of stay, and place of residence. Drawing on Otto Jespersen, Hertzler (1965, pp. 185–195) describes eleven factors that will yield "uniformation of language": war and military service; intermarriage; a common religion; the language used in government; the rise of administrative, trade, and cultural centers; universal education; technological and economic factors; physical and social mobility; and social psychological factors such as language loyalty and prestige of certain languages.

Rather than attempt to provide a new list of factors relevant to the linguistic outcome of race and ethnic relations, this study considers the quantitative importance of a minimal number of forces. Language behavior is viewed as a form of adaptation to a set of institutional and demographic conditions in the society, namely, population composition, both linguistic and ethnic, the degree of segregation, the occupational forces generated by the industrial structure of the society, and age. Although education is of great importance in societies in which schooling is widespread, its role in the maintenance of a group's language will be viewed as at least partially influenced by the forces described earlier, such as population composition.

No attempt has been made to differentiate between groups in terms of possible differences in their propensity to retain their languages. For one, "language loyalty" is impossible to determine until the social context of language contact is described and taken into account. As Haugen (1953, p. 280) observes, "The strongest possible motive for language learning is the need of associating with the speakers of the language. Any facts we can find about linguistic retentiveness are thus in large measure bound to reflect the degree of social isolation of the group." Whether some groups are particularly likely to retain their tongues above and beyond these social forces, Haugen notes that "it seems doubtful whether we can assemble data which will be delicate enough to disentangle this factor from the others" (p. 281). It is risky to use the degree of language shifting as a measure of the group's willingness to adopt a new language, for this becomes nothing more or less than circular reasoning. The point is not to question the possibility that groups will differ in their inherent retentiveness, nor is it simply that this cannot be determined without taking the social context into account, but rather that there are certain social limitations on linguistic maintenance which operate above and beyond the group itself.

There are then two critical problems: the forces leading to bilingualism and the language transferred to children of multilingual parents. In the first problem bilingualism is viewed as a dependent variable. Granted that some second-language learning must take place in a language-contact setting, its actual frequency is influenced by the partial alternatives of economic and social segregation. The interrelations between bilingualism and segregation are critical because segregation can reduce the degree to which bilingualism is necessary by reducing the amount of interaction between language groups. Attention will be paid to the level of communication necessary for the city or region to function, given the nature of the economy and the distribution of the mother-tongue groups both spatially and by economic niches.

The second problem faced is in determining the influence bilingualism has, as an independent variable, on mother tongues of the next generation. In the final analysis the behavior of bilinguals will decide whether a society consisting of several language groups will become unilingual or instead remain multilingual for generations or even centuries. Bilingualism provides the necessary mechanism for intergenerational shifts in mother tongue since parents cannot pass on a tongue to their children unless they speak it themselves. Linguists seem to be fond of citing cases where each parent addressed their child in a different tongue or where a governess used a language not spoken by either parent, but normally the child's mother tongue will be a language which is spoken by both parents.

The family of procreation is usually the family of socialization. This means that if both mates share the same mother tongue, then the only reasonable chance that a new mother tongue will be passed on to their offspring is when both mates have acquired some second language. If the parents have different mother tongues but are bilingual in the other's language, it is unclear what language will become the first tongue of their children. If the parents have different mother tongues but only one parent is bilingual, the chances are good that the mother tongue of their children will be the one language shared by the parents. It is unlikely that the parents will have different mother tongues and neither learn the other's language, although this is a matter that students of marital bliss might wish to investigate. Basically, if it is assumed that the tongue passed on to offspring will be a language that both parents understand, it is necessary for mates who share the same mother tongue to be bilingual before they are likely to transmit a different mother tongue to their children.

In brief, if one of the native languages used in a multilingual setting is to disappear and therefore the society veer toward unilingualism, the native speakers must first acquire a second language for communication. Thus the forces influencing the frequency of bilingualism are a natural first interest. However, since bilingualism per se does not necessarily lead to loss of the speaker's native tongue, a critical second step involves the transfer to the next generation of a mother tongue that is the second language of their parents. In this sense, and not to be confused with its technical meaning in linguistics, bilingualism may be viewed as being either "replacive" or "nonreplacive" for the children of bilinguals. This distinction also implies that the forces influencing second-language learning may differ from those which determine mother tongue shift in the next generation.

CANADA

Because it is a multilingual setting with several different linguistic processes occurring simultaneously, Canada is suitable for a case study of the sociological context of language contact. English and French are both official languages and have stood the test of contact for several centuries without the collapse or disappearance of either. Yet Canada is not standing still; it is a nation of vast and diverse immigration. Fully a quarter of its population are of neither British nor French stock, but are of German, Ukrainian, Italian, Dutch, Polish, Jewish, Norwegian, Asiatic, and other origins. Except for isolated pockets of these groups, on the farms and in the small towns and leading metropolises they are giving up their native languages, mostly becoming English-speaking Canadians. At one and the same time Canada is the scene of both linguistic diversity and unity, linguistic maintenance and decline, politically recognized and politically ignored tongues, subordinate indigenous peoples, and subordinate migrants.

The nation's diversity is an asset in determining the influence of such institutional factors as the official languages of government, the school system, and the like on linguistic maintenance; for example, French is an official language, whereas Ukrainian is not. Hence the importance that official recognition has for the survival of a tongue can be examined. In similar fashion one can compare the fate of French in communities with supportive school systems as opposed to its survival in areas in which this language is neither the medium of instruction in the schools nor a mandatory second language. Since the autonomy and power of provinces in Canada is far greater than that reserved for states in the United States, the influence of some political policies on linguistic maintenance can be inferred.

One uncomfortable feature in interpreting Canada's linguistic processes is the Dominion's proximity to the United States. Its southern neighbor, to say the least, is more than a passing acquaintance. Ranging from the dominance of the automobile industry by Canadian subsidiaries of Detroit to the popularity of American films, television shows, magazines, and swarms of tourists, the linguistic situation is influenced by the United States. Were Mexico on Canada's southern border, there would be no problem, since Spanish is not a critical language in Canada. Although the influence of the United States in the maintenance and promulgation of English is probably significant, it is difficult to gauge. We are safe when considering other tongues, since Canada's strong ties to the United States and its political alliance with the United Kingdom are certainly not pillars of strength for the French, Ukrainian, German, or Dutch languages. When these languages survive, it is in spite of the United States, not because of it.

As might be expected in any case study, there are institutional elements which cannot be considered. Canada does not maintain, for example, a policy of extreme coercion with respect to language. Therefore, the influence of this type of policy on linguistic pluralism cannot be determined. On the other hand, the difficulties of linguistic pluralism are sometimes seen as a peculiarity of the economically less developed countries. This is certainly not the case for Canada; it ranks high by any standard: in natural resources, level of living, length of life, and urbanization. When explanations are sought for the maintenance of languages, it cannot be in terms immediately generalizable to technologically backward nations.

Census Data

Of no trivial consideration in the selection of Canada is the fact that its censuses have relatively good language data. Coverage of mother tongue goes back to 1921 and reports on official language (the ability of respondents to speak English, French, both, or neither tongue) are available since 1901. Ethnic coverage is also fairly detailed and available for even earlier periods.

Both the mother-tongue and official-language questions used in the Canadian census provide some difficulties. Mother tongue in recent years is defined as "the language first learned in childhood and still understood. In the case of infants the language commonly spoken in the home was recorded" (Dominion Bureau of Statistics, 1962, Bulletin 1.2-11, p. xi). Prior to 1941, mother tongue was the language first learned in childhood and still *spoken*, an even more restrictive definition. Thus, by either definition of mother tongue, Canadian census procedure allows for the omission of the first learned language if the person no longer retains some minimal knowledge of it at the time of enumeration. This runs counter to the normal view of mother tongue as simply the first learned language in childhood, without regard to the respondent's current ability in the tongue. It has been necessary at times to assume that the mother tongue reported is indeed the first learned language of the respondents without the kind of qualification used in the Canadian census. Empirical evidence exists to support this approach: at least for English and French, there is a relatively small net shift in the mother-tongue composition of males classified by age cohorts between the 1951 and 1961 censuses despite the possibility of doing so under the Canadian census qualification (Lieberson, 1966, Table 3).

"Official language" provides a more serious difficulty for which there is no easy answer. The Canadian population questionnaire uses these simple questions: "Can you speak English? French?" or in its French form "Parlez-vous anglais? français?" Four classes of current official language status are developed: those who speak English only; French only; both English and French; or neither official language. It should be noted that these items do not refer to other languages, for example, someone fluent in English and Italian would be classified as "speaking English only."

The main objections to this variable stem from the ambiguous nature of the question and the subjectivity of the response, for example, the possibility of distortion due to nationalistic feelings or ethnic pride on the part of either the respondent or the interviewer. Tackling the ambiguity and subjectivity of the question first, this would be no problem if mono- and bilingualism were two discrete categories, since the respondent would either speak a tongue or not. If ability in a second language is viewed as ranging on a continuum from absolutely no knowledge to Bloomfield's (1933, p. 56) oft-quoted, "native-like control of two languages," the appropriate answer to the Canadian census question is unclear for those well-intentioned respondents whose second-language ability lies somewhere between polar types.

The linguists are by no means encouraging on this matter; as Mackey (1962, pp. 51–52) notes, "the concept of bilingualism has become broader and broader since the beginning of the century" Haugen (1953, p. 7), includes all those who can at least "produce *complete, meaningful utterances* in the other language. From here it may proceed through all possible gradations up to the kind of skill that enables a person to pass as a native" (author's italics). More recently, Diebold (1961, p. 99) has extended the notion of bilingualism to include even more minimal skills which he calls "incipient bilingualism." Diebold then "suggests to the sociologist that much of his census data concerning bilingualism may be faulty, especially in concealing in the category 'monolingual' some very real measure of bilingualism" (p. 111). One of the few sociologists to venture into this maze is Hertzler (1965, p. 415) who proposes the term "plural lingual facility" for describing "various degrees of practical or existent (though not 'perfect' or 'equal') facility in more than one language." By restricting bilingualism to the most proficient type of "plural lingual facility," its technical meaning would be less ambiguous, but we would hardly be any closer to a practical solution.

The point is well taken that linguistic ability in a second or several languages may vary from a very minimal level to exceptional facility, but how does one handle data based on the Canadian census question on official language ability? First, it should be noted that residents of multilingual communities receive sufficient exposure and contact with speakers of both tongues that they may rapidly find out if they can indeed communicate in French and/or English. In other words, in cities such as Montreal, no matter how isolated the resident, he will learn in short order whether he can communicate in these tongues. Second, such a minimal level of bilingualism as included in the term "incipient," though of value in enriching our understanding of the great range of language possibilities in contact situations, is of minimal significance for sociological purposes where the issues are interpersonal communication, use of a second language at work, use in the family, and the like. It is even more irrelevant in considering which language is passed on to the children since an incipient bilingual is unlikely to transmit his second language as the mother tongue of his offspring. If the respondent indicates whether or not he can communicate in the language, then for our sociological purposes this would be ideal, granted that there would still be some ambiguity in terms of the "domains" in which the respondent was thinking of, for example, shopping in a store vs. use at a party (where those attending were sober).

If we can assume that there is a linear relationship between the percentage of respondents indicating ability to speak a given language or languages in each area of Canada and the actual percentage who do under any criterion of "bilingualism," then much of the analysis which follows is valid despite the possibilities of inadvertent errors due to the nature of the question or extraneous factors such as ethnic militancy.

There is no doubt that the two language questions as well as the ethnic question are subject to more response variance than, say, age, sex, or marital status. Based on his experiments within a multilingual area during the 1961 census, I. P. Fellegi (1964, p. 1037) a statistician with the Dominion Bureau of Statistics, reports higher values for his "index of inconsistency" and correlated response error than for many other census questions. He notes that "These questions are quite emotionally charged in Canada, and as it turns out, the interviewers did not seem to be detached." Granted that the census has a lower response variance for other characteristics, the results for our variables are not so bad by normal standards of research. The following is the 95 percent confidence interval for estimates of 10,000 persons with these characteristics in the experimental area around Cornwall, Ontario (based on Fellegi, memorandum):

	English	French
Ethnic group	±450	±350
Mother tongue	±220	±350
Official language	±130	±460

It should be noted that the response variance measures only the extent to which different census estimates would differ from their average; it does not take into account systematic errors such as that created if the respondents were to repeatedly overestimate their linguistic ability in a given tongue (Fellegi, unpublished memorandum, p. 5).

In short, the Canadian census question on current linguistic abilities is, like most censuses, hardly optimal in the sense that it is ambiguous and may be subject to systematic over- or underreporting. On the other hand, the response error, although high for census questions, is still not unbearably great. Ryder (1955) who is critical of ethnic origin data in the Canadian census, proposes the substitution of a two-generational mother-tongue question. In view of the exposure to both languages in many parts of Canada, the question is less subjective and vague since respondents would have a good idea of whether or not they can use the language. This is particularly the case for those parts of Canada that are of greatest interest to us, namely, where both tongues are viable contenders. Of course, nothing can be done about differences between respondents in their interpretation of the minimal level necessary to answer "yes" to a question on current linguistic ability or the possibilities of respondent and interviewer attitudes influencing the results. For the gross purposes of this study, however, it would seem reasonable to make the crude assumption that there is an interareal correlation between linguistic ability as measured in the census and actual numbers that would be obtained if a more precise measure of bilingualism was used. Finally, in spite of these difficulties, Canadian censuses provide one of the broadest and most useful bodies of language data currently available.

AN OVERVIEW

The demographic and institutional pressures affecting the linguistic situation in Canada are described in Chapters 2 and 3, respectively. The official languages have more or less maintained their relative positions in Canada throughout this century. Although the French are shifting to English in many provinces, the concentration of French Canadians in Quebec coupled with the strong retention of French in this province has had the net effect of maintaining the basic demographic position of French as Canada's second national language. This is true despite the fact that English-speaking Canadians are far less likely to learn French than are French-speaking Canadians to learn English.

The stable positions of English and French in Canada have been the product of a balance between dynamic forces in opposing directions. For example, there has been no important immigration from France for two hundred years, whereas sizable numbers have migrated from Britain and other parts of Europe in the past century. The Ukrainians, Germans, Dutch, Italians, and other ethnic groups—Canada's "third force"—have favored English over French by an overwhelming margin, but there has been a stream of outmigrants nearly as large from Canada to the United States which has included relatively more English-speaking residents of Canada than French speakers.

Migration flows between provinces of Canada have moved French Canadians out of Quebec into areas of the Dominion in which their descendents are more likely to be English-speaking. In recent decades, however, the actual number of French migrants from Quebec to elsewhere in Canada has been small and thus the net effect of this process on French-language maintenance is minor. Montreal attracts a sizable part of the French Canadian exodus from rural Quebec, thus ensuring that they will remain in a milieu which is compatible with French.

Fertility has been higher among the French than other Canadians, thus permitting the French language to maintain its demographic position even when some French-Canadian offspring are raised as English-speaking. So far this has also offset the strong propensity of other ethnic groups to shift to English as their mother tongue. During the last century the British component of the population has declined at the expense of a rising proportion of Canadians who are of some other ethnic origin, but the French ethnic component of the population has remained steady in recent decades.

Government, education, and the economy are described in Chapter 3 as the institutions most significant for linguistic maintenance. With regard to government policy the British North America Act provides for French and English equality in the Federal government and in the province of Quebec. In practice, many units of the national government favor English. Opportunities in the military, for example, are far greater for an English-speaking monoglot than for his countryman who knows only French.

All provinces outside Quebec are free to formulate their own linguistic policy and thus the position of French varies greatly between provinces and over time in the same province. Quebec has maintained strict equality of the two tongues, but it is an overwhelmingly French-Canadian state and its government currently provides an important instrument for the expression of French-Canadian interests. No other province recognizes French as an official language on a par with English, although this was the case in some of the western provinces when French Canadians comprised a numerically important segment of the early settlers. A decline in the French-Canadian numerical position, however, led to the demise of French equality with English in these areas.

One of the most crucial policy areas reserved for the provinces is education. Schooling in Quebec is available in either tongue from grade school through higher education, but French educational opportunities are not as good elsewhere. They are reasonably adequate in New Brunswick and Ontario, although there are some complaints, but definitely inferior to English-language training in most of the remaining parts of Canada. Generally, opportunities for an education in which French is the medium of instruction tend to be better in those provinces where French Canadians comprise either a sizable proportion of the total population (New Brunswick) or are numericaly important in an absolute sense (Ontario). A concentration of French Canadians in some communities leads to greater opportunities for French-language training than in areas where they are widely dispersed.

Most provinces provide only limited training in French, ensuring that all French Canadians will acquire English in the schools. In several instances, for example, French-language instruction can be made available up to an hour per day in the early grades. The Catholic–Protestant conflict over publicly supported parochial schools probably makes it all the more difficult to establish French education in some parts of Canada. On the other hand, French is widely available as a second language in high schools and sometimes in earlier grades. Many English-speaking children take such courses, but in the absence of a practical need for the language, do not retain their knowledge.

Canada's industrial, commercial, and financial worlds are dominated by Canadians of British origin and important American and British companies who together make English the language of big business and industrial power. As one goes up the hierarchy, English is increasingly the language of communication. Accordingly, in many facets of Quebec's economic life, the ambitious French Canadian faces far greater pressure to learn English than does an English monoglot to learn French. Further, English is the language of technology in Canada, providing an additional incentive for bilingualism among French Canadians.

The causes of bilingualism are examined from an ecological perspective in Chapter 4 and 5. The first of the two chapters surveys a wide variety of factors operating throughout Canada; the second concentrates on various industrial and occupational influences in Montreal.

The age- and sex-specific rates of bilingualism among the French and English mother-tongue group in Canada provide an outstanding opportunity to draw inferences about the causes of bilingualism, particularly when traced over decades. Early childhood accounts for a relatively small degree of bilingualism in Canada as a whole. There is a very sharp rise in second-language acquisition during the school ages. This suggests that the neighborhood effect is not a significant cause of bilingualism in

Canada as a whole, but that the pressures associated with schooling do create an important impetus to bilingualism. Until early adulthood, both boys and girls with the same mother tongue do not differ very much in their bilingualism. However, beginning in the early adult years, bilingualism increases much more rapidly among men than women. This suggests the operation of a significant occupational inducement to bilingualism in Canada generally. There is a later phase in which each mother-tongue cohort displays a net unlearning of their second language between decades. This net decline occurs earlier for women than men, and may be interpreted as reflecting the former's lower rates of participation in the labor force.

Cohorts are also traced in Chapter 4 for five specific cities, representing a wide range of linguistic contact settings. In cities where French is a numerically weak mother tongue, a high degree of bilingualism among its native speakers takes place at a very early age. Here community context is a powerful influence along with the pressures occuring in school. In cities where the French are a small minority, the occupational pressures for learning English are superfluous since virtually everyone is bilingual prior to entrance into the work force.

French-mother-tongue children in two cities differ considerably in the occurrence of bilingualism. Yet, several decades later, as adults, the rates are similar in the two cities. This suggests that causes of bilingualism operated differently in the two cities, although their net effect was similar by the time adulthood is reached.

A systematic examination of a number of Canadian communities indicates different patterns of male–female bilingualism rates for the two major mother-tongue groups. The gap between French-mother-tongue men and women is minimal in cities where the French are a small minority —undoubtedly reflecting the "overdetermination" of bilingualism described above. But their absolute gap widens as the percentage of residents with French-mother-tongue composition increases. Although the pressures to become bilingual for the French declines with more favorable linguistic composition, the amount of decline is much greater for women than for men. The widened gap is due to the dominance of English in the economic world, a dominance that does not recede as rapidly with French numerical increases as do the factors that influence female bilingualism.

The same factor accounts for the pattern among the English-mother-tongue group. In cities where French is a minor tongue, bilingualism is minimal for the English, although slightly higher for men. However, even in cities where French is a fairly sizable minority language, the sex gap is slight. The absolute gap between men and women increases in places where French is the majority mother-tongue. Thus, the bilingualism gap between men and women in both mother-tongues is greatest in communities where French is the mother-tongue of the majority.

Residential segregation has a definite influence on the frequency of bilingualism. Among both the English and French, bilingualism tends to be inversely related to the magnitude of the group's isolation in the city. But more than that, the influence of a neighborhood's composition on bilingualism is modified by the city's total linguistic composition. A given concentration of native English speakers in Montreal will generate more bilingualism than an equivalent neighborhood in Toronto. There is some indication that female rates of bilingualism vary more sharply between neighborhoods than do the rates for men with the same mother tongue. Women, being less influenced by the labor-market demands, are more responsive to local residential pressures than are men. All of this indicates that segregation is a determinant of bilingualism, but like the other forces described in Chapter 4, its influence interacts with other community factors.

The classified directories, *Yellow Pages*, published by telephone companies in Canadian cities, provides a valuable clue to the linguistic pressures and opportunities operating on the various services and industries listed. In many cities, an advertiser has the option of listing under the English and/or French rubric. Accordingly, it is possible to use these listing practices to determine the linguistic orientation of the activity; for example, physicians may be classified into those listing under the English rubric "Physicians & Surgeons," those who place their name under the French rubric "Médecins & Chirurgiens," and those who list under both categories.

None of the cities examined have *Yellow Pages* that are exclusively in French, even when the community is overwhelmingly French in mother-tongue composition. On the other hand, it is quite common to find cities whose directories are exclusively in English. Analysis of intercity variations in telephone directory listing practices discloses that English is generally favored and French underrepresented when the linguistic composition of the communities is taken into account. Dividing the categories into those that are consumer and nonconsumer oriented, the French suffer a decided disadvantage in the latter set of listings. The competitive market for consumers is such that both groups receive reasonably adequate treatment in the listings, but once one moves back from the consumer world the dominance of English is striking.

Much of Chapter 5 is devoted to a further elaboration of the occupational and industrial influences on bilingualism in a specific setting, metropolitan Montreal. Several major problems are considered: the influence of bilingualism on income separately for each mother-tongue group; the job market, as measured by the want-ads in French and English language newspapers; and the linguistic orientation of various specific services and industries listed in Montreal's *Yellow Pages,* both now and 25 years ago.

The telephone book listings reflect the linguistic demands and breadth of the market served. Not only are consumer industries more likely to list in French than are nonconsumer services, but there is variation within the former category; for example, grocers in Montreal often list in only one language, undoubtedly reflecting linguistic residential segregation in the city and the restricted spatial market served by any single grocery. By comparison, bowling alleys are much more likely to be bilisted since the residential area served by bowling alleys is much larger and hence more likely to draw upon significant numbers of both English- and French-speaking customers. In similar fashion physicians located downtown or with specialized practices draw upon a more diverse set of patients than the neighborhood general practitioner. This, too, is reflected in comparisons between downtown and neighborhood doctor's listings, as well as between specialists and general practitioners. Indeed, general practitioners of 25 years ago who listed in only one language are now much more likely to be bilisted if they are currently specializing. This is particularly striking when these doctors are compared with singly listed general practitioners of 25 years ago who still do not specialize.

For some activities, such as the shoe industry, an analysis is made of listing practices in the retail, wholesale, and manufacturing domains, as well as the suppliers of material and equipment for the manufacturers. The different listing practices in these sectors point to a weak position for French in the manufacturing and nonconsumer facets of employment in Montreal. Nevertheless the position of French has improved considerably when compared with *Yellow Pages* of 25 years ago.

Want ads in local newspapers, although they represent a biased and distorted sample of the job market, do provide some clues to the linguistic pressures operating among the work force. Many job ads in both the English and French language newspapers specify a need for knowledge in the other official language. Particularly striking is the demand for knowledge of English in the white-collar world; for example, 94 percent of the listings for stenographers in the French newspaper required a knowledge of English. By comparison only 37 percent of the advertisements for stenographers in the English language paper listed bilingualism as a criterion for employment. The want ads can be used to measure the various employment domains in which bilingualism is a particularly frequent prerequisite to employment. By comparing ads in the two papers for the same type of work it is also possible to get at the differential pressures for bilingualism.

In general, the native speaker of French in Montreal earns less than someone whose mother tongue is English. This difference remains even after a number of standard controls are used such as education, occupation, and sex. Among the French-mother-tongue participants in the labor force, those also able to speak English earn considerably more than their monolingual compatriots. On the other hand, there is very little income difference between monolingual and bilingual workers if their mother tongue is English.

Educational attainment and bilingualism are associated among the French-mother-tongue group, but bilingualism does not vary at all by education among the native speakers of English. For the French in the labor force higher educational achievement means greater likelihood of being able to speak English, but nothing of this sort holds for the English. Indeed, bilingualism among the least educated French is more frequent than bilingualism among the college-educated component of the English-mother-tongue group.

The income advantages for bilingualism and the consequent pressure this entails is nicely illustrated for the French-mother-tongue group in Montreal. Holding educational achievement constant, one finds that the percentage of native French speakers who are bilingual varies from occupation to occupation in direct relation to the income advantage that bilingual French enjoy over French monoglots. In effect, the greater the income gap between bilinguals and monolinguals with French mother tongue, the greater the proportion of French in the occupation who can also speak English. By contrast, among the English, there is no persistent association between the income gap and their percentage able to speak French. The gains accruing to French bilinguals in the work world of Montreal are considerably greater than the advantages for the British who learn French.

The impact of bilingualism on language maintenance in the next generation is approached in Chapters 6 and 7 as a problem distinctive from the causes of bilingualism. To be sure, in the absence of parental bilingualism, mother-tongue continuity is almost insured between generations. But the bilingual parent may raise his child in either of two languages.

Differences between major French cities in intergenerational shift is related to the mother-tongue composition and frequency of bilingualism in these centers. An understanding of the mechanisms whereby these two variables influence mother-tongue maintenance, however, is still another matter. Moreover, neither factor is very adequate for explaining variations between cities where French is the mother tongue of only a small proportion of the residents. In these cities, bilingualism is uniformly high and French-mother-tongue composition varies only slightly, but mother-tongue retention varies widely. At best, it is difficult to visualize why a very small difference in mother-tongue composition should produce such a wide difference in the behavior of bilinguals toward their children. Likewise, it is unclear how the frequency of bilingualism could explain such wide variations in retention since bilingualism is very nearly equal in all of these communities. Accordingly, much of Chapter 6 is devoted to interpreting variations in retention ratios among the French in "lesser cities," namely, places in which no more than 10 percent of the residents are native speakers of French.

Several institutional factors are found to influence the likelihood of mother-tongue retention among the children of French bilinguals. Availability of French as a medium of instruction in the schools is an important distinguishing feature between lesser cities with high and low retention. Maintenance of the parental mother tongue is more likely in cities where French is the medium of instruction in at least one elementary school. Lesser cities with high employment in manufacturing also have higher retention ratios. Such jobs very likely lead to a weaker mastery of English than do white-collar forms of employment that are more common in non-manufacturing industries. Communities whose Catholic population consists largely of French Canadians tend to have higher levels of retention among French bilinguals. This may reflect the higher probability of matings between French speaking spouses, or it may also reflect a stronger French influence on the Catholic church in the community and the consequences this has for the support of the French language.

Other influences on intergenerational shift are considered as well in Chapter 6. Some commonly held factors have no bearing on language maintenance; for example, political differences between the provinces. Others provide clues to the way composition influences language maintenance in the major French centers; for example, the retention of French in important centers is related to the difference between male and female rates of bilingualism among the French-mother-tongue residents. Both the lower rates of bilingualism among women as well as the absolute level of bilingualism influences the probability of a bilingual French-Canadian man marrying a woman who could also use English in raising their children. French-mother-tongue parents will be far less likely to use English in raising their children if one of the mates cannot speak the tongue. This factor helps to explain the rates of intergenerational shift in various major French cities, but is of no value for the lesser cities since nearly all of their French residents can also speak English.

The focus in Chapter 7 remains on the forces influencing mother-tongue maintenance, but is not restricted to the lesser cities. Some of these factors provide a more elaborate understanding of how composition influences retention. The pattern of residential segregation, for example, has an impact on intergenerational shift, but this influence interacts with the community's population composition. Cities with low retention ratios among the French bilinguals are also places where these people are especially likely to interact with English-speaking residents.

Even more significant, the residential patterns of the bilingual and monolingual segments of each mother-tongue group are themselves to be understood in terms of the community's linguistic context. In general, the bi- and monolingual components of the English-mother-tongue residents are not as sharply differentiated from one another as are the two components of the French-mother-tongue population. Because of the economic pressures for the acquisition of English, the French bilingual tends to differ greatly from his monolingual compatriot along various socioeconomic dimensions such as occupation, education, and income. The English, occupying a dominant position, are not so different from one another socioeconomically, regardless of whether they learn French. This, in turn, means that residential segregation between the French bilingual and monolingual segments will tend to be more sizable than segregation between the analogous segments of the English-mother-tongue group. Cities where French is most vulnerable to linguistic loss between parent and child, that is, where the pressures to learn English are strongest, are the very places where the two linguistic segments will be most isolated from one another. In effect, the residential segregation pattern between the two components of a mother-tongue group not only influences retention among the children of bilinguals, but itself reflects other sociolinguistic forces within the community.

There is further evidence to support the contention that bilingualism and mother-tongue retention are not simply the products of the same causes. Mother-tongue shift among the children of bilingual French parents has increased in recent years, but this change has been accompanied by a drop in the frequency of bilingualism among the French group. Likewise, there is no association between changes in bilingualism and the retention of French over time in various Canadian cities, although cross-sectional correlations are found.

Chapter 7 ends with an effort to develop a model of linguistic retention that incorporates several demographic factors. Only one variable, the index of "communication advantage," is of value in explaining both intercity differences in retention at a given point in time as well as longitudinal changes within these communities during a decade. This index measures the relative number of ethnic compatriots a French-Canadian child can communicate with in English as contrasted with French. For both logical and statistical reasons, the present mother-tongue composition of the French ethnic group is by itself not a useful variable in explaining the rate of language maintenance among bilinguals.

The causes of bilingualism are intentionally considered separately from the causes of mother-tongue shift (Chapter 4 and 5; 6 and 7, respectively). This reflects the proposition that the causes of one phenomenon are not merely interchangeable with the causes of the other. Chapter 8 provides added empirical justification for this approach. Both the availability of French medium schooling and the frequency of employment in manufacturing industries influence mother-tongue maintenance, but they have no effect on the occurrence of bilingualism in lesser cities. The four different ways a factor may influence bilingualism and/or intergenerational mother-tongue shift are outlined. Accordingly, these two dependent variables will often respond differently to a given ecological condition.

Chapter 8 also considers an issue raised in this chapter, namely, the influence of language on ethnic-group maintenance. The role of language as a bond between and within the British and French ethnic groups is examined for all of the metropolitan areas in 1961. Cohesion within the British group based on a common mother tongue is extremely high (the probability is close to 1.0 in most cities that two randomly selected British residents will have the same mother tongue). A bond based on a common mother tongue is far less likely among the French ethnic group in many of these urban areas. Moreover, in a number of these centers, a common mother tongue between a British and a French ethnic resident is more likely than within the latter ethnic group. This does not hold, of course, for such major French centers as Montreal, Quebec, or Trois-Rivières. But the French ethnic group in many Canadian cities is split into major English- and French-mother-tongue components. This in turn creates a very weak mother-tongue bond within the French ethnic group.

Bilingualism, which largely means the acquisition of English among those with a French mother tongue, ironically raises the probability of mutually intelligible communication within the French ethnic group to close to 1.0 However, not only does the high communication potential within the French ethnic group depend on the acquisition of English by the French-mother-tongue component. but English is the required medium of communication in a very sizable proportion of the random contacts within the French ethnic group in most of the metropolitan areas. The price paid for a linguistic bond within the French ethnic group therefore often involves a further undermining of the role of the French language as a medium for in-group communication.

It is reasonable to expect ethnic continuity to be related to the magnitude of the group's mother-tongue maintenance. This proposition is almost self-evident. However, empirically the issue is the importance of mother-tongue continuity for preventing assimilation when compared to other features which also differentiate ethnic groups. Mother tongue is compared with religion, a factor which also differentiates many ethnic groups. Comparisons between different ethnic groups in the same city as well as the same ethnic group in different cities both indicate that mother tongue is at least as important as religion, if not more important, in its retardation of assimilation.

The final chapter, in short, elaborates both empirically and theoretically on two major propositions: first, that mother-tongue shift and bilingualism are not caused by the same factors; second, that mother-tongue maintenance is not merely an influence on ethnic assimilation but a highly significant force when compared with other factors commonly held to play a role in differentiating ethnic groups in contact.

2

Demographic Processes

Were English and French language trends in Canada during this century to be summarized in one word, it would be "stability." Among those 5 years of age and older, between 1901 and 1961, the percentage able to speak English either alone or with another tongue increased from 78 to 81, a change of 3 percent. During this period, the population able to speak French, either monolingually or along with English, remained unchanged at 32 percent. Although English is far more widely used and known than French, the latter tongue has held its own throughout this century. Because of shifts between censuses in the base populations for which data are reported, it is necessary to "splice" the detailed changes between decades shown in Table 1 in order to make comparisons consistent. With but minor fluctuations, about two-thirds of the population speak English only and about one-fifth speak only the French official language. The one noteworthy change is the jump in the bilingual segment of the Canadian population which occurred around the time of World War I. Here too, there has been a high degree of stability since then with about 12 percent currently able to speak both languages. Keeping in mind that Canada's population has more than tripled during this century, the stability of these language figures indicates each language group has been able to grow at about the same rate as Canada itself.

An index proposed by Greenberg (1956, p. 112) describes "the probability that if two members of the population are chosen at random, they will have at least one language in common. Following Lieberson's terminology (1965a, p. 13), this basic statistical tool for describing the degree a population can participate in mutually intelligible speech will be referred to as H_w. The range of H_w runs from 1.0 (where every possible pair of speakers shares at least one common tongue) to 0 (the unlikely extreme where every speaker possesses a different mother tongue and has not learned the language of anyone else). Applying this measure to Canada, the degree of mutual intelligibility appears very stable through a number of decades. After an increase around World War I due to the rise

TABLE 1

Official Language Percentage Distributions and H_w, by Decades, 1911–1961

Official Language	Ten Years of Age and Older			All Ages[a]			
	1911	1921	1931	1931	1941	1951	1961
English only	68.0	68.1	69.6	67.5	67.2	67.0	67.4
French only	19.3	13.2	13.6	17.1	19.0	19.6	19.1
English and French	7.4	16.7	15.1	12.7	12.8	12.3	12.2
Neither	5.2	2.0	1.8	2.7	1.0	1.1	1.3
H_w	.634	.781	.777	.716	.725	.715	.717

[a]Newfoundland included in 1951 and 1961. Exclusion of this province in these years would have only a minor effect.

in bilingualism, Greenberg's H_w measure for all of Canada has stabilized at about .72, that is, randomly paired Canadians could expect to share a common official language 72 percent of the time. Since H is computed here on the basis of the total Canadian population and because interaction will obviously be more likely within the local community, the actual degree of mutual intelligibility in normal interaction is understated. However, it does serve to summarize the striking stability of potential communication in Canada through an official language; the range in H_w between 1931 and 1961 is only .009.

There is evidence that mother-tongue composition also has remained stable, although marred by a change in the Canadian census definition in 1941. Looking at the entire population, regardless of age, between 1931 and 1961 English is the mother tongue of just under 60 percent of Canada's population and French is the mother tongue of nearly 30 percent (see Table 2). Comparisons between the population 10 years of age and older for 1921 (the earliest data available) and 1961 would appear to deny this stability since English has dropped from 62 to 56 percent at the expense of a rise in "other" mother tongues. This is due to the large increase in immigration in these years from the European continent as well as the fact that exclusion of infants and small children affects the Canadian-born more than the foreign-born.

Between 1931 and 1961 the mother-tongue composition of just the Canadian born population actually increased from about 55 to 60 percent English. On the other hand, English was the mother tongue of 61.5 percent of the foreign born in 1931, but only of 46 percent in 1961. This decline is due to the relative increase since World War II of non-English immigrants. Since French-speaking immigrants have never been of great significance (French was the mother tongue of 3 percent of the foreign born in both 1931 and 1961), its position is less affected. Therefore the mother-tongue composition of Canada is rather stable in most comparisons, with the one exception largely due to sizable immigration.

Not only is English dominant over French in a simple numerical sense (10.7 million versus 5.1 million mother-tongue speakers in 1961) but the former is also stronger on the basis of a second criterion of dominance, "the extent to which a given language is learned by native speakers of other languages in the country" (Ferguson, 1962, p. 11). Slightly more than half of the population whose mother tongue is not English know this language; whereas, in 1961, not quite 5 percent of the population whose native tongue is not French are able to speak French. To put it crudely, if the language learned by a child in his home was not English, there is a 50-50 chance that English will also be spoken. By contrast only 1 out of 20 persons speak French as an additional tongue if it was not the

TABLE 2

Mother Tongue Percentage Distributions, by Decades, 1921–1961

Mother Tongue	Ten Years of Age and Older[a]			All Ages[b]			
	1921	1931	1961	1931	1941	1951	1961
English	62.2	58.5	.562	57.0	56.4	59.1	58.5
French	26.7	25.6	.283	27.3	29.2	29.0	28.1
Other	11.2	15.9	.155	15.7	14.5	11.8	13.5

[a]Yukon and Northwest Territories not available for population 10 years of age and older in 1921 and 1931. Both of these areas and Newfoundland excluded in 1961.

[b]Newfoundland included in 1951 and 1961. Exclusion of this province in these years would have only a minor effect.

language first learned at home. Even with respect to second-language adoption, there has been virtually no change through the years. In 1931 54 percent of those with a different mother tongue had learned English and 4 percent of the non-French mother-tongue population knew French. On the basis of estimating procedures reported in Lieberson (1966), in 1961 no more than 6 percent of Canada's English-mother-tongue population spoke French in 1961, whereas at least 32 percent of the French-mother-tongue population could speak English.

Because language learning is both age-related and reversible, it is important to recognize that these figures are only rough approximations of the amount of bilingualism occurring in a particular age group. These figures include people of all ages and so a cross-sectional percentage of non-English speakers who are currently able to speak English includes small children who will learn English later in their life span as well as many older people who used to know this tongue. Accordingly, such percentages greatly underestimate the degree of second-language learning that takes place among the middle age groups. Later in this volume a more detailed examination of second-language learning as related to age is presented. For the present purpose of measuring linguistic dominance, use of cross-sectional percentages is adequate.

It would be erroneous to infer from the stability of these figures that Canada's linguistic situation is static with the exception of the temporary shifts introduced by large-scale immigration. It is far more correct to describe the Canadian scene as an equilibrium based on counterbalancing forces. In all provinces except Quebec English is replacing French as the language of the French-Canadian ethnic group. Father Richard Arès (1964 a, b) examined the linguistic composition of French Canadians from 1931 to 1961 in each province and found a persistent trend toward English. In Prince Edward Island, for example, French was the mother tongue of three-fourths of the French Canadians in 1931, but now slightly more than half are native speakers of English. Likewise, slightly more than half can now speak only English, whereas in 1931 less than 20 percent spoke only the English official language (Arès, 1964a, p. 108). Table 3 shows the decline of French in each of these provinces during that 30-year period. To be sure, ethnic intermarriage through the years may complicate the picture, since origin is attributed to the father's side, but it is unlikely that the decline of French over such a short period of time could be attributed solely to this factor. In Quebec, however, only 1.6 percent of the French ethnic population reported English as their mother tongue in 1961.

Actually the decline of French in each of the provinces is somewhat deceptive, since an overwhelmingly large proportion of French Cana-

TABLE 3

Linguistic Characteristics of the French Ethnic Group by Provinces: 1931 and 1961[a]

Province	Percent with French Mother Tongue		Percent Able to Speak English Only	
	1931	1961	1931	1961
Prince Edward Island	77.3	44.5	18.8	51.9
Nova Scotia	67.7	42.8	28.5	52.6
New Brunswick	94.9	87.6	4.3	10.0
Quebec	99.4	98.2	0.4	0.8
Ontario	77.4	61.4	20.2	33.6
Manitoba	86.0	67.2	10.7	29.1
Saskatchewan	78.5	54.4	16.5	41.1
Alberta	70.4	46.8	22.6	48.8
British Columbia	48.5	33.7	44.7	61.4

[a]From Arés (1964 a, b).

dians is in Quebec (currently, somewhat more than 75 percent). Since 98 percent of French Canadians in Quebec retain the French mother tongue, the overall association between language and ethnic origin remains high in Canada: in 1961 90 percent of Canada's French-Canadian population have French for their mother tongue.

English, by contrast, is the mother tongue of nearly 99 percent of all persons reporting British origin in 1961. Moreover, its position among the British population has hardly changed in the last four decades. It is worth noting that a fairly large segment of the British ethnic population later acquire English if their mother tongue was some other tongue. In 1961, for example, nearly two-thirds of the small number of British ethnics with French or some other mother tongue were also able to speak English. By contrast, a far smaller segment of the French ethnic population whose mother tongue is not French later acquire their group's language as a second tongue; for example, in 1961 only 16 percent later learned French. This means that not only are the French ethnic members more likely than the British to lose their native mother tongue, but a far larger proportion of lost British ethnics are "recaptured" in the sense that they later acquire at least a speaking knowledge of their ethnic tongue. In terms of a third demographic criteria for measuring linguistic positions, namely, a language's tenacity among the appropriate ethnic group, English is clearly stronger than French. Nevertheless the linguistic weakening among French Canadians located outside Quebec is sufficiently compensated for by other demographic forces to produce the remarkable stability found in Canada's linguistic composition during this century.

Several features in the demographic situation merit consideration in this survey of the linguistic problem in Canada. For one, the close association between ethnic group and mother tongue suggests that ethnic composition will greatly affect the linguistic distribution. Second, as Father Arès's study suggests, the location and concentration of the ethnic and linguistic populations of Canada must be taken into account, since both group size and the degree of communication will influence the chances of language maintenance. Further, the foreign-born in Canada are of great importance, not simply because they are a sizable part of the population but because any preference on their part for one of the official languages will obviously tip—although not necessarily "tilt"—the linguistic balance. Finally, it is necessary to consider the means by which these diverse forces have led to the linguistic equilibrium found in Canada.

ETHNIC ORIGIN

Although the British are the largest single ethnic group in Canada, the British and French ethnic groups are much closer in number than are their languages. In part this is due to the favoring of English over French by other ethnic groups as well as the greater linguistic loss among the French ethnic group compared with their British countrymen. Also of great importance is the sizable immigration of new ethnic groups through the years as well as differential fertility. The net result has been a steady decrease in the British-Canadian numerical advantage over the French. Canada's ethnic composition in 1901 was 57 percent British, 31 percent French, and the remaining 12 percent divided among numerous groups of which Germans constituted nearly half. In every decade since, although the French ethnic proportion has remained constant, the position of the British has declined at the expense of increases among other ethnic groups. Thus in 1961 44 percent of the population were British, 30 percent French and a quarter of all Canadians were members of other ethnic groups. The inclusion of Newfoundland in the last two decades, because it is overwhelmingly British, only understates the decline of the British ethnic group in the remainder of Canada.

This third force—composed of German, Ukrainian, Dutch, Italian,

Jewish, indigenous Indians and Eskimos, and many other groups—plays an important role in influencing the linguistic situation because of their sizable and mounting numbers. Keep in mind there are now about three Canadians of French origin for every four of British derivation. The language choices of Canada's "other" ethnic groups, shown in Table 4, is overwhelmingly in favor of English. In 1921 about a quarter had English mother tongue, whereas less than 1 percent reported French. Although nearly half reported an English mother tongue by 1961, French is still the mother tongue of less than 2 percent. The rather sizable portion of other ethnic groups with nonofficial mother tongues is due, among other reasons, to the foreign-born segments and their rate of assimilation. Through the years, as Canadian-born generations become a larger part of these other ethnic groups, a drop in the proportion with other mother tongues occurs, but it is English that gains, not French.

Linguistic differences in Montreal between the Canadian-born residents and those born elsewhere demonstrate both the intergenerational shifts toward English and the great attraction of this language even in a pre-dominantly French-Canadian city. Among Canadian-born who are of neither British nor French origin, somewhat more than half report their mother tongue is English, whereas 5 percent of their ethnic compatriots born elsewhere (excluding the United States) have an English mother tongue. By contrast French increases from being the mother tongue of 4 percent of the foreign-born to only 14 percent among the Canadian-born of "other" origin. With the exception of the Italian population of Mon-treal, English gains very well among the Canadian-born members of the ethnic groups specified in Table 5. Comparisons between Canadian-born and American-born members of the ethnic groups now living in Canada indicate, however, that the presence of such a large French-speaking

TABLE 4

Mother Tongue Composition of "Other" Ethnic Groups, 1921–1961

Year[a]	English	French	Other	Total
1921	25.3	0.4	74.3	100.0
1931	22.7	0.9	76.5	100.0
1941	28.7	1.4	69.9	100.0
1951	44.1	1.4	54.6	100.0
1961	47.3	1.7	51.1	100.0

[a]Data for 1921 based on population 10 years of age and older; all ages in other years.

TABLE 5

Mother Tongue Percent Distribution by Birthplace and Ethnic Origin, Population 15 Years of Age and Older, Montreal Metropolitan Area, 1961

Ethnic Group	Born in Canada				Born in United States				Born Elsewhere			
	English	French	Other	Total	English	French	Other	Total	English	French	Other	Total
British	93.9	6.0	0.1	100.0	95.8	3.9	0.3	100.0	98.2	0.8	1.0	100.0
French	2.1	97.8	0.1	100.0	18.7	81.1	0.2	100.0	4.7	91.1	4.3	100.0
German	65.0	24.1	10.9	100.0	86.1	5.3	8.7	100.0	3.4	0.9	95.7	100.0
Italian	15.6	34.4	49.9	100.0	54.9	8.8	36.3	100.0	0.4	1.3	98.3	100.0
Jewish	78.7	1.2	20.1	100.0	89.1	—[a]	10.9	100.0	9.3	3.3	87.4	100.0
Ukrainian	30.4	5.5	64.1	100.0	65.5	17.2	17.2	100.0	2.3	0.8	96.9	100.0
All Other	58.9	14.4	26.7	100.0	77.9	8.0	14.1	100.1	7.1	5.8	87.1	100.0
Other than British or French	55.6	14.1	30.3	100.0	80.1	5.4	14.6	100.0	5.0	3.6	91.4	100.0

[a] A dash indicates none reported in the category indicated.

population in Montreal does alter linguistic behavior to some extent. In all cases a larger percentage of the American-born have English mother tongue than the Canadian-born and, with one exception, a larger percentage of Canadian born report French mother tongue than do the American-born.

Other ethnic groups help advance the English language in another way as well. Among those without an English mother tongue, around 90 percent acquire English as a second language. Thus nearly all members of other ethnic groups can speak English whereas, by contrast, around 4 or 5 percent can speak French if it was not their mother tongue. Indeed, other ethnics with a non-French mother tongue are only slightly more likely to learn French than is the British component of Canada's population. Quite understandably, this preference for English is related to the high concentration of French Canadians in Quebec and thus the insignificance, numerically speaking, of French in many parts of Canada. The preference for English by other ethnics is only partially due to this factor since English is the mother tongue of other ethnics twice as often as French even in Quebec.

In summary, the French ethnic population is virtually the sole carrier of the French mother tongue, whereas the British are assisted by the other ethnic groups in Canada who generally favor English over French by an enormous margin. In 1961 97 percent of all Canadians with a French mother tongue were members of the French ethnic group.

TERRITORIAL DISTRIBUTION

Although the French ethnic group constitutes 30 percent of Canada's population, they are a far smaller segment in all but two provinces. In addition to Quebec, which is 80 percent French Canadian, the 200,000 French living in neighboring New Brunswick are nearly 40 percent of that province's population. Well over one million French Canadians reside outside Quebec's protective embrace and are a prime target for linguistic assimilation, since they are usually vastly outnumbered by the British and other Canadians. The largest number outside Quebec is in Ontario, 650,000, but they are only 10 percent of that province's population.

During the last 50 years the concentration of the French ethnic population in Quebec has remained stable. In 1871 86 percent of the French Canadians in the four original provinces of Canada lived in Quebec. This declined steadily through 1911, when Quebec held 78 percent of Canada's French Canadians. Currently about 77 percent of Canada's

French population lives in Quebec. With respect to language, however, Quebec currently holds a larger percentage than ever of the French-mother-tongue population and monolingual French speakers. About 93 percent of the population able to speak only French resided in Quebec in 1961; 61 percent lived in Quebec in 1911. Although Quebec has declined in its share of the total Canadian population, it remains the major center of the French ethnic group and has more than held its share of French monoglots. "Le glacier québécois," as Henripin (1960) calls it, has melted only slightly.

As might be expected from the French mother-tongue and ethnic concentration in Canada, English is acquired by a very large proportion of the population with some other mother tongue who live outside of Quebec and New Brunswick. In 1961, for example, between 85 and 94 percent of the residents in other provinces could speak English (Table 6). Second-language learning of English is roughly of the same magnitude in these provinces since 1921. Quebec, by contrast, consistently ranks as the province with the lowest percent learning English. Indeed, the distance between Quebec and the other provinces has increased through the years. New Brunswick occupies an intermediate position; the learning of English is more frequent among the non-English mother-tongue population of New Brunswick than in Quebec, although the other provinces have considerably higher rates than New Brunswick.

Acquisition of French among those with a different mother tongue is virtually nil outside Quebec; only 2 to 4 percent in New Brunswick and an even smaller percentage in other provinces could speak French as a second language in 1961. Although New Brunswick contains a sufficient French-speaking component to allow about half those not raised in English to remain ignorant of this tongue, there is hardly any learning of French by those whose native tongue is different. Even Quebec in recent years has a somewhat higher percentage learning English than French as a second language. In short, English is either the mother tongue or second language for 97 percent or more of the residents in all provinces except New Brunswick, where 81 percent speak English, and Quebec, where a third know English. French is the mother tongue or the second language of less than 10 percent of the population in all provinces except New Brunswick (38 percent) and Quebec (87 percent).

Spatially, the French language has not only maintained its position during this century but has actually expanded. At one time a number of the eastern counties in Quebec itself were largely in the hands of the English, but as Ross (1943, 1954) has shown French Canadians expanded into these areas and replaced the English. In a process in some respects analogous to racial invasion of urban neighborhoods in American cities the

TABLE 6

Second-Language Learning by Decade and Province of Residence, 1921–1961

Year	Percent Learning English among Those with a Different Mother Tongue			Percent Learning French among Those with a Different Mother Tongue		
	Quebec	New Brunswick	Other Provinces[b]	Quebec	New Brunswick	Other Provinces[b]
1921[a]	43.0	65.0	76.8–96.5	31.6	3.5	2.0–3.7
1931[a]	42.3	65.7	82.5–97.5	31.3	2.9	1.1–2.4
1931	33.1	52.2	77.9–88.0	28.4	2.5	0.9–2.0
1941	29.2	49.6	88.7–93.4	31.2	2.7	0.6–1.6
1951	27.0	46.9	85.5–93.6	31.8	3.5	1.1–2.3
1961	27.4	48.2	84.6–94.3	32.7	3.9	1.1–2.8

[a]Population 10 years of age and older.
[b]Excluding Newfoundland.

earlier British settlers have all but left. Although the movement began as early as 1860, the available linguistic data allow us to trace these trends over the 60 years of this century from 1901 to 1961.

A number of technical difficulties are encountered because of the creation of new counties, merger of old counties, and other shifts in boundaries within Quebec and Ontario in particular. These problems are discussed in an appendix to this chapter. The number of county units examined may not correspond exactly with the number of counties presently in each province. Also, the reader should keep in mind that county trends should not be confused with trends among the total populations of the provinces since the counties are given equal weight regardless of their population size.

There is a close association between the 1901 and 1961 positions of both English and French in the counties of each province, with the linguistic position in 1901 explaining much of the intercounty variance in 1961 (see Table 7). Although these correlations are rather high, there are some definite shifts in the direction of French in Quebec. For the average Quebec county in 1901, 87 percent were able to speak French and 39 percent knew English. By 1961, the mean percentage able to speak French had risen to 92 percent, but English speakers fell to 26 percent. Of course, there is great variation from these arithmetic means; the standard deviations range from 10 to 22. Because of bilingualism, the percentage speaking English and French exceed 100.

TABLE 7

Linguistic Ability by Counties, 1901–1961

Province and Number of County Units	r_{21}	b_{21}	a	r_{43}	b_{43}	a
Nova Scotia (17)	.96	.5	52.6	.99	.9	.7
New Brunswick (13)	.90	1.2	−18.4	.99	1.1	5.1
Quebec (53)	.83	.7	− 1.5	.83	.5	51.2
Ontario (46)	.87	1.3	−27.1	.94	1.1	1.3
Canada (132)[a]	.96	1.1	−14.5	.98	1.0	3.3

X_1=percent speaking English in 1901, 5 years of age and older
X_2=percent speaking English in 1961, all ages.
X_3=percent speaking French in 1901, 5 years of age and older.
X_4=percent speaking French in 1961, all ages.
[a]Includes three Prince Edward Island county units.

The French language has expanded on its strong initial position in Quebec at the expense of a decline in English speakers in many parts of the province. Comparisons between 1901 and 1961 show a drop in the percentage speaking English in most counties (Table 8). Although the inclusion of children under 5 in the 1961 figures tends to bias the results in the direction found since small children are less likely to be bilingual, the growth of French during this same period as well as the magnitude of some of these changes indicates there has been a basic increase in French at the expense of English in many counties of Quebec.

The initially strong position of French in Quebec, 34 of 53 counties had 90 percent or more French speakers in 1901, has been improved through the ensuing years; for example, of the three counties with 30–40 percent French speakers in 1901, the lowest one currently has more than 50 percent speaking French (Table 8, bottom panel). Only three counties in Quebec have dropped a class; these were among those with more than 90 percent French-speaking in 1901. Since the possibility of bilingualism exists, the percentages speaking French and English are theoretically independent of each other, that is, both could go up or down jointly.

The overall linguistic pattern is far different in Ontario, although there are some important exceptions. Of 46 county units, 41 had more than 90 percent English speakers in both 1901 and 1961. Likewise less than 10 percent of the residents in 37 Ontario counties were able to speak French in both years. There are several counties in Ontario in which French has been able to increase its position during this century. French has also made some advances during this century in several other Ontario counties, but the spatial expansion of French westward into Ontario has not been very great.

In parts of New Brunswick, Quebec's southeastern neighbor, French has increased with some loss in English speakers. Five of the six county units with more than 10 percent French speakers in 1901 have increased their proportion of French-speaking residents. At the same time, several counties in New Brunswick have witnessed some decline in the percentage speaking English in this period. Nova Scotia's linguistic situation, by contrast, has been fairly static in this period. It is noteworthy, however, that the five counties with more than 10 percent able to speak French in 1901 have been able at least to hold their own so far.

In summary, the French language was important in all parts of Quebec by the turn of this century. Since then, its position has strengthened in those counties where a sizable segment of non-French speakers were found; English has suffered losses in some parts of the province. The expansion of French is particularly notable in those parts of Quebec which border on New York State, Vermont, and Maine. In Ontario and New Brunswick, French has done very well in those counties where it was

TABLE 8

Comparison Between Counties of Quebec in Linguistic Abilities: 1901–1961

Percent Speaking English 1961

1901[a]	0.0 9.9	10.0 19.9	20.0 29.9	30.0 39.9	40.0 49.9	50.0 59.9	60.0 69.9	70.0 79.9	80.0 89.9	90.0 100	Sum
0– 9.9											–
10.0–19.9	8	3									11
20.0–29.9	4	6	1	3							14
30.0–39.9		5	3	1	2						11
40.0–49.9			4	1							5
50.0–59.9				1		1					2
60.0–69.9			1			2					3
70.0–79.9					1	2					3
80.0–89.9					2			1			3
90.0–100								1			1
Total	12	14	9	6	5	5	–	2	–	–	53

Percent Speaking French 1961

1901[a]	0.0 9.9	10.0 19.9	20.0 29.9	30.0 39.9	40.0 49.9	50.0 59.9	60.0 69.9	70.0 79.9	80.0 89.9	90.0 100	Sum
0– 9.9											–
10.0–19.9											–
20.0–29.9											–
30.0–39.9						1	1	1			3
40.0–49.9									1		1
50.0–59.9								1			1
60.0–69.9									2	1	3
70.0–79.9								2	2	1	5
80.0–89.9										6	6
90.0–100									3	31	34
Total	–	–	–	–	–	1	1	4	8	39	43

[a]1901 data based on population 5 years of age and older.

fairly widespread in 1901, but there have been no noteworthy gains in counties where French was weak in the beginning of the century.

It is tempting to explain Canada's dual language situation in terms of the isolation of French speakers in Quebec. Although this is hardly a factor to be overlooked, the problem is far more complex. For one, the development of French-Canadian isolation is itself a dynamic process which occurred over a number of decades. Second, in monolingual nations such as the United States there were enormous concentrations of distinctive linguistic groups in many cities and over vast rural areas without in most cases the same persistency of their tongues. There are quantitative questions even for the spatial isolation interpretation. What would happen to French if Quebec was half the size it is, if native speakers of English made up 40 percent of the population, or if the economy was different?

Mother-Tongue Composition of Cities

An examination of second-language learning in Canadian cities illustrates how linguistic composition is an important, but only partial, determinant of the outcome of linguistic contact. Figure 2.1 indicates that the proportion of a city's population with English mother tongue influences the degree others learn English. The graph suggests a line in which the second-language learning of English is about 10 percent in cities with hardly any English-mother-tongue speakers and then rises rapidly. The curve levels out at cities where 70 percent or more of the residents are native English speakers. In these centers about 90 percent of the non-English mother-tongue population acquire the English language.

Inspection of an analogous graph for French indicates that French-mother-tongue composition likewise influences the degree it is learned by others in the city (Figure 2.2). The curve for French learning rises very gradually in cities with a small or moderate proportion of residents with French mother tongue and then reaches much higher levels as French-mother-tongue composition increases.

These graphs show not only that mother-tongue composition influences second-language learning, but that other forces operate as well. Looking back at the first graph, the level at which 80 percent or more of the population learn English is first reached with two cities in which slightly less than half the residents have English mother tongue. By contrast, somewhat more than 80 percent of the non-French population learn French in only one Canadian city, Rivière-du-Loup, where all but 123 of 10,835 residents have a French mother tongue. Indeed, comparison of the two graphs show that the influence of mother-tongue composition on second-language learning is very different for the two tongues. Throughout, acquisition of English is far greater than that of French when the mother

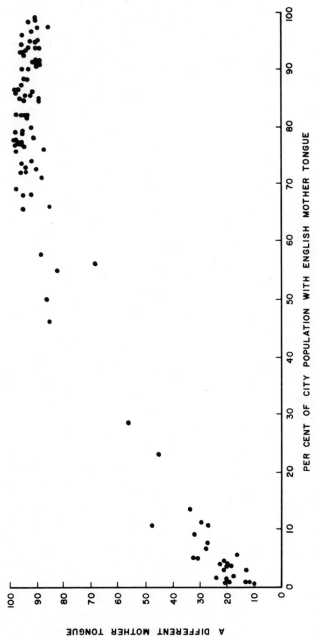

FIGURE 2.1 *Acquisition of English by language composition in cities, 1961.*

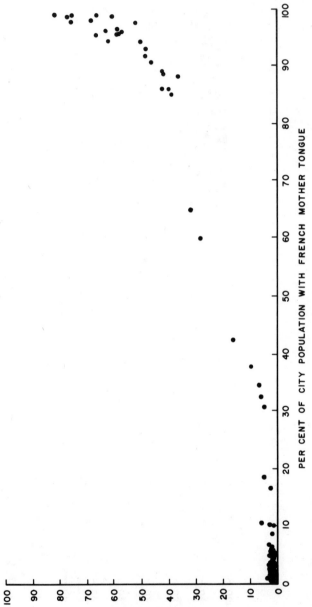

FIGURE 2.2   *Acquisition of French by language composition in cities, 1961.*

tongue strength of the language is taken into account. In Rivière-du-Loup, for example, nearly 20 percent of the native French speakers have learned English, despite the fact that French is the mother tongue of 99 percent of the residents.

These differences are summarized in Table 9, in which columns 1 and 2 show, respectively, the English-mother-tongue composition and the percent of residents with a different mother tongue who learn English; columns 4 and 3 indicate the French mother-tongue composition and the degree French is learned by those with another mother tongue. The differences are impressive to say the least; for example, in cities where English is the mother tongue of less than 10 percent of the residents, about a fifth of the remaining population learn English as a second language. By con-

TABLE 9

Influence of Mother Tongue Composition on Second-Language Learning in Leading Urban Areas, 1961[a]

English—Mother-Tongue Composition (1)	Mean Percent Learning English Among the Non-English Mother-Tongue Population (Number of Cities) (2)	Mean Percent Learning French Among the Non-French Mother-Tongue Population (Number of Cities) (3)	French—Mother-Tongue Composition (4)
less than 10%	21.1 (21)	1.8 (66)	less than 10%
10–20	34.7 (4)	3.7 (5)	10–20
20–30	51.0 (2)	—[b]	20–30
30–40	—[b]	7.0 (4)	30–40
40–50	85.6 (2)	15.8 (1)	40–50
50–60	79.3 (3)	28.3 (1)	50–60
60–70	92.8 (5)	31.8 (1)	60–70
70–80	94.1 (22)	—[b]	70–80
80–90	94.1 (19)	40.2 (6)	80–90
90+%	91.4 (25)	61.5 (19)	90+%

[a]Data based on all metropolitan and urban areas as well as other cities of 10,000+ population.
[b]No cases falling in the category indicated.

trast in cities where French is an equally weak mother tongue, an average of less than 2 percent acquire French. In cities in which English is the mother tongue of 90 percent or more of the residents about 90 percent of others also learn English. By contrast only 60 percent of non-French mother-tongue residents learn French in communities whose native speakers of French comprise 90 percent or more of the residents. The absolute differences are even greater in cities where the positions of English and French are more nearly balanced.

Considerably more attention is paid to variations between cities in second-language learning and linguistic maintenance later in this study, but for the moment it is sufficient to suggest that composition is only a partial explanation of linguistic responses in communities, a conclusion shared by Weinreich (1957) in his examination of a related problem, bilingualism in India. These results also provide substantial support for the contention that English is dominant over French, even after territorial distribution is taken into account.

In passing the reader should also note the striking bimodal distribution of both English and French in the communities shown along the abscissas of Figures 1 and 2. There are many cities in which 15 percent or less of the residents have English for their mother tongue (all but one of which are in Quebec), and there is an even larger concentration of Canadian cities in which English is the mother tongue of at least 70 percent of the residents. Hardly any cities fall between these two extremes.

FERTILITY

Populations grow or decline through differences between fertility and mortality, immigration and emigration. Mother tongue, because of the peculiar prerequisite of the Canadian census takers that it still be understood or spoken, is in the ambiguous position of being not quite an irreversible ascribed status, but neither is it fully reversible. It is safe to assume that nearly all people retain a reasonable knowledge of their first-learned language if they reach adulthood still able to use it. There is good reason to believe that mother tongue, even as defined in the Canadian census, is not reversible (Lieberson, 1966, Table 3). By contrast knowledge of some additional tongue, particularly when acquired in school (as this author can readily attest), can easily be lost later in life. Differences in fertility are consequently more directly relevant to the maintenance of a language *qua* mother tongue than to the maintenance of a language per se. This is due to the fact that usage of a language may increase or decrease without any changes in the vital processes, whereas differentials in fertility, mortality, and migration will be the main determinants of a mother tongue's relative size.

La revanche des berceaux, "the revenge of the cradle," is more than a clever phrase; it is a reality of great importance to French-language maintenance. There were probably no more than 10,000 immigrants to New France during the entire period of the French colony, yet by 1763 New France had a population of about 70,000, suggesting "a rate of fertility among the highest ever reached, even among small populations occupying practically limitless areas" (Keyfitz, 1960, p. 130). Observing that immigration from France after the Peace of Paris was negligible, Keyfitz goes on to estimate the annual rate of growth necessary to yield a population of 890,000 found in Lower Canada (presently Quebec) by 1851. He concludes that the population grew at an extremely high compounded rate of 2.7 percent annually, with a crude fertility rate of at least 52 per thousand. Growth in the number of French from 1.3 million in 1881 to 4.3 million in 1951 also implies a high rate of increase each year, particularly when we consider that there was considerable French Canadian emigration to the United States during this period.

What is of importance is not so much the rapid growth of the French Canadian population through high fertility rates but rather their rate of growth compared with the English-speaking segments of Canada. In his excellent analysis of the French-Canadian demographic situation Henripin (1960, p. 160) observes that around 1850 non-French fertility was probably almost as high as that for French Canadians. One of the difficulties is that for many years there were no direct fertility data available for specific ethnic or linguistic groups, but only for provinces. Comparisons between Quebec and either Ontario or the remainder of Canada are taken as roughly equivalent to, or at least suggestive of, differences between French Canadians and British Canadians.

From the mid-nineteenth century until late in the 1930s fertility dropped for both groups, but far more rapidly for the Ontario population. The net effect was a more rapid increase through fertility for French Canadians. Although fertility has risen since 1940 in both areas, the increase has been sharper for Ontario than Quebec. It is important to keep in mind that the absolute differences between the two provinces are still far more in favor of the French than were the differences during at least a good part of the nineteenth century. Ethnic data available for these provinces during recent decades indicate that the provincial comparisons understate the actual British–French differences in fertility (see Henripin, 1960, Table 6, p. 163).

Gross reproduction rates, shown in Table 10, provide a rough measure of ethnic differences in fertility in recent decades. Based on age-specific fertility rates, this measure indicates the number of girls that would be borne by 1000 women going through the childbearing ages. Although the magnitude shifts from decade to decade, women of French origin clearly outproduce other Canadian women by a comfortable margin in all three periods. The lowest difference in gross reproduction rates, recorded for 1951, still involves 450 more births per thousand French-Canadian women. Since French Canadians probably have higher mortality, particularly in the early years of life, these gross reproduction rates overstate the net excess of French births. Apparently, age-specific fertility rates are not available for ethnic groups in Canada in 1961. However, there is some evidence to suggest that the French advantage in fertility has continued to decline (Garigue, 1962).

Keeping in mind that our central concern is with the implications of fertility for language maintenance, in a sense all of this discussion is only an indirect measure of the crucial issue, namely, the reproduction of each mother tongue in the next generation. Because of the close correspondence between the French ethnic group and the French-mother-tongue population, it is reasonably certain that this analysis reflects differences in mother-tongue fertility. Moreover in a most careful study Enid Charles (1948) has directly compared the fertility of English-, French-, and other European-mother-tongue women who had completed the childbearing ages in 1941. Taking education, present residence, birthplace, and religion into account, Catholic French-mother-tongue women exceeded others by a high margin; for example, those with low education who were born on a farm and currently live in rural areas had given birth to an average of 8.3 children by the end of their childbearing period. Protestant English-mother-tongue women of similar background reported only four children. Since the trends are toward more education and urban living, it is worth noting that such differences are still favorable to the French among urban college women as well, albeit of a lower magnitude (Charles, 1948, Table 31, p. 68).

TABLE 10

Gross Reproduction Rates by Ethnic Origin, 1931–1951

Year	Ethnic Origin	
	French	Other
1931	2240	1304
1941	1866	1173
1951	2015	1564

Although it is true that higher fertility among the French-speaking population must occur to offset the gains made by English through migration, higher fertility among French-mother-tongue women will not necessarily maintain the language's position as a mother tongue in Canada. French-Canadian women must also have children who are French-speaking. Since a sizable segment of the French-Canadian population can also speak English, high fertility could not prevent a decline in the French language if the offspring were raised as native English speakers. Indeed, this is essentially what happened in the linguistic shift to English in the United States by groups whose native tongues were different. Mother tongue is never an achieved status, since it is not up to the child to decide what language his parents will choose to use with him in the home. Moreover, mother tongue is not quite an ascribed language in families in which the parents can speak more than one tongue, since there is an option in the language that may be used with the child. The question thus comes down to comparing the French-mother-tongue position among small children with its standing among women in the childbearing ages.

The number of children with French mother tongue has risen in each decennial census since 1931. Although the increase between 1931 and 1941 was very slight, one must keep in mind that this was counter to an absolute drop in the total number of small children in Canada during this period (Table 11). In recent decades the increase has been more substantial in that the number of children under 5 years of age with French mother tongue was 660,000 in 1961 compared with 370,000 in 1931. Moreover, until 1961 the percentage of small children with French mother tongue exceeded by a comfortable margin the percentage of women in the childbearing ages with this mother tongue. In 1961, for the first time, there were proportionately more French-mother-tongue women than children. In other words, although the number of Canadian children with French mother tongue increased by nearly 100,000 from the preceding decade, this gain failed to keep up with the percentage of children necessary to match the percentage of women in childbearing ages with French mother tongue. Computation of age-specific fertility rates for the various census years indicates that this decline is not due to age variations among women in the childbearing ages.

In short, the French-mother-tongue population is growing in Canada, at least in terms of the number of small children in each decade with this language. However, in the two decades from 1941 to 1961 the percentage of small children with French mother tongue has dropped to the point at which it was slightly below the percentage of women in childbearing ages with French mother tongue (29.2 versus 29.6 percent). This shift may reflect a relative decline in French-Canadian fertility and/or an increase

TABLE 11

Mother Tongue Composition of Small Children and Women in the Childbearing Ages, 1931–1961

Year and Mother Tongue	Number		Percent Distribution	
	Children Under 5 Years	Women 15–44 Years	Children Under 5 Years	Women 15–44 Years
1931				
English	543,481	1,331,398	50.6	57.7
French	372,216	628,919	34.6	27.3
Other	158,718	346,211	14.8	15.0
Total	1,074,415	2,306,528	100.0	100.0
1941				
English	544,344	1,480,397	51.8	55.8
French	382,747	791,029	36.4	29.8
Other	124,763	379,802	11.9	14.3
Total	1,051,854	2,651,228	100.0	100.0
1951[a]				
English	1,060,301	1,796,638	61.6	57.9
French	558,289	928,305	32.4	29.9
Other	103,519	378,864	6.0	12.2
Total	1,722,109	3,103,807	100.0	100.0
1961[a]				
English	1,410,792	2,065,140	62.5	55.5
French	659,844	1,100,954	29.2	29.6
Other	185,765	555,557	8.2	14.9
Total	2,256,401	3,721,651	100.0	100.0

[a]Newfoundland included.

in the degree children of French-mother-tongue women are raised in English. In either respect its continuation in future decades could weaken the position of French in Canada. Although language maintenance between generations is examined more closely in Chapters 6 and 7, keep in mind that French has thus far maintained its position in Canada through fertility and, moreover, the number of children with this mother tongue actually increased in each decade. In examining the linguistic characteristics of small children it is important to recognize that assimilation on an individual basis need not lead to group assimilation. Within limits, a sizable proportion of an ethnic population can assimilate and yet the group maintain itself or even grow in size (Lieberson, 1963, p. 9).

In all decades women with "other" mother tongues have not maintained their position among small children. Although fairly close in 1931, in recent years the gap is in the neighborhood of 2 to 1. In 1961, for example, 8 percent of small children had mother tongues that were neither English nor French, whereas 15 percent of adult women were native speakers of some nonofficial language. Although the number of children increased since 1951, it is unlikely that these other languages have a rosy future in Canada, since the rise is probably due to the enormous immigration in recent years to the Dominion.

The number of English-mother-tongue children has jumped greatly since the end of World War II. It is only in the postwar decades that this language's position among small children exceeded its standing among women of childbearing ages (Table 11). English is helped by the fact that many of the other mother-tongue women have children whose first-learned language is English.

In brief, French-Canadian fertility during this century has generally been higher than the British rates. Up until very recently, this also meant that the percentage of small children with French mother tongue exceeded the percentage expected on the basis of the French language position among mothers in Canada. Women with other mother tongues do not contribute their proportionate share of children with similar native tongues. Very likely this is due to a shift in the next generation to English. Now for the first time French is slightly underrepresented among small children compared with its position among women in the childbearing ages. The opposite trend holds for English. However, since the *number* of French-mother-tongue children has been increasing, the maintenance of French as a native tongue in future generations is in no immediate and direct danger. If this process continues, it would mean a drop in the relative strength of the French language in Canada, which in turn could increase the degree of bilingualism necessary among French Canadians and provide a greater threat to loss of the native tongue in future generations. So far in this century, however, fertility differences have generally been very favorable to the French language.

INTERNATIONAL MIGRATION

The importance of 7 million migrants to Canada since 1900 (Department of Citizenship and Immigration, 1963a, Table 3), although by no means a trivial number under any circumstances, can be readily appreciated when one considers that the current population is in the neighborhood of 20 million. While it is true that for a significant number of immigrants Canada was hardly more than a temporary domicile before entrance into the United States, nevertheless, the impact of immigration on the linguistic balance in Canada is of great significance. First, French speakers made up only a minor proportion of immigrants. Second, Britain itself has been an extremely important source of immigration to Canada. The British constituted 35 percent of the 2.7 million migrants from overseas between 1926 and 1962; the French ethnic group amounted to only 2 percent. Although it is true that if information had been available on the ethnic origins of immigrants from the United States for the entire period, the French segment would have been higher, it is important to keep in mind that more than half the United States' emigrants to Canada during 1946–1962 were of British ethnic origin and less than 10 percent were French (Department of Citizenship and Immigration, 1963b; and tables made available to the author by the Department of Citizenship and Immigration).

In discussing the impact of immigration on the linguistic balance in Canada, it is well to confess at the outset that international migration statistics are a demographic no man's land. Particularly in earlier years, difficulties and inconsistencies in terminology, inadequate distinctions between country of birth and last permanent residence or between temporary and permanent visitors, the relative ease with which the Canadian–United States border can be crossed without official permission and notation, and many other problems make this a difficult matter to discuss (e.g., Price, 1965). Keyfitz (1950, p. 48), for example, estimates 300,000 migrants from Canada to the United States on the basis of life tables for a decade in which United States government statistics indicate 3000.

Using a modified English life table, Keyfitz calculates that Canada received 7.1 million immigrants between 1851 and 1950, whereas its emigrants (largely to the United States) amounted to 6.6 million (1950, p. 62). This suggests that the direct increment due to migration, ignoring the offspring born in Canada, was only about 500,000 in an entire century. In five of the nine decades beginning with 1851 there was actually a net loss in Canada due to migration (p. 50). Although Canada was something like the "Grand Central Station" of international migration, it would be a mistake to infer that international migration has not had a significant impact on the linguistic composition of the nation. As we shall see, the net effect has been to greatly help the English language.

The second side of migration is the sizable movement of Canadian residents to the United States. At the beginning of the present century the number of Canadian-born living in the United States equalled 25 percent of the Canadian-born population found in Canada itself. The record number of Canadian-born reported in the United States was about 1.3 million in 1930, which would comprise 16 percent of the Canadian-born population in the 1931 Census of Canada. The number of Canadian-born in the United States has declined in each decade since the peak in 1930, but there are presently close to 1 million residing in the United States. Considering that the migration of non-Canadian-born to the United States from the Dominion are not included in these figures, the influence of emigration to the United States is clearly of great importance. Gains due to net migration will increase the strength of one language and raise the necessity for either greater bilingualism or more isolation among the speakers of the other tongue.

Canadian-born living in the United States, beginning with the 1890 census, were classified into two categories, French and other, largely on the basis of whether their mother tongue was French. Using this classification, the mother-tongue composition of Canadians living in the United States can be inferred for each decade through 1960. Inspection of Table 12 indicates that generally about a third to a quarter of the Canadian-born population living in the United States were native French speakers, but more or less declining from a peak at the beginning of this century to only 20 percent in 1960 (column 1). By comparing either the linguistic or ethnic composition of the Canadian-born population living in Canada (columns 2 and 3), it is clear that French Canadians are underrepresented among the Canadian-born living in the United States. At the beginning of the 1930's, for example, 29 percent of the Canadians living in the United States were French, compared with 34 to 35 percent of the Canadian-born population remaining in Canada. Truesdell (1943, p. 47) drew a similar comparison, but unfortunately with the entire Canadian population, rather than with those living in Canada who were also born there.

In view of the obvious advantages in America for those fluent in English, it is reasonable to assume that French Canadians unable to speak English are less likely to emigrate than are their bilingual compatriots. Viewed by itself, a sizable emigration flow to the United States has helped the French-language position in Canada. Not only are the French Canadians underrepresented among Canadians living in the United States, but the relatively greater drain on English-speaking Canadians is probably understated considering that these figures do not include foreign-born who lived in Canada prior to migrating to the United States.

What can be inferred about the net influence of international migration on Canada's linguistic balance? Although the difference between the number of immigrants and emigrants is relatively small, the impact has been very sizable and most favorable to English. For one, a large segment of the immigrants to Canada were either native speakers of English or immigrants who learned English after arrival. Not only are there very few

TABLE 12

French Component of the Canadian Population Residing in the United States Compared with Canada, 1890–1961

Year	Percent of Canadian-born Population Living in United States Who Are French (1)	Year	Percent of Canadian-born in Canada	
			With French Mother Tongue (2)	Who Are French Ethnic (3)
1890	30.8			
1900	33.5			
1910	32.2			
1920	27.5	1921	N.A.[a]	34.8
1930	29.0	1931	34.2	35.3
1940	26.2	1941	34.6	35.9
1950	24.0	1951	33.5	35.6
1960	20.2	1961	32.7	35.4

[a]Data not available.

immigrants from France or native French speakers, but the immigrants did not learn French as often as English. Although French Canadians comprise a smaller part of the Canadian-born population living in the United States than their proportion in Canada would lead us to expect under conditions of random outmigration, nevertheless, from a quarter to a third were native French speakers. This means that French gained little from immigration but lost a sizable number through migration to the United States. Thus, although the number of emigrants from Canada is somewhat smaller than the number of immigrants, Canada sent out more French speakers than were received.

Based on Canadian censuses, the net outmigration of Canadian-born from Canada is estimated at about 1.6 million between 1871 and 1941, whereas the net migration into Canada of the foreign-born is about 2 million (Keyfitz, 1950, p. 60). Assuming that 30 percent of the net loss of Canadian-born were native French speakers and that only about 10 percent of the foreign-born immigrants became carriers of the French language, then this tongue lost about 300,000 due to international migration during this period. Since Thomas (1954, p. 251) estimates that net migration of Canadian-born to the United States was probably close to 2 million between 1871 and 1930, if anything these calculations are conservative with respect to the loss of French speakers in Canada.

More recently Keyfitz (1960, p. 136) estimated that between 1851 and 1951 French Canadians had 7.6 million births, 2.9 million deaths, and a loss of 1.2 million through emigration. For the non-French, there were 11.8 million births, 6 million deaths, 7.2 million immigrants, and 5.3 million emigrants. Excluding the addition of Newfoundland, this means a gain for the French of 3.5 million, or 30 percent of the total growth of Canada. Thus the net effect of linguistic and ethnic differentials in mortality, fertility, and international migration is more or less to maintain the linguistic balance of Canada. The outlook for the future is by no means certain since shifts may occur which would change this demographic balance; for example, a drop in migration to Canada of foreign groups or a rise in the French-speaking component would hurt the position of English. On the other hand, a drop in emigration from Canada to the United States or a rise in the French-Canadian fraction among emigrants would reduce the position of the French language.

Location and Language of Immigrants

Not only is the immigrant population of Canada composed of a sizable number of English speakers from Great Britain and only a minor number of French speakers but the remaining immigrants favor English by a considerable margin; for example, the official language distribution among the foreign-born residing in Canada in 1961 is English only, 85.9 percent; French only, 2.2 percent; bilingual, 7.6 percent; and neither English nor French, 4.4 percent. Even recognizing that far more of the immigrants arrive with an English mother tongue than French, it is clear that most of the others favor the former. This is a long-standing matter; in 1911, for example, 84 percent of the foreign-born knew English, whereas 5 percent were able to speak French.

One factor contributing to the linguistic behavior of immigrants is their avoidance of Quebec. For each decade between 1881 and the present the percentage of immigrants residing in Quebec has ranged from 9.3 to 13.7 of Canada's foreign-born. By contrast about a third of the Canadian-born population live in Quebec. Possibly reflecting the competition with French Canadians for less skilled and lower paying jobs, immigrants not only tend to avoid Quebec, but among those residing in the province there are proportionately few in the areas where French is most dominant.

Using data for three provinces in which sizable numbers speak French—New Brunswick, Quebec, and Ontario—the distribution by counties was analyzed for the foreign-born arriving shortly before the 1961 census. The index of dissimilarity measures the degree to which the spatial distributions of two populations are similar or dissimilar to one another. Expressed in the form of frequency distributions, the index measures the proportion of one or the other population who would have to relocate (in this case by counties) in order for the two frequency distributions to be identical. The index ranges from 0 (identical distributions) to 100 (complete segregation such that one population is found only where the other is absent). Greater details on this measure are given in Duncan and Duncan (1955) and Lieberson (1963). For Quebec in 1961, the index of dissimilarity between recent immigrants and the English-speaking population is 20, whereas the index between immigrants and the monolingual French speakers is 63. Rather clearly, the spatial distribution by counties of immigrants in Quebec is far closer to that of the English-speaking residents of the province. Similar results are obtained for Ontario and New Brunswick in 1961, as well as for the three provinces in most earlier decades (see Table 13).

These results could be due largely to the fact that the British-born, who are almost entirely English-speaking, are a major segment of the immigrant population of Canada. Classifying the foreign-born by mother tongue in 1941, 9 percent of those with English mother tongue and 60 percent of those with French mother tongue are located in Quebec. But what is most important is the fact that among immigrants in Canada with some other mother tongue and who would therefore have no linguistic reason to favor English-speaking areas over Quebec, a mere 10 percent reside in the latter province. There is little doubt that linguistic characteristics influence French immigrants to locate in Quebec. On the other hand, immigrants whose native tongue is neither English nor French avoid Quebec to the same degree as those whose mother tongue is English.

There are five immigrant groups in 1941 which have at least a thousand members whose mother tongue is French. These are immigrants from the British Isles, the United States, Belgium, France, and a residual "other" European category. The British Isles and the United States may raise some eyebrows. It should be noted that the French mother tongue segment of the British immigrants amounts to only one-tenth of 1 percent of that group. The French segment of the American-born immigrant population is far more sizable, comprising 15 percent of Americans in Canada. This is probably a function of the French-Canadian movement between the two nations described elsewhere.

Cities of 30,000 and more were divided into two categories: those in which less than 5 percent of the Canadian-born population had French mother tongue and those in which more than 15 percent reported French mother tongue. With the exception of Windsor, most cities in the latter category have a much larger percentage of Canadian-born residents with

TABLE 13

Indexes of Dissimilarity Between Immigrants and Monolingual English and French Speakers, by Counties, New Brunswick, Quebec, Ontario, 1901–1961[a]

	Foreign-Born versus Monolingual Speakers of	
	English	French
1901		
New Brunswick	26.1	61.4
Quebec	32.6	43.0
Ontario	40.8	57.4
1931		
New Brunswick	23.0	57.8
Quebec	16.6	57.6
Ontario	26.5	77.2
1941		
New Brunswick	17.8	73.6
Quebec	15.5	55.9
Ontario	23.0	82.7
1951		
New Brunswick	14.9	67.7
Quebec	14.9	60.6
Ontario	15.8	79.3
1961		
New Brunswick	16.4	70.8
Quebec	20.0	63.1
Ontario	24.0	74.8

[a]Comparisons between decades may not be fully comparable because of changes in the number of county units. Likewise the indexes of dissimilarity are partially redundant because of the fact that some of foreign-born are included again in the monolingual English or monolingual French categories. The part–whole effect is minimal.

French mother tongue; Sudbury was next with 38.8 percent and Ottawa-Hull, Montreal-Outremont-Verdun, Quebec, Sherbrooke, and Trois-Rivières were all greater than that. The results, shown in Table 14, indicate that the heavily English-mother-tongue cities persistently capture far greater proportions of English-speaking members of the immigrant groups. The French-mother-tongue segments of the same groups are far more likely to locate in the cities with a sizable native French population. Among some of the ethnic groups, the "other"-mother-tongue segment

TABLE 14

Percentage Distributions of Foreign-born by Mother Tongue and Canadian-born in Cities of Different Linguistic Composition: 1941

Percent of Canadian-born in Cities with French Mother Tongue	Foreign-born			Canadian-born
	English Mother Tongue	French Mother Tongue	Other Mother Tongue	
Less than 5	80.4	15.3	68.5	50.9
More than 15	19.6	84.7	31.5	49.1
Total	100.0	100.0	100.0	100.0

tends to occupy an intermediate position between their English and French compatriots. While this suggests that part of the linguistic patterns of mother-tongue groups can be viewed as a function of ethnic composition, the fact remains that immigrants whose native tongue is neither English nor French locate in those parts of Canada where French is unimportant. Accordingly, the immigrants and their children shift to English and provide a strong and increasingly important source of strength to this language in Canada.

INTERNAL MIGRATION

Although the proportion of foreign immigrants located in Quebec is nowhere so large as the province's position among the Canadian-born population, an even smaller segment of internal migration is directed into Quebec. Only about 13 percent of the population moving from one province to another in the 10 years preceding 1941 ended up in Quebec. By contrast, about 18 percent of those who moved to Canada in the same period from a foreign country were located in Quebec. An examination of recent interprovincial migration between 1955 and 1961 discloses that Quebec still receives a proportionately small number of migrants from other parts of Canada. Among the population alive in 1961 who had moved during the preceding five years, only 67,000 were found in Quebec, compared with 80,000 and 87,000 in the provinces of Alberta and British Columbia. Compared with Quebec, Ontario attracted more than twice the number of migrants.

The inability of Quebec to "pull" residents from other provinces is, however, not so serious as it might appear, since its residents are also the least likely to move to another part of the Dominion. Of those located in Quebec in 1956 who were still alive and residing in Canada in 1961, 98.4 percent remained in Quebec. This is the highest degree of retention in the nation, although it should be noted that most provinces are not radically lower in their holding power over such a short period.

Of the 8.8 million Canadians who were born in some province outside Quebec and who were living in Canada in 1961 15 percent were not located in the province of their birth. Among those born in Quebec only 5 percent were located in some other province. Although the number of Canadian-born living in Quebec was less than the number of Quebec-born in the country, the difference, 45,000, is rather small. Quebec's loss through internal migration is of rather minor significance, since relatively few either leave or enter the province. Moreover the impact of interprovincial migration for linguistic maintenance in Quebec is even more insignificant now than earlier in the century. In 1911, for example, the differences in the retention percentages for Quebec and the remaining provinces was somewhat less (respectively, 94 and 88 percent) and Quebec's net loss with the remaining provinces of Canada was −84,000.

The linguistic impact of internal migration on the concentration of French speakers in Canada is also minimized, although not eliminated, by the great selectivity among Canadian-born migrants. Among the Quebec-born population with French-mother-tongue 98.6 percent resided in Quebec in 1941; whereas only 82 percent of the English-mother-tongue population born in Quebec were still located in the province of their birth. In other words, native English speakers are more likely than the French to leave Quebec for other parts of Canada. This is shown in the first column of Table 15, which indicates the percentage with French mother tongue among the Quebec-born living in different provinces. Among those born and currently residing in Quebec 87.7 percent are native French speakers, whereas the figure is considerably lower for natives of Quebec in many other provinces. New Brunswick is an important exception, but of course this is the one other province in which native French speakers form a sizable proportion of the population. Since other-mother-tongue speakers are relatively unimportant, it can be readily seen that the English-mother-tongue population is overrepresented among the migrants from Quebec to other parts of Canada. Only a third of the Quebec-born population living in Nova Scotia, for example, report that their mother tongue is French. This is far less than the proportion with French mother tongue among their fellow Quebecers who remained in Quebec.

In similar fashion, the French-mother-tongue component of each province is far more likely to migrate to Quebec than are the English. In some instances, the selectivity is overwhelming, for example, nearly half the Ontario-born residents of Quebec are native French speakers, yet less than 10 percent of Ontario's nonmigrants report French as their mother tongue. Although the magnitude of selectivity is not as high in all provinces as in Ontario and some of the prairie provinces, there is no exception to the rule that native French speakers are more likely to move to Quebec. However, despite this selectivity, French-mother-tongue speakers comprise a greater proportion of outmigrants from Quebec than they do of Canadians immigrating to the province (compare columns 1 and 2 of Table 15). This represents a net loss through internal migration of the French-mother-tongue population and is due to the fact that French is a far smaller segment of the population in most provinces outside of Quebec. Thus, although the selectivity process favors French, it is insufficient to compensate for the higher French-mother-tongue base in Quebec; for example. whereas only 30 percent of the Quebec-born population living in British Columbia are

TABLE 15

Percent with French-Mother-Tongue, by Province of Birth and Residence, 1941

Province or Territory	Born in Quebec, by Province of Current Residence (1)	Residents of Quebec, by Province of Birth (2)	Both Born and Currently Residing in the Province (3)
Prince Edward Island	37.6	19.7	11.5
Nova Scotia	34.9	10.1	7.2
New Brunswick	73.7	55.0	35.7
Quebec	87.7	87.7	87.7
Ontario	54.3	44.5	7.8
Manitoba	55.5	27.8	8.9
Saskatchewan	62.1	41.7	5.1
Alberta	59.0	36.9	4.1
British Columbia	29.4	8.8	0.6
Yukon and N.W.T.	72.0	11.6	1.3

native French speakers, this is still greater than the French-mother-tongue percentage of British Columbians living in Quebec. Since there is more outmigration than inmigration to Quebec, the net effect is a loss of native French speakers in the province (40,000 in the period ending in 1941). As long as the number crossing the provincial boundary remains relatively small, the net effect is negligible. Data are not available for examining these trends for recent decades.

Rural Outmigration

The ability of Quebec's cities to absorb the exodus of its rural population has been critical in allowing the province to retain its French-speaking population so successfully. In 1941 the Quebec-born population between 5 and 54 years of age living in the rural areas of the province numbered 980,000. Taking into account the mortality experienced during the ensuing decade by means of the Quebec life tables for 1940–1942 and 1950–1952 as well as changes in the census definition of "rural," there was a net outmigration from rural areas of about 190,000 between 1941 and 1951. However, the inmigration of the Quebec-born population to the province's cities during the decade for the same ages is estimated to be 90,000. Thus nearly half the net migration of the Quebec-born residents from rural areas was captured by the cities in the province. Between 1951 and 1961 there was an even greater exodus of rural residents; the Quebec-born population 15 to 64 years of age living in rural Quebec in 1961 was 270,000 less than the number 10 years earlier after mortality is taken into account (by means of the 1955-1957 Quebec life table) and adjustments are made for changes in the definition of "rural." In this decade the Quebec-born population living in the urban parts of the province increased by 230,000 in the relevant ages. Therefore an overwhelming part of the rural exodus in the most recent decade is not lost to the province or to a milieu incompatible to French; rather, most relocate in the province's cities. Given this sizable flow from Quebec's rural areas, the ability of the urban areas to provide economic opportunities is critical to the maintenance of French in the province.

APPENDIX

COMPARABILITY BETWEEN COUNTIES, 1901–1961

Shown below is a list of county units in 1901 coupled with comparable spatial units in 1961. In many instances it was necessary to splice or combine the counties in one period in order to maximize comparability with the other decade under consideration. For many counties in Ontario it is exceptionally difficult to achieve comparability for analyses of changes between 1901 and 1961. Accordingly, it was often necessary to subdivide the counties in 1901 and make the crude assumption that linguistic composition was uniform throughout the county.

Most changes in county boundaries occurred in the earlier decades of this century. Anyone using these matched sets of boundaries for other research purposes, however, should note that no effort was made to maximize comparability between 1901 and any of the decades preceding 1961. For comparisons between the initial year and decades before 1961 it is necessary first to examine changes occurring between the year under study and 1961. Likewise comparisons between 1901 and decades after 1961 should be relatively simple, provided the investigator first considers whether any county boundary changes have taken place since 1961.

1901	1961

Prince Edward Island

1901	1961
Kings	Kings*
Prince, East; Prince, West	Prince*
Queens, East; Queens, West	Queens*

1901	1961

Nova Scotia

1901	1961
Halifax, City and Co.	Halifax
Shelburne and Queens	Shelburne; Queens
All other counties unchanged	

New Brunswick

1901	1961
St. John, City and Co.	St. John
Sunbury and Queens	Queens; Sunbury
Victoria	Victoria; Madawaska
All other counties unchanged	

Quebec

1901	1961
Equivalent area not available	Abitibi
Bagot	Bagot*
Beauce; Compton	Beauce; Compton; Frontenac*
Bertheir	Bertheir*
Brome	Brome*
Chambly and Verchères	Chambly; Verchères
Champlain	Champlain*
Châteauguay	Châteauguay*
Chicoutimi and Saguenay	Chicoutimi; Saguenay; Lac-St-Jean
Drummond and Arthabaska	Drummond; Arthabaska*
Hochelaga; Jacques-Cartier; Laval; Maisonneuve; Montreal, Ste. Anne, City; Montreal, Ste. Antoine, City; Montreal, St. Jacques, City; Montreal, St. Laurent, City; Montreal, Ste. Marie, City	Montreal and Jesus Islands
Labelle	Labelle; Papineau*
Laprairie and Napierville	Laprairie; Napierville*
L'Assomption	L'Assomption*
Maskinongé	Maskinongé*
Mégantic	Mégantic*
Missisquoi	Missisquoi*
Nicolet	Nicolet
Pontiac	Pontiac; Témiscamingue
Quebec, Centre, City; Quebec, East, City; Quebec, West, City; Quebec, County	Quebec
Richelieu	Richelieu*

1901	1961

Quebec (continued)

Richmond and Wolfe	Richmond; Wolfe
Rimouski	Matane; Rimouski
Rouville	Rouville*
St. Jean and Iberville	St. Jean; Iberville*
Shefford	Shefford*
Trois-Rivières and St. Maurice	St. Maurice*
Wright	Hull*
Yamaska	Yamaska*
All other counties unchanged	

Ontario†

Addington (9,925/24,490); Lennox	Addington; Lennox
Addington (14,565/24,490); Kingston City; Frontenac	Frontenac
Algoma	Algoma; Kenora; Manitoulin; Rainy River; Thunder Bay*
Bothwell (16,333/25,223); Kent; Elgin, West (8,995/23,195)	Kent
Bothwell (8,890/25,223); Lambton, East; Lambton, West; Middlesex, West (2,321/15,843)	Lambton
Brant, South; Wentworth and Brant, North (6,176/18,717); Oxford, South (5,257/21,797)	Brant
Brockville; Leeds, South; Leeds and Grenville, North (889/13,647)	Leeds
Bruce, East; Bruce, North; Bruce, West	Bruce
Cardwell (7,788/13,060); Peel	Peel
Cardwell (2,161/13,060); Simcoe, East (33,846/39,277); Simcoe, North; Simcoe, South (16,018/19,271); York, North (3,326/18,778)	Dufferin
Carleton; Lanark, North (5,003/18,180); Ottawa, City; Russel (14,884/35,166)	Carleton
Cornwall and Stormont	Stormont
Durham, East; Durham, West	Durham
Elgin, East; Elgin, West (14,200/23,195); Middlesex, East (2,138/26,609)	Elgin
Essex, North; Essex, South	Essex
Grenville, South; Leeds and Grenville North (8,190/13,647)	Grenville

1901	1961

Ontario† (continued)

Grey, East (20,368/25,387); Grey,
North; Grey, South — Grey

Haldimand and Monck (17,044/20,052);
Norfolk, South (4,189/20,899) — Haldimand

Haldimand and Monck (3,008/20,052);
Lincoln and Niagara (2,490/27,566);
Welland — Welland

Hastings, East; Hastings, North;
Hastings, West — Hastings

Hamilton, City; Wentworth and Brant,
North (7,862/18,717); Wentworth,
South (18,956/24,432) — Wentworth

Huron, East; Huron, South; Huron,
West; Perth, South (2,367/17,861);
Middlesex, North (5,964/17,455) — Huron

Lanark, North (13,177/18,180);
Lanark, South; Leeds and Grenville,
North (4,568/13,647) — Lanark

Lincoln and Niagara (25,076/27,566);
Wentworth, South (5,476/24,432) — Lincoln

London, City; Middlesex, East
(24,471/26,609); Middlesex, North
(11,491/17,455); Middlesex, South;
Middlesex, West (13,522/15,843) — Middlesex

Muskoka and Parry Sound; Ontario,
North (6,802/20,689); Simcoe, East
(5,431/39,277) — Muskoka; Parry Sound

Nipissing — Nipissing; Sudbury; Timiskaming°

Norfolk, North (12,437/18,657);
Norfolk, South (16,710/20,899) — Norfolk

Norfolk, North (6,220/18,657); Oxford,
North (20,965/25,357); Oxford,
South (16,540/21,797); Wentworth
and Brant, North (4,679/18,717) — Oxford

Northumberland, East; Northumberland,
West; Peterborough, West (929/
17,005) — Northumberland

Ontario, North (13,887/20,689);
Ontario, South; Ontario, West
(9,728/16,695) — Ontario

Ontario, West (6,967/16,695); Toronto
Centre, City; Toronto, East, City;

1901	1961

Ontario† (continued)

1901	1961
Toronto, West, City; York, East; York, West; York, North (15,452/ 18,778)	York
Oxford, North (4,392/25,357); Perth, North; Perth, South (15,494/17,861); Wellington, North (2,839/23,801)	Perth
Peterborough, East (19,292/22,290); Peterborough, West (16,076/17,005); Victoria, North (698/16,258)	Peterborough
Peterborough, East (2,998/22,290); Victoria, North (3,561/16,258)	Haliburton
Renfrew, North; Renfrew, South; Nipissing (483/36,551)	Renfrew
Russell (20,282/35,166)	Russell
Victoria, North (11,999/16,258); Victoria, South	Victoria
Waterloo, North; Waterloo, South	Waterloo
Wellington, Centre (16,164/20,570); Wellington, North (15,715/23,801); Wellington, South	Wellington
Appears to be no population in area which developed into Cochrane	Cochrane
All other counties unchanged	

*County units which are approximately but not fully equivalent for the two decades are shown with an asterisk.

†Fractions shown in parentheses for some Ontario counties give the approximate proportion of the 1901 population which were located in the counties listed under the 1961 equivalents.

3

Institutional Forces

French-speaking Canadians in general insisted on the need for institutions which could safeguard and promote the French language and culture and give it full expression. In Sudbury this opinion was put in the following terms, "In order to have a culture (I am referring to the French minority in Ontario in particular), in order to be French, we need a French environment, we need French institutions, we need to be able to live in French." . . .

In Saskatoon a school teacher spoke strongly against what he considered to be the futile idea of trying to build a protective wall around a culture by means of institutions: "I don't think a culture is safeguarded or maintained. I don't think you can lock it behind walls. I don't think you can preserve it. It must live on its own power."

Royal Commission on Bilingualism and Biculturalism,
1965, pp. 63–64.

Can an ethnic or linguistic group which is threatened by superior numbers maintain itself if the necessary institutions are provided? Or is it true, as the schoolteacher suggests, that no language or culture can be preserved merely through the existence of institutions created out of artifact and law rather than demand? Recent developments in American race relations clearly show that political and legal institutions can sharply change the ongoing racial practices. On the other hand, the futile attempts of most immigrant groups in the United States to preserve their languages and other cultural characteristics by schools, churches, and societies show how easily one can overemphasize the role of many institutions in the survival of racial and ethnic groups. A balanced view would require some sort of intermediate position.

The pressures generated by government, education, and industry are

probably the most important institutional influences on linguistic maintenance in a nation. Although the exact role of these institutions involves
empirical questions which will be treated later, no overview of Canada
would be complete without some description of the institutional forces
operating in the Dominion. Showing whether an institution is compatible
or not with the maintenance of a language, as interesting as this may be,
is still different from demonstrating just how important its effect is in
quantitative terms. That the postage stamps of Canada are bilingual, to
take an extreme illustration, is of interest factually and symbolically, but
is hardly of great import for the maintenance of French or English.

FEDERAL GOVERNMENT

Although Upper and Lower Canada (Ontario and Quebec) were united
in 1841, modern Canada is an even more recent political entity, being
based on the British North America Act of 1867. Section 133 of the B.N.A.
Act allows for the usage of either English or French in the Canadian Parliament, Federal courts, and the courts and parliament of Quebec. The
two languages are also used in government documents and crown corporations of both the Federal and Quebec governments.

The nature of the British North America Act is itself disputed and
deeply involved in the British–French polemic. For some the Act is
regarded as a pact between the two founding groups, British and French.
This implies full linguistic equality in all phases of Canadian life throughout the nation. Others reject the equal partnership implied by this view
and contend the Act is a compact between provinces (*Montreal Star*, May
1, 1964, p. 25). From this perspective, the special privileges of French
Canadians and their language are restricted to Quebec and the provisions
explicitly made in the Act.

Nevertheless there are various unwritten and unofficial understandings
about the role of French Canadians in the government. Speakers in both
houses of parliament are alternately French- and English-speaking. Likewise English- and French-speaking judges take turns serving as Chief
Justice. The first Canadian-born Governor-General was English and the
second was French (Dufresne, 1965, p. 3). At one time French and English
Canadians also took turns serving as mayor of Montreal (Wade, 1955, p.
638). Starting with preconfederation politics, typically the prime minister
and his chief lieutenant have been of different ethnic groups, for example,
Baldwin and La Fontaine (Engelmann and Schwartz, 1967, p. 43–45).

Despite the laws of confederation and these informal practices, the
equality of the two tongues in the Federal government is not fully

achieved. Indeed, one of the major current complaints of French Canadians deals with the inferior position of their language in the national government. The Royal Commission on Bilingualism and Biculturalism (1965, pp. 73–74) noted that "French-speaking Canadians insistently brought up . . . their role in the Federal Civil Service, where the dominant working language is English." One particularly sore spot was the transportation services run by the national government where French Canadians encounter conductors and flight crew members unable to speak French. "Complaints of this kind were so numerous," noted the Commission, "so consistent and so familiar that nothing would be accomplished by piling quotation on quotation." Thanks to French Canadian pressures, many of these difficulties are being eliminated.

In Porter's (1958, p. 491) survey of the ethnic composition of the upper level of the Federal government bureaucracy, the "bureaucratic elite," he found only 13 percent were French Canadian, far below the group's proportion of the entire population of Canada.

It appears that recent turmoil in Canada has created greater interest in the Federal government requiring employees to be able to converse in French. Although a Canadian can correspond with the Federal government in either official language, French Canadian civil servants had to write or translate all letters and reports into English. The government has been engaged in an effort to increase the number of French-Canadian civil servants as well as train English-speaking workers in French in order to increase bilingualism. In this connection, it is worth noting that the Pearson cabinet included a rather large number of French-Canadian ministers.

As the following quotations from the *Montreal Star* (May 7, 1964, p. 36) indicate, the armed services was another area of government activity in which French is hardly the equal of English:

Departmental officials have long conceded that the French-speaking member of the armed forces doesn't have the same opportunities as the English-speaking serviceman for advancement . . . English is the working language of the Defense Department and the armed forces. A serviceman must be able to speak not only passable but good English to get ahead in the armed forces.

· · ·

None of the services has ever had a French-speaking chief of staff. No French-speaking Canadian has ever reached the top ranks in the Navy or RCAF.

· · ·

The three-battalion Royal 22nd Regiment operates entirely in French, but when it communicates . . . with other regiments it does so in English. There is no unit in the Navy or Air Force which uses French.

If a soldier wishes to remain in the Royal 22nd—and thus confine his service career to the infantry corps—the highest rank he can hope to attain is lieutenant-colonel.

If he wants to serve successfully in another unit or become a staff officer, he has to have an excellent command of English.

One attempt to overcome this situation was the founding of Le Collège Militaire Royal at St. Johns, where instruction is bilingual.

Not only are the armed forces viewed as institutions which "deliver up French Canadians to English unilingualism," but the schools available for servicemen's children outside of Quebec often provide no instruction in the French mother tongue (Royal Commission on Bilingualism and Biculturalism, 1965, p. 75).

Radio and Television

The national government plays an important role in these media not only as a result of its licensing powers, but because many radio and television stations are owned by the Federal government through the C.B.C. or, if privately owned, participate in the C.B.C. networks. The treatment of English and French in these forms of communication is of great importance. As Stanley (1960, p. 335–337) observes, the development of radio in the 1920's and 1930's meant that the sanctuary for French provided in the home could be penetrated for the first time.

In the mass media French encounters a difficulty which is repeated with respect to other institutions as well; namely, the position of French in Quebec is both strong and unchallenged by institutional developments but the position of French in many other parts of the Dominion is not supported by the institutions, or at least not without a fight. Whereas bilingual radio was initially supported by the Canadian government in Quebec, establishment of French-language stations in western Canada was by no means an easy task. For the most part, efforts to obtain free time for French-language programs on existing stations met with only limited success. It was not until 1946 that the first French-language station began to broadcast in western Canada, and this was supported by private funds. In turn, additional stations were constructed in the west, although often opposed by English Canadians.

Since many of the radio and television stations are owned by the government, requests for French-language stations are based on the bilingual equality recognized in the acts of confederation, but the compact occurred long before radio existed and obviously there is no mention of broadcasting. This has opened the way to counterarguments that the position of French is guaranteed in only Quebec.

As of 1962, there were four government owned and 23 privately run

French-language radio stations affiliated with the C.B.C. (*Canada Year-book*, 1962, p. 854). Of these 18 were in Quebec, two each in New Brunswick and Ontario, three in Saskatchewan, and one each in Manitoba and Alberta. There were also 14 French-language television stations affiliated with the C.B.C., 5 of which were owned by the government. One of these is found in Moncton, N.B., two in Ontario (Ottawa and Sturgeon Falls), and one in Winnipeg, and the remainder are located in Quebec. In effect, television and radio coverage for French Canadians is very good in the province of Quebec, where the greatest concentration exists, and in a number of French-Canadian centers elsewhere in the nation, but coverage is understandably poor in parts of Canada where the French Canadians are small in number and widely scattered. The proportion of radio and television stations in the C.B.C. French network located outside Quebec is as great or greater than the proportion of French Canadians located in these provinces, but the dispersion of French Canadians over such a large area means that a smaller percentage of non-Quebecers will be able to receive French-language broadcasts.

The Royal Commission on Bilingualism and Biculturalism (1965, pp. 71–72) encountered little complaint about either French- or English-language radio and television programming in Quebec, but, as might be expected, they often met with protests from French Canadians in other parts of Canada. Some of these questions, however, are in flux. A French-language FM radio station has been installed for use in metropolitan Toronto, an area in which there are 26,000 French-mother-tongue speakers, but only 3,000 who cannot also speak English.

PROVINCIAL GOVERNMENT

Although the position of French in the Federal government is hardly one of equality, at least as critical are the policies of the provinces. It is safe to say that the provinces of Canada have greater autonomy than states in the United States (Epstein, 1964, p. 47). The concentration of French Canadians in Quebec has meant not only that the government of one of the most populated provinces of Canada is solidly in the hands of the French, but has provided this group with a powerful instrument for the expression and negotiation of their interests with the remainder of Canada.

Provincial government is particularly important since Section 93 of the B.N.A. Act places control of education in the hands of each province. French Canadian interest in obtaining French-language schooling has not only been viewed with antipathy in a number of provinces, but has been aggravated by the religious issues between parochial and secular schools,

Roman Catholic vs. Protestant. The nature of the school systems available for French Canadians is certainly one of the sharpest points of friction for those located outside the protective embrace of Quebec. On the other hand, the autonomy given to the provinces has enabled Quebec to be a powerful instrument for the maintenance of the French language and culture. As Stanley (1960, pp. 346–347) observes, concern in Quebec exists over the invasion of the Federal government into the domain currently under provincial control. On the other hand, French Canadians located elsewhere in Canada look to the national government as a means for overcoming the objections and obstacles found in their local municipal and provincial governments.

Not only are French Canadians numerical minorities in all of the provinces outside Quebec but, with the exception of New Brunswick, they form rather small percentages of the population. As a consequence the recognition of French as an official provincial language and the availability of publicly supported schools where French is the language of instruction is largely out of the hands of French Canadians in most of Canada. Conditions in the provinces range from Quebec, where the linguistic rights of both the English and French are officially recognized and protected, to British Columbia, which is adamant in refusing French-Canadian or Catholic interests. In New Brunswick, although English is the only official language, French is sometimes used on an unofficial basis in the legislature, civil service, schools, and courts by the sizable French minority (*Montreal Star*, April 11, 1964, p. 5).

Contemporary Education

Unless otherwise indicated, the status of French education summarized below is based on letters received from departments of education in various provinces and a manuscript prepared by Charles Bilodeau which was revised in October, 1963 (Department of External Affairs, Reference Paper No. 84). No attention is paid to English-language education, since such needs are generally met throughout the nation.

In Quebec all grades are denominational, either Roman Catholic or Protestant, with the medium of instruction being either French or English. The latter tongue is used in nearly all Protestant schools and French is the usual language of instruction in Catholic schools. In addition, English is taught as a second language beginning with the fifth grade in schools in which French is the medium of instruction. French is taught as a second tongue beginning with grade 3 in schools in which English is the language of instruction.

In Ontario there are about 27 bilingual high schools and a large number of separate grade schools available for French-language instruction. As of September 1956, there were 2305 French-speaking teachers employed in the elementary schools of the province (Ontario Department of Education, 1956, p. 9). Although these separate schools are tax-supported, they do not receive their share of the taxes (Lamontagne, 1960, p. 363). According to the *Montreal Star* (April 20, 1964, p. 27), several important complaints remain about French education in Ontario, particularly on the secondary level. The French-Canadian Education Association has noted the absence of French textbooks for grades 11 to 13 and their shortage in the preceding two grades. Secondary education is largely in English, although provincial regulations permit instruction in French. A shortage of French-speaking teachers is attributed to the lack of French-language high schools. One of the basic requests is for French-language schools rather than just French classes.

There are no French-language schools in Prince Edward Island, although there are no specific provincial rules about this matter. French is a required subject in the junior and senior high schools, and some elementary schools introduce French at the third-grade level. In a small area of the province instruction is given in both French and English.

The basic language of instruction in publicly supported schools is French in those parts of Nova Scotia in which the Acadian French are concentrated, although English instruction begins in the second or third year of elementary school. Basic instructional materials are available in French, with the exception of senior high school texts in mathematics, the sciences, and history. In parts of Richmond County, where the numbers of French- and English-mother-tongue children are fairly balanced, instruction tends to be in English. Although there is no required second language in the public schools, a French course is taken by nearly all English-speaking children from grades 7 through 12. The language of instruction to be used in the schools is decided by the local school authorities which tend to favor English unless the population is almost completely French.

Publicly supported schools in which French is the language of instruction are available in New Brunswick, both on the elementary and secondary levels. In most instances they represent separate schools rather than special classes in the same school. This is made possible by the high concentration of French Canadians in parts of New Brunswick. In addition, French is a compulsory course for students in English-language schools from grades 5 through 10. It is optional in later grades and is sometimes available for earlier years. As is the case for Nova Scotia, the language of instruction is determined by the local school boards.

There are no publicly supported schools in the prairie provinces of Manitoba and Saskatchewan with French as the language of instruction.

The School Acts of both provinces require that English be the language of instruction. Saskatchewan law permits local districts to provide French-language instruction for not more than one hour a day in all grades beginning with the first year of elementary school. In a recent year boards in 54 communities with important French-Canadian constituencies took advantage of this one-hour option. French language is also offered as an optional subject in grades 9 through 11 and is taken by about 60 percent of the students in order to meet the University language requirements for entrance. Likewise French is the most common second-language course in Manitoba schools. It is offered also in grades 1 through 12 at the option of the local school board. There are two programs offered in French courses, one primarily for native French speakers and another for students whose native tongue is not French.

In the third prairie province, Alberta, English is also the mandatory language of instruction. However, local school boards are permitted to use French as the language of instruction in grades 1 and 2 provided that at least one hour a day be devoted to English language instruction. Beginning with grade 3, English must be the language of instruction. Up to two hours per day in grade 3 and no more than one hour per day in later grades may be devoted to instruction in French. French is offered in all high schools of the province and, although an optional subject, it is the most common second language taken by the students.

In Newfoundland and British Columbia the number of French Canadians is rather small. There are no publicly supported French-language schools in British Columbia. French is taught as a required second language in the eighth grade of all secondary schools. Newfoundland, which has no rule that prevents French Canadians from establishing publicly supported schools, has instruction in English throughout the province. There are two exceptions in newly established communities where both English and French are languages of instruction in the same school. French is offered as a second language for those planning to go beyond high school and it may be taken in the elementary schools as well.

In brief, this review of current Canadian education indicates that there is a wide range of practices in the provinces, ranging from conditions of almost maximum support for native French speakers to conditions in many provinces which strongly undermine French by providing only minimal work in this language and by making English the basic language of instruction. In interpreting the influence of school systems on linguistic maintenance, it is important to distinguish between schools where a French-language course is offered French Canadians from systems which provide complete instruction in the French tongue. In the former case knowledge of English is required for most classwork and therefore native

French speakers may be handicapped. In the latter type of system French is a self-sufficient tongue and its native speakers are not penalized, at least in the schools. In any regard either system is more likely to facilitate French than schools in which no instruction is offered in that tongue except in the later grades when French is available as a foreign language.

Earlier Developments

The development of French linguistic instruction and official language status in the various provinces of Canada is not to be taken for granted or viewed as a property of haphazard structural variations; rather, to some degree these developments may themselves be seen as a by-product of demographic forces. Particularly in the newer parts of Canada, demographic changes led to a number of significant shifts in the position of French.

French explorers and fur traders were the first to open up western Canada. Along with French-speaking hybrids, the Métis, they were of sufficient number and strength after the Riel rebellion that the Manitoba Act of 1870 provided for separate schools and official equality of the French language with English. Stanley (1960, p. 322) describes the early days of the new province of Manitoba:

In the first legislature, almost half of the twenty-four members were French-speaking, and it was a French Canadian, Marc Girard, whom the Lieutenant-Governor called upon to form the first provincial ministry. In 1871 a school system was established which took as its model that of the province of Quebec, with its two governing boards, Protestant and Roman Catholic. In its early days Manitoba was a bilingual province; French and English were spoken in its towns and villages, taught in its schools and heard in its legislative chambers.

As the early French Canadian settlers became swamped by the English and other ethnic groups, the position of their language was weakened and destroyed. The section of the original constitution of Manitoba which provided for official equality of French with English was repealed in 1890 by the legislature and the dual educational system was also ended. These acts were fought on the provincial and national level, leading to a compromise in 1896 (the Laurier-Greenway agreement) by which elementary teaching might be provided in French. In turn, however, the legislature eliminated even these privileges in 1916 (Stanley, 1960, pp. 324–325).

In one form or another, this process was repeated in the newly created provinces of Alberta and Saskatchewan. Through the Northwest Territories Act of 1875 and an act of 1877, the official language status of French as well as English was guaranteed by parliament. The legislature abolished the use of French for debates in the Northwest Territories only 15 years later (Scott, 1960, p. 99). Likewise the guarantees of the Saskatchewan Act of 1905 were, in the words of Stanley (1960, p. 331),

". . . battered, broken, and breached by the repeated assaults of hostile provincial legislation. All that was left to the western French Canadians of the equal status of former years was a state of uneasy truce in Manitoba (where French was taught on sufferance in defiance of the law), one hour a day of instruction in the French language in the schools of Saskatchewan, and one hour daily in Alberta after the first two primary grades."

In the annexation of the Territory of Keewatin to Manitoba no guarantee of the educational rights of the numerical minority was included, although separate schools had existed prior to annexation (Wade, 1955, p. 616).

These policies sprang not only from antipathy toward the French and Catholicism, but also reflected a general expectation of assimilation into the English-speaking world. Describing the education of foreign groups who had settled en masse in the western provinces, the Superintendent of Education in 1900 called "especial attention to the fact that the best work accomplished in these schools is done by English speaking teachers practically unacquainted with the language of the colony." (Report of the Council of Public Instruction of the Northwest Territories, 1900, p. 25).

In the junior, middle, and senior forms of most schools in Saskatchewan in 1911, about as many or more students were registered for Latin as French (Annual Report of the Department of Education of the Province of Saskatchewan, 1911, pp. 19–20). The fact that a sizable segment of the nation's population was French appeared to have no great effect on the propensity to learn the tongue in western Canada during this period. One is tempted to interpret these conditions as a product of attitudes toward the French, but it should be kept in mind that the expression of these attitudes was made possible by demographic shifts which greatly undermined the initially high proportion of prairie settlers who were French Canadian.

In Ontario, for example, French has been subject to a number of assaults through the years, but it is in a reasonably strong position in the school system today. In the second decade of this century restrictive actions in Ontario raised a furor among French Canadians generally and seriously undermined enlistment efforts among this group during World War I (Wade, 1955, ch. 11). Of perhaps greater significance was the introduction of Regulation 17 by the Ontario Department of Education in 1912 which "imposed English as the sole language of instruction in the elementary schools, with minor exceptions, and placed the bilingual Catholic schools under English Protestant inspectors. The study of French was confined to one hour a day." (Wade, 1955, pp. 627–628). The province also withdrew financial support for the Ottawa separate schools (Wade, 1955, pp. 634–636). The increase of French Canadians from a handful in 1863 to over 600,000 by 1961 created " 'a new condition in Ontario' and a group not lightly to be denationalized by the stroke of a Protestant pen." (Kirkconnell, 1960, pp. 53–54). Recognizing that there are a number of criticisms which French Canadians make of their position in the school system of Ontario, the fact remains that numerous battles over the role of French in the province's school system did not lead to the same defeat as occurred in areas where the French Canadians were numerically less important.

Current Educational Problems

Debate on the provincial school systems continues through the present time, often hinging on whether the provinces, which clearly have jurisdiction over schooling, are obliged to follow the "spirit" of confederation by granting public funds for the maintenance of separate schools. One difficulty revolves about teacher's colleges in the Maritimes, Ontario, and the Prairie provinces. They are needed for the training of teachers for French areas and for a supply of French-language teachers for English schools (Royal Commission on Bilingualism and Biculturalism, 1965, p. 66). Both New Brunswick and Ontario have bilingual teacher's colleges, but there is some demand in at least New Brunswick for an exclusively French institution. One additional problem is that many French-Canadian teachers in Quebec will not accept positions elsewhere because of the absence of French institutions.

French is taught as a second language to a rather sizable segment of the Canadian population, regardless of their mother tongue. During the 1957–1958 school year, nearly 70 percent of the high school students in seven provinces were enrolled in a French course. Considering that New Brunswick, Ontario, and Quebec were excluded, the figure for all of Canada would have been even higher (Dominion Bureau of Statistics, 1960, pp. 34–35, 95–103). Whether due to the French-Canadian separatist movement or other forces, course offerings in French have expanded in recent years. Witness the following excerpts from the "Back to School" supplement of a Montreal newspaper (*The Gazette*, August 25, 1964, pp. 46–47):

Expansion of French instruction into elementary schools continues in many parts of the country, with Newfoundland and British Columbia the notable exceptions. French as a second language is available as early as grade three in Prince Edward Island and grade four in Manitoba and Alberta.

. . .

Referring to Manitoba

Some schools will introduce courses in French for grade one and two pupils who speak it as a first language. As last year, French will be taught as a second language from grade four up.

.   .   .

Referring to Regina

The separate schools report teaching of oral French in an increased number of schools.

.   .   .

[In] Calgary public and separate schools . . . the teaching of French will extend from grade four to senior high school.

.   .   .

Edmonton public schools are expanding the oral French program to the extent of teacher availability, with a 20-per-cent increase in both teachers and students expected.

An important difficulty in the development of bilingualism among native English speakers is clearly the inadequate French-language teaching facilities and programs available in many provinces. The Royal Commission on Bilingualism and Biculturalism (1965, p. 68) encountered many Canadians who deplored the poor teaching techniques and the lack of qualified teachers. It should be noted, however, that the absence of any functional utility in bilingualism for many Canadians, both French- and English-mother-tongue speakers, no doubt minimizes the need and desire to retain a second tongue which is in many parts of Canada of rather minimal daily use. "A number of English-speaking people, like some French-speaking Quebecers," observed the Commission (p. 68), "told us that their main handicap to learning the second language was the lack of opportunity to speak it outside the classroom." The point is that a large number of Canadians are exposed to the second official language in the course of their elementary and secondary education. For many, however, there is no real need to acquire this second language since it is hardly used in their daily lives. As a consequence at least part of the failure to develop widespread bilingualism in Canada is due, both directly and indirectly, to the linguistic composition of the communities as well as the position of each language in the local and regional economic life.

No review of recent educational developments would be complete without at least brief mention of technical education in Quebec, a long-standing subject of criticism, particularly on the part of English-speaking Canadians. The major objection hinges on the emphasis of a classical education and training for classicial professions at the expense of providing little technical training to meet the current demands of industry and commerce for newer skills. French Canada has also criticized itself, at least the critique of French-Canadian education and language by Brother Jean-Paul Desbiens in 1960 broke all publishing records in Quebec (*The Gazette*, August 31, 1964, p. 2). Education in Quebec is undergoing a thorough reexamination and will no doubt move in the direction of the demands created by modern industry and trade (witness, for example, the report of the Royal Commission of Inquiry on Education in the Province of Quebec, 1963, 1964). It is difficult to determine how severe these earlier shortcomings were, although Hughes (1943) provides ample demonstration of the problems, but it is clear that French-Canadian technical disadvantages will decline in the near future.

The position of each language in the Federal and Provincial governments may change in the near future. Some of the difficulties faced by French-speaking Canadians in the Federal government would be eliminated if recent proposals by the Royal Commission on Bilingualism and Biculturalism (1967) and the Trudeau government are put into effect. On the other hand, the position of English is under reexamination by some of Quebec's intellectuals and politicians, with a unilingual French Province as the possible outcome. In Montreal's suburb of St. Leonard, for example, an effort was made in the autumn of 1969 to eliminate the unique usage of both English and French languages as instructional mediums in the Catholic school system (*Calgary Herald*, September 10, 1969, p. 20).

INDUSTRY

The linguistic pressures generated by industry in Canada are very much in favor of English. Not only is English the technical language of Canada, but it is the tongue spoken by those who run and control big business. First, there is an enormous investment of American and British companies in Canada. Second, even in Canadian-owned industries, the English-speaking Canadians are dominant. The economic subordination of French Canadians occurs in a major French center such as Montreal. Drawing upon Jamieson's study of directors of Montreal firms in 1935, Hughes (1943, p. 203) reports that 768 out of 861 directors of 83 large companies were English. English tends to be the language of technology which adds further influence, as the following quotation suggests: "If I get a job as a technician with the Bell Telephone and want to get to the top then I must speak English because the electronic and electrical instruments come from the United States." (Royal Commission on Bilingualism and Biculturalism, 1965, p. 77).

Based on an examination of the ethnic origins of Canadian directors in 170 dominant corporations in the economy, Porter (1961, p. 493) concludes that economic power is almost exclusively held by those of British origin:

Of the 760 persons here considered, only 51 (6.7 per cent) can be classified as French Canadians although this group makes up about one-third of the population. Of those French Canadians who have made their way to the boards of the larger corporations, one-third are lawyers and 14 others have important political affiliations. The rest are mainly those with directorships in the two small French-Canadian banks. There are no more than a handful who . . . could be classed as top-flight industrialists.

With an overwhelming concentration of economic power in the hands of English speakers, it is clear that the avenue to the top is in this tongue. "Everyone knows that here [Chicoutimi], where the population is 98 per-cent French Canadian, big business has made English the working lan-guage and anyone who wants to work his way up at the plant has to use English" (Royal Commission on Bilingualism and Biculturalism, 1965, p. 77). Brazeau (1958) and Keyfitz (1963) have both described some of the linguistic disadvantages faced by French Canadians in industry.

Based on an admittedly small sample of English speakers, de Jocas and Rocher (1961, pp. 466–477) report substantial differences in intergenera-tional occupational mobility patterns between the two linguistic groups in Quebec's urban centers. They find, for example, that English-speaking sons tend to shift from manual to nonmanual occupations to a greater degree than do the French. Likewise sons of French-Canadian farmers who change occupations are likely to become unskilled workers, whereas sons of English-speaking farmers tend to enter white-collar occupations. There is also an unusually low degree of occupational inheritance among English-Canadian sons of unskilled workers in Quebec. In summary, comparing French and English Quebecers, "The former go up the scale, so to speak step by step, while the latter seem to move more rapidly to the top occupational levels." (de Jocas and Rocher, 1961, pp. 476–477). Undoubtedly at least part of these differences in mobility patterns reflect occupational advantages held for English speakers compared with those whose native tongue is French.

In addition to the control of large Canadian corporations by English-speaking Canadians, it is important to recognize the fact that many seg-ments of industry are in the hands of Americans and the British. At one time British investment far exceeded that made by the United States, whereas currently the opposite situation exists. In either case major seg-ments of the Canadian economy are linked to and part of an English-language system. Granted that there is considerable variation between sec-tors of the economy in their degree of foreign control, nonresident owner-ship of business as a whole (manufacturing, petroleum, mining, merchandising, railways, and utilities) was 34 percent in 1959. Coupled with the fact that United States investments alone comprise more than three-fourths of all foreign investments (*Canada Year Book*, 1962, pp. 1081–1082), this indicates the tremendous English-speaking influence in Canada's industry and commerce derived from American and British activities. Although these data on foreign ownership are not the most pertinent and actually provide only indirect evidence of the language pressures generated in industry, one need only skim through Canadian magazines and newspaper advertisements to readily appreciate the degree industrial activities in the nation are in the hands of American subsidiaries.

The role of French as a business language may increase through such policies as Quebec's ownership of power-producing stations and the formation of a provincially sponsored investment company, Société Generale de Financement du Quebec (Siekman, 1965, pp. 161–162); however, so far the linguistic forces generated by large-scale industry strongly favor English. Witness the novelty of the event reported below:

"You know, they are building Manicouagan in French," a proud Quebecker said today.

He meant that the blueprints and specifications for the multi-million-dollar hydroelectric plant under construction on the Manicouagan River were in French as well as English.

"You have no idea, but there is something precedent-breaking in a French-Canadian engineer getting to read building plans in his own language," a visitor was told. "The government has gone to great pains to make it possible this time" (*New York Times*, March 17, 1965).

The effect of economic and industrial pressures on the maintenance of the French mother tongue as well as second-language learning is a topic that will be considered carefully later in this volume. However, it is important to note that composition here too will play an important role; for example, despite the fact that English is the dominant economic language in say both Vancouver and Montreal, the work-world chances for a monolingual French speaker in the latter city are still far greater than in Vancouver.

THE PRINTED WORD

Of 11 French-language daily newspapers in 1963, all but two are located in Quebec. There are three in both Montreal and the city of Quebec, and one each in Granby, Sherbrooke, and Trois-Rivières. Of the two located outside the province, one is in Moncton, N.B., center of an important concentration of French Canadians, and the other is in Ottawa. which borders on the French-Canadian center in Hull, Quebec (*Canada Year Book*, 1965, p. 850).

Although population concentration and composition play important roles in providing the necessary readership base for a successful daily newspaper, it appears that French-language newspapers labor under greater handicaps than do those printed in English. Looking at what the Canadian census describes as "Other Major Urban Areas," that is, constellations of communities that are too small to be "Census Metropolitan Areas," it is clear that those communities which have sizable French settlements are less likely to have daily newspapers. Of the 10 urban areas in which French Canadians constitute 15 percent or less of the residents, at least nine have daily newspapers, all of which are in English. Of the seven urban areas in which French Canadians make up 85 percent or more of the poulation, five have no daily newspaper, one has a French-language paper, and the other has both an English and a French daily.

While the non-French communities within this class of urban centers tend to be somewhat larger, it is clear that there is an additional factor operating. Moreover, it is not to be explained simply in terms of proximity to the dailies of larger urban centers—these urban areas are not part of larger census metropolitan areas. Moreover, several of the English newspapers are located in cities no farther from Toronto than are some of the newspaperless French communities from Montreal. It is not possible at this point to determine whether these differences are due to difficulty in obtaining advertisements or other economic handicaps which French-Canadian papers face.

Another way of thinking about the linguistic differences is that there are 100 English-language daily newspapers in Canada in 1963, of which 47 are published in cities of less than 30,000 population. By contrast all 11 of the French dailies are published in cities with more than 30,000 residents.

CONCLUSIONS

From an impressionistic viewpoint, attitudes toward the French by other Canadians sometimes remind one of the paternalistic attitude toward Negroes on the part of many whites in the United States. The linguistic demands are complicated by supercilious views of French Canadians on the part of their countrymen as well as, in part, by the Protestant–Roman Catholic clash. The distance between English- and French-speaking Canadians is demonstrated by the existence of cultural exchange programs between the two groups, for example, Visites Interprovinciales, which provides opportunities for the groups to get to know each other better (Gagnon, 1952, pp. 1–2).

In some respects, both French- and English-speaking Canadians are equally subject to cultural influences emanating from English-speaking America. Much is translated into French and therefore, while French Canadians may become Americanized to some degree, they need not lose their tongue while doing so, although many English words enter the French language, *franglais*. Looking at the Sunday comics of a French-Canadian paper, as I did with *La Presse*, an important Montreal daily, one is impressed with how virtually all 12 pages of comics are American imports, but not a word of English appears. Thus, although Donald Duck, The Little King, and Mandrake the Magician are spread into French Canada, they are known as "Donald le Canard," "Le Roitelet," and "Mandrake le magicien." To be sure, French newspaper advertisements will often have a phrase or word or two in English; for some reason many companies insist on giving their names or those of their products only in English, for example, "Miss Clairol Hair Color Bath" appears at the end of an entirely French advertisement. Likewise, most cigarette packages manage to be not quite fully bilingual (see Elkin, 1961). The point remains that much of the American culture reaching French Canadians is transmitted in the latter's language and therefore is less of a threat than might appear otherwise.

In addition, there are various elements of the French-Canadian world in which language serves to insulate French Canadians from American culture to a greater degree than their English-speaking countrymen. In network television, for example, generally a far smaller proportion of French-language programs are produced in the United States and more tends to be produced in Canada itself. Proximity to the United States, coupled with volume advantages which American publications possess even when they publish Canadian editions, greatly threaten English-language magazines of Canadian origin. Based on the O'Leary Royal Commission report, Irving (1962, p. 225) points out that 92 of the 96 periodicals in Canada with newsstand circulations of more than 10,000 copies a month are American. "The most important of the three general problems faced by the mass media in Canada is unquestionably our proximity to the rich and powerful United States of America. We share with such multilingual countries as Switzerland and Belgium the difficulties inherent in being next-door neighbor to a much larger country with a common language." By contrast, this is of considerably less threat to French-Canadian publications.

The presence of American tourists helps to increase the number of bilinguals among French Canadians in resort areas. In 1963 there were 31 million American residents in Canada, of whom more than 10 million remained for one or more nights (*Canada Year Book*, 1965, pp. 949–950). Although less than 10 percent of all foreign automobiles entered or left Canada through the province of Quebec, American tourists have a notable impact in the city of Quebec and Montreal. Many tourist services, however, probably require only a minimal knowledge of English and, moreover, the percentage of French Canadians affected is probably not too great.

Education, industry, government, and, to a lesser degree, the mass media are the most important institutions in determining whether a language will maintain its position among native speakers and its ability to gain new speakers. In each instance, French is handicapped. However, since these handicaps are based in part on the linguistic composition of the areas of Canada, it will be necessary to take demographic factors into account before gauging their quantitative importance for linguistic maintenance.

Population composition's direct influence on institutions is most clearly seen in the realm of education and the official language status of French in provincial affairs. Witness the strong position of French in Quebec's educational system and the deterioration of the French language's educational and political status in the western provinces after French Canadians became vastly outnumbered by English-speaking countrymen. To be sure, the nature of the educational systems in the various provinces are by no means solely a function of composition, for example, English fares better in Quebec than does French in some of the other provinces.

By way of summary the compatibility or incompatibility of various institutions in Canada with the maintenance of monolingual speech communities, bilingualism, and linguistic transfer across generations from parents to children can be readily determined. A listing of such features in itself is only a partial accomplishment, since the critical question remains unanswered: namely, what influence do these institutional practices have on linguistic maintenance independent of the demographic environment in which they occur? In later chapters some preliminary answers are given.

II

BILINGUALISM AND MOTHER-TONGUE MAINTENANCE

4

Some Causes of Bilingualism

It is best to recognize, at the outset, that bilingualism is caused by a wide variety of factors. Not only do the causes range from the very subtle and personal, on the one hand, to broad aggregative characteristics on the other extreme, but they also differ in their overall significance and impact on bilingualism. What is most important at this stage is not systematic inclusion of all the possible causes; such a mixture represents no real contribution to any systematic understanding of multilingualism. Nor is there much to be gained by a Durkheimian devastation of alternative approaches. Unless the data are exceptionally good and the methods extraordinarily appropriate, very little can be accomplished to change anyone's predispositions. The cruel truth is that more than one perspective can often provide a satisfactory interpretation. The aim of the game, in dealing with the social factors influencing bilingualism, is to replace conjecture with substantive information in as orderly a way as possible. In turn, one must examine the causes of linguistic retention among the children of bilinguals, careful to use the same set of causal factors. By following this strategy it should be possible to determine the significance of the ecological forces—broadly conceived—that influence the creation of bilingualism and their impact on mother-tongue maintenance in the next generation.

AN ETHNIC EFFECT

Ethnic origin influences the propensity to learn the official languages in Canada, particularly the acquisition of French by those with some other native tongue. In all provinces in 1961, as well as in most earlier periods, the French language has a much stronger attraction for French Canadians than for other ethnic groups whose members possess some other mother tongue. Among nonnative speakers of French in New Brunswick, for example, members of the French ethnic group are far more likely

91

to learn French than are either the British or those of other ethnic origin (in 1961, 18 percent versus 2.6 and 4.1 percent, respectively). This holds for the two preceding decades as well, but not so much for 1931 and even less for 1921 (see Table 1).

Except for Quebec, however, where in recent decades somewhat more than 50 percent of the French learn their ancestral language if they possess another mother tongue, "linguistic recovery" is not terribly strong for the French. In many of the other provinces the recovery rates run little higher than 10 percent. There is neither an upward nor downward trend over time in these recovery rates. Bilingualism in Canada fails to recapture the vast majority of those French Canadians raised in a competing mother tongue. Through much of Canada, once a child of French origin has been raised in some other tongue, he is lost to the French language. Even in Quebec, where the overwhelming majority of the French ethnic group have French as their mother tongue, only about half the strays are recovered through bilingualism.

Several features of French language acquisition are more meaningful when contrasted with analogous figures for the learning of English among nonnative speakers (see Table 2). Even a casual comparison between the two tables indicates that English is acquired as a second language far more frequently. The recovery power of English among the British is much greater than the analogous pattern for the French ethnic group. In Saskatchewan, for example, 84 percent of the British with some other mother tongue can speak English, whereas less than 10 percent of the French can speak their ancestral tongue if they were raised in some other language. Indeed, with the exception of Quebec since 1941, acquisition of English as a second language is far more likely among the French ethnic group than is acquisition of French. (Bear in mind that this refers only to those with a different mother tongue in each case.)

In some cases the recovery of English among the British ethnic group is less complete than the acquisition of English by other ethnic groups. Even the French in several provinces have a higher rate of bilingualism in English than do the British in 1961. Of those whose mother tongue is not English in Saskatchewan, for example, nearly 90 percent of the French ethnic group learn this language whereas 84 percent of the British recover English. No explanation is readily apparent for these surprising differences, but one should not lose sight of the fact that the recovery of English is extremely high among those of British descent. Except for Quebec, the return to English for the British is much higher than the recovery power of people of French origin. Patterns of bilingualism in recent decades in Canada have very much favored the English language. Exposure to the risk of intergenerational switching to English is high because of bilingual-

TABLE 1

Acquisition of French Among Those with Another Mother Tongue, by Province and Ethnic Group: 1916 to 1961[a]

Province and Year	Percent Learning French			Province and Year	Percent Learning French		
	British	French	Other		British	French	Other
Newfoundland				Manitoba			
1951	0.4	5.8	0.9	1916	2.1	4.1	3.4
1961	0.4	4.2	3.3	1921	2.9	16.1	3.6
				1931	1.5	7.5	2.1
Prince Edward				1941	1.2	8.5	1.4
1921	1.9	—	4.3	1951	1.3	12.4	1.5
1931	1.0	3.5	2.5	1961	1.5	9.6	1.6
1941	0.6	1.3	1.1	Saskatchewan			
1951	0.8	7.0	3.2	1916	1.7	6.9	1.7
1961	0.7	6.0	1.8	1921	2.3	9.4	2.1
				1931	1.2	9.0	1.2
Nova Scotia				1941	0.8	4.1	0.8
1921	2.0	1.0	2.8	1951	0.8	9.4	0.9
1931	1.1	1.9	1.6	1961	0.9	8.3	0.9
1941	0.8	4.8	1.1	Alberta			
1951	1.0	7.1	1.0	1916	2.2	9.5	9.4
1961	1.1	7.7	1.3	1921	2.9	6.0	2.6
				1931	1.8	9.0	1.6
New Brunswick				1941	1.1	5.1	1.1
1921	3.4	0.3	6.7	1951	1.2	8.3	1.2
1931	2.7	5.7	5.4	1961	1.4	7.4	1.3
1941	2.1	16.3	4.2	British Columbia			
1951	2.4	21.8	3.6	1921	4.0	6.1	2.8
1961	2.6	18.0	4.1	1931	2.5	4.2	1.9
				1941	1.7	5.4	1.1
Quebec				1951	1.8	7.2	1.4
1921	29.8	32.4	38.8	1961	2.0	7.0	1.9
1931	28.8	27.9	38.1	Yukon			
1941	27.6	53.8	36.6	1941	3.2	12.8	1.2
1951	26.7	56.4	37.2	1951	2.6	11.5	1.5
1961	26.6	51.8	37.0	1961	3.0	7.4	2.6
Ontario				Northwest Territories			
1921	2.5	3.5	2.8				
1931	1.6	1.1	2.4	1941	7.4	25.0	9.5
1941	1.4	7.1	1.7	1951	4.4	24.8	3.2
1951	1.8	12.0	2.3	1961	5.4	13.8	2.3
1961	2.2	11.9	2.8				

[a]Data for 1916, 1921, and 1931 refer to the population 10 years of age and older; for other periods, the data are for all ages. Years shown for each province are the only years available.

TABLE 2

Acquisition of English Among Those with Another Mother Tongue, by Province and Ethnic Group: 1916 to 1961[a]

Province and Year	Percent Learning English			Province and Year	Percent Learning English		
	British	French	Other		British	French	Other
Newfoundland				Manitoba			
1951	93.1	93.3	43.9	1916	90.5	84.2	74.5
1961	61.7	89.3	65.3	1921	97.1	90.0	88.2
Prince Edward				1931	94.1	88.3	91.7
1921		96.5	95.7	1941	94.1	88.3	91.7
1931	99.5	97.2	96.3	1951	94.4	87.0	90.0
1941	97.1	91.0	99.8	1961	83.8	86.9	93.1
1951	94.5	89.3	94.5	Saskatchewan			
1961	70.0	84.2	93.5	1916	96.4	86.7	78.3
Nova Scotia				1921	82.5	89.9	87.2
1921	68.6	86.1	90.8	1931	98.6	92.8	89.7
1931	99.0	86.0	92.6	1941	95.8	91.0	93.6
1941	98.5	83.3	96.7	1951	95.5	89.5	92.8
1951	98.0	80.7	95.3	1961	84.0	89.6	94.7
1961	91.3	84.8	92.7	Alberta			
New Brunswick				1916	98.3	89.7	83.5
1921		64.1	94.7	1921	96.9	90.8	88.7
1931	66.3	64.0	96.1	1931	98.8	90.0	87.8
1941	67.3	47.2	94.5	1941	97.4	89.1	93.4
1951	61.5	45.1	90.6	1951	94.7	84.9	90.3
1961	59.9	46.2	87.0	1961	87.2	87.5	95.2
Quebec				British Columbia			
1921		41.1	84.7	1921	94.3	98.0	74.3
1931	57.3	38.8	85.3	1931	99.7	98.2	81.4
1941	56.3	25.6	84.0	1941	96.4	97.7	90.1
1951	50.2	24.1	75.5	1951	99.4	98.1	93.1
1961	49.9	24.0	66.4	1961	83.7	91.5	94.3
Ontario				Yukon			
1921	90.5	86.8	91.1	1941	100.0	98.5	93.0
1931	96.4	84.5	90.5	1951	92.2	97.7	89.2
1941	94.9	78.3	95.8	1961	96.9	91.4	97.4
1951	92.9	77.2	90.8	Northwest Territories			
1961	74.7	77.3	90.1	1941	88.7	86.8	25.1
				1951	68.5	85.1	30.1
				1961	70.4	91.9	44.0

[a]Data for 1916, 1921, and 1931 refer to the population 10 years of age and older; for other periods, the data are for all ages. Years shown for each province are the only years available.

ism. Also recovery is much greater for the British than the French among those who have been raised in a mother tongue other than their ancestral language.

Mother Tongue

As noted in Chapter 2, the percentage of the French ethnic group with French mother tongue declined sharply between 1931 and 1961 in a number of provinces. Tables 3 and 4 below provide a detailed examination, decade by decade, of the mother-tongue composition of the French and British ethnic groups, respectively, in each province. The most striking feature is the steady deterioration of French as the mother tongue of the French ethnic group in most provinces (see Table 3). English is the native language of half or more of the French Canadians living in Newfoundland, Prince Edward Island, Nova Scotia, British Columbia, and the Yukon; it is the mother tongue of at least 30 percent of the French Canadians in all but two of the remaining provinces. The notable exceptions are Quebec and New Brunswick, although there is evidence of a steady deterioration in the latter province as well. What is most important, however, is the persistent trend for the decline of French. With the exception of the prairie provinces between 1916 and 1921, in all provinces and in all other periods the position of French is declining (see Arès, 1964 a, b).

With almost equal persistence, the position of French as a mother tongue among the British has increased (see Table 4). However, the level of linguistic gain is extremely low in all provinces except Quebec. Moreover, the changes are small. In Nova Scotia, for example, French was the mother tongue of less than 0.05 percent of the British in 1921, 0.1 percent in 1931, 0.2 percent in 1941 and 1951, and 0.3 percent in 1961.

The deterioration of the French-mother-tongue position in all parts of Canada except Quebec, when compared with the enormous strength of English as the mother tongue of the British, suggests an extremely important conclusion about the relationship between bilingualism and mother-tongue retention. Although there is no clear-cut temporal trend found in the magnitude of bilingualism among the French-mother-tongue group, the position of French as the mother tongue of the French ethnic group is steadily deteriorating. What this suggests, in an admittedly crude fashion, is that trends in bilingualism and mother-tongue maintenance need not run together. The forces causing bilingualism are not necessarily the same or of equal importance as the forces influencing the mother tongue transferred by bilingual parents to their children. The rates of bilingualism among the French-mother-tongue group are stable in recent decades, yet the English-mother-tongue composition of French Canadians increases steadily. For the moment, until a more adequate

TABLE 3

Mother-Tongue Composition of the French Ethnic Group, by Province: 1916 to 1961[a]

Province and Year	Percent Distribution			Province and Year	Percent Distribution		
	English	French	Other		English	French	Other
Newfoundland				Manitoba (*continued*)			
1951	78.1	21.8	0.1	1931A	11.2	87.1	1.7
1961	85.2	14.7	0.1	1931	12.1	86.0	1.8
Prince Edward				1941	14.6	84.7	0.7
1921	2.0	98.0	0.0	1951	22.5	76.0	1.5
1931A	19.5	80.5	0.0	1961	30.3	67.2	2.4
1931	22.7	77.3	0.0	Saskatchewan			
1941	29.1	70.9	0.0	1916	10.1	88.5	1.4
1951	46.4	53.6	0.0	1921	6.8	91.7	1.5
1961	55.2	44.4	0.4	1931A	17.1	80.3	2.6
Nova Scotia				1931	18.9	78.5	2.6
1921	4.4	95.5	0.1	1941	23.4	75.4	1.2
1931A	29.0	70.7	0.2	1951	32.7	64.9	2.4
1931	32.1	67.8	0.2	1961	43.2	54.5	2.3
1941	39.6	60.3	0.1	Alberta			
1951	49.2	50.7	0.2	1916	13.7	83.5	2.8
1961	56.9	42.8	0.2	1921	11.3	87.1	1.6
New Brunswick				1931A	23.5	72.3	4.1
1921	0.8	99.2	0.0	1931	25.5	70.4	4.1
1931A	4.6	95.4	0.0	1941	29.8	68.0	2.2
1931	5.0	94.9	0.0	1951	39.5	56.9	3.6
1941	6.6	93.4	0.0	1961	49.8	46.8	3.4
1951	9.1	90.9	0.0	British Columbia			
1961	12.2	87.6	0.3	1921	12.7	85.8	1.5
Quebec				1931A	46.1	52.8	1.1
1921	0.1	99.9	0.0	1931	50.5	48.5	1.0
1931A	0.5	99.5	0.0	1941	53.7	45.4	0.9
1931	0.6	99.4	0.0	1951	56.9	41.2	1.9
1941	1.0	99.0	0.0	1961	64.8	33.7	1.5
1951	1.4	98.6	0.1	Yukon			
1961	1.6	98.2	0.2	1931A	22.8	76.8	0.4
Ontario				1941	35.3	64.4	0.3
1921	4.9	94.3	0.8	1951	53.8	44.8	1.4
1931A	21.0	78.5	0.5	1961	59.1	40.0	0.9
1931	22.2	77.4	0.4	Northwest Territories			
1941	25.1	74.4	0.5				
1951	31.3	68.3	0.4	1931	13.0	85.6	1.4
1961	37.7	61.4	0.9	1941	14.6	84.5	0.9
Manitoba				1951	22.6	53.6	23.8
1916	5.1	94.6	0.4	1961	37.9	57.8	4.3
1921	1.6	97.8	0.6				

[a]Data for 1916, 1921, and 1931A refer to the population 10 years of age and older; for other periods, the data are for all ages. Years shown for each province are the only years available.

TABLE 4

Mother-Tongue Composition of the British Ethnic Group, by Province: 1916 to 1961[a]

Province and Year	Percent Distribution			Province and Year	Percent Distribution		
	English	French	Other		English	French	Other
Newfoundland				Manitoba (*continued*)			
1951	99.9	0.0	0.1	1931A	99.4	0.1	0.5
1961	99.8	0.0	0.1	1931	99.4	0.1	0.4
Prince Edward				1941	98.7	0.4	1.0
1921	100.0	0.0	0.0	1951	98.9	0.4	0.7
1931A	98.1	0.1	1.8	1961	98.9	0.4	0.7
1931	98.4	0.2	1.4	Saskatchewan			
1941	99.0	0.2	0.8	1916	99.5	0.0	0.5
1951	99.6	0.2	0.2	1921	99.6	0.0	0.4
1961	99.6	0.2	0.2	1931A	99.2	0.1	0.7
Nova Scotia				1931	99.3	0.1	0.6
1921	100.0	0.0	0.0	1941	98.7	0.2	1.1
1931A	92.6	0.1	7.3	1951	99.2	0.2	0.6
1931	93.6	0.1	6.3	1961	99.2	0.2	0.6
1941	97.0	0.2	2.7	Alberta			
1951	98.3	0.2	1.4	1916	99.6	0.0	0.4
1961	98.9	0.3	0.8	1921	99.7	0.0	0.3
New Brunswick				1931A	99.1	0.1	0.8
1921	99.9	0.1	0.0	1931	99.2	0.1	0.8
1931A	99.0	0.9	0.1	1941	98.8	0.2	1.0
1931	98.7	1.2	0.1	1951	99.3	0.2	0.5
1941	98.3	1.5	0.2	1961	99.2	0.2	0.5
1951	98.3	1.6	0.1	British Columbia			
1961	98.0	1.8	0.2	1921	99.8	0.0	0.2
Quebec				1931A	99.4	0.0	0.5
1921	98.5	1.4	0.1	1931	99.5	0.0	0.5
1931A	95.2	4.4	0.4	1941	99.2	0.1	0.7
1931	94.0	5.7	0.3	1951	99.5	0.1	0.4
1941	91.9	7.4	0.7	1961	99.4	0.2	0.4
1951	91.3	8.4	0.3	Yukon			
1961	90.2	9.4	0.4	1931A	97.8	0.0	2.2
Ontario				1941	99.1	0.2	0.8
1921	99.8	0.0	0.2	1951	98.9	0.2	0.9
1931A	99.6	0.1	0.3	1961	99.1	0.2	0.7
1931	99.7	0.1	0.2				
1941	99.3	0.3	0.5	Northwest Territories			
1951	99.5	0.3	0.2	1931	97.1	0.8	2.1
1961	99.4	0.4	0.3	1941	95.4	0.4	4.2
Manitoba				1951	93.1	1.1	5.8
1916	99.7	0.0	0.2	1961	96.0	0.6	3.4
1921	99.8	0.0	0.2				

[a]Data for 1916, 1921, and 1931A refer to the population 10 years of age and older; for other periods, the data are for all ages. Years shown for each province are the only years available.

understanding of the causes of bilingualism is secured, the matter will rest with these crude data, but a more careful empirical examination of this thesis will be made in later chapters.

URBAN-RURAL DIFFERENCES

Bilingualism is more frequent among urban dwellers than rural residents. About 14 percent of the former are able to speak both official languages in 1961, nearly twice the rate for the rural parts of Canada, 8 percent. Even in the rural areas there is a difference between those living on farms as opposed to other rural residents. Bilingualism is found among only 6 percent of the rural farm residents, as contrasted with 9 percent of the rural nonfarm inhabitants. These differences reflect the greater linguistic heterogeneity in urban areas as well as the wider range of contacts occurring in cities.

The rural–urban differences hold for bilingualism in either English or French. Over half (54 percent) of Canada's urban residents can speak English if this was not their mother tongue. By contrast 44 percent of the rural population in 1961 know English as a second language, with the rate similar among both the farm and rural nonfarm residents (44.0 and 43.8 percent, respectively). Likewise, the acquisition of French is more common among urban residents than inhabitants of rural areas. About 5.6 percent of urban residents with a mother tongue other than French are able to speak this language in 1961. In relative terms this is considerably higher than the 2.2 percent for rural inhabitants.

The acquisition of bilingualism in either English or French is more likely to occur in urban areas as opposed to rural locations. A compact and isolated settlement is harder to create in a large city. Residential segregation is common enough in Canada's urban centers, but this form of isolation is less successful in preventing out-group contacts in various nonresidential domains. In particular, a population that is highly isolated residentially will still face interaction with other groups in the course of employment, shopping, and daily travel. In rural areas linguistic concentration assures a more isolated set of contacts in these other contexts. Of course, urban residential segregation can have an effect on bilingualism, but its impact is not as strong as is isolation in rural locations. In this regard, Haugen's analysis (1953, 283–288) of mother-tongue retention among the second generations of various immigrant groups in the United States discloses greater mother-tongue tenacity among rural residents than urban dwellers. However, it is unclear for the moment whether the greater strength of mother tongues in rural areas is a product of lower rates of bilingualism or different rates of intergenerational switching among the offspring of bilingual parents.

AGE, SEX, AND BILINGUALISM

Most of the demographic factors influencing bilingualism were examined in Chapter 2; there is no need to review them at this point. However, there is much to be learned about the causes of bilingualism through an examination of the patterns for different age groups. This is particularly fruitful when the data are available, as they are in Canada, for more than one decade by both age and sex.

There are two major ways of inferring the causes of bilingualism through age– and sex–specific rates. One is to trace a given cohort through the years, observing the net effects on bilingualism of the various stages in the life cycle. This longitudinal analysis focuses on the changes in bilingualism experienced over time by a given group of people who belong to a common generation (for an illustration of this technique applied to bilingualism in Montreal, see Lieberson, 1965a). On the other hand, it is possible to study the changing situation faced by different cohorts entering a given age period. In other words, what was bilingualism like among teenagers in 1941, as contrasted with both more recent and earlier groups of teenagers? (I shall exercise my sociological prerogative to leave for linguists the question whether teenagers speak any known language.) This latter approach focuses on the changing conditions of bilingualism in each age and sex niche in the society; the former emphasizes the experiences of a given age- and sex-specific group as they enter new stages of their life cycle. Much can be learned about the causes of bilingualism from both perspectives.

Several difficulties, of varying degrees of importance, complicate both forms of analysis. Newfoundland became part of Canada in 1949; thus data for Canada as a whole in 1951 are not fully comparable to the results obtained for 1941 when Newfoundland was still independent. Two sets of data are presented for 1951: one excludes Newfoundland and is therefore comparable to 1941; the second includes this new province and is therefore comparable to the Canada of 1961. More serious is the difficulty due to the absence of statistical controls on the population entering or leaving Canada between censuses. In this regard the longitudinal analysis is not an examination of true cohorts in a population closed to emigration or immigration. Temporal fluctuations in immigration to Canada occur as well. with relatively large numbers entering in post-World War II years compared with the 1930's.

Because the cross tabulations between mother tongue and official language necessary to a study of bilingualism are not generally available, procedures are employed to obtain the minimum and maximum percentages acquiring each official language as a second tongue. Formulas for these procedures are described in an earlier paper (Lieberson, 1966, p. 265). The Dominion Bureau of Statistics did run off some cross tabulations between mother tongue and official language for a few cities in 1961. Comparisons with the minimum and maximum percentages, based on the formulas referred to above, indicate that the lower end of the range for the French-mother-tongue group and the higher end of the range for the English-mother-tongue population provide the best estimates of bilingualism for the respective groups. Accordingly, unless otherwise indicated, the data presented in this chapter follow the minimum formula for the French-mother-tongue group and the maximum formula for the English. For a more detailed discussion of the estimating procedures employed see the appendix to Chapter 6.

Cross-Sectional Analysis

Bilingualism among the English- and French-mother-tongue groups has been moving in opposite directions during the last few decades. For both the male and female segments of the English-mother-tongue group, bilingualism increased between 1941 and 1951, and again between 1951 and 1961. Among males with English mother tongue, the percentage able to speak French is greater in 1951 than in 1941 (except for those between the ages of 5 and 14, see Table 5). With several exceptions the acquisition of French is even more frequent in 1961 than in 1951. The patterns of change during these years are virtually identical for English-mother-tongue women.

By contrast bilingualism declined during both decades for males with French mother tongue. The ability to speak English among women also declined between 1941 and 1951, but no consistent pattern is evident during the past decade (see Table 5). Among males with French mother tongue bilingualism is lower in virtually every age category in 1951 compared with the levels in 1941. The most striking change is the relatively sizable drop among those in the preschool ages, where 8.6 and 4.8 percent were bilingual in 1941 and 1951, respectively. In the vast majority of age grades, the new cohorts in 1961 have even lower rates of bilingualism than their predecessors in 1951. The same pattern of declining bilingualism is found between 1941 and 1951 for French-mother-tongue women. Between 1951 and 1961, the pattern breaks down, with increases observed among the 5–9 age group, the new cohorts entering the late teens and early 20's, and in nearly all those 40 and older. So, if anything,

TABLE 5

Bilingualism by Age, Sex, and Mother Tongue, Canada: 1941, 1951, and 1961[a]

Age	English Mother Tongue: Percent Learning French								French Mother Tongue: Percent Learning English							
	Male				Female				Male				Female			
	1941	1951A	1951B	1961	1941	1951A	1951B	1961	1941	1951A	1951B	1961	1941	1951A	1951B	1961
0– 4	1.0	1.2	1.0	0.8	1.0	1.2	1.1	1.0	8.6	4.8	5.0	4.1	8.5	5.0	4.9	3.8
5– 9	2.3	2.1	2.1	1.9	2.4	2.2	2.1	2.1	13.0	10.1	9.8	10.7	13.1	10.3	10.4	10.7
10–14	3.7	3.6	3.3	3.3	3.9	3.8	3.5	3.8	19.8	17.2	17.5	17.8	19.5	17.1	17.4	17.3
15–19	5.2	6.1	5.8	6.6	5.9	6.3	6.0	7.5	37.0	35.3	35.4	35.0	33.2	33.1	33.1	34.2
20–24	6.1	7.4	7.0	9.0	5.7	6.4	6.1	7.7	50.7	49.1	49.2	48.9	41.4	39.0	39.1	40.3
25–29	6.4	7.8	7.6	10.2	5.4	5.8	5.7	7.9	55.2	56.8	55.4	53.7	43.1	40.8	40.6	38.6
30–34	6.9		8.0	10.4	5.3		5.7	7.8	57.7		57.1	55.6	42.3		41.0	38.8
35–39	7.0	8.3	7.9	11.2	5.2	5.8	5.6	7.7	59.8	57.4	57.3	57.0	40.9	40.1	40.7	40.2
40–44	7.4		8.0	9.5	4.6		5.3	7.4	61.9		57.6	57.5	41.4		39.2	40.1
45–49	7.3	8.1	8.1	9.4	4.5	5.3	5.2	6.8	61.1	58.6	58.2	55.7	39.7	37.0	37.8	39.7
50–54	6.2		7.9	9.1	3.9		4.9	6.5	59.7		58.9	54.6	37.9		36.4	37.9
55–59	5.3	7.3	7.9	8.4	3.5	4.2	4.4	5.9	57.4	55.5	56.7	53.7	36.5	33.8	34.6	29.9
60–64	4.7		6.4	8.1	3.2		3.8	5.0	54.9		53.6	52.6	34.0		32.6	33.2
65–69	4.2	5.1	4.9	6.8	3.0	3.4	3.2	4.3	52.3	50.5	51.0	49.1	32.0	30.8	30.9	31.1
70–74	4.0		4.3	5.6	2.9		3.1	3.9	48.1		46.5	45.0	28.9		28.8	29.4
75–79	3.6		3.9	4.0	2.6		3.0	3.0	45.7		43.8	42.6	27.5		26.3	28.0
80–84	3.2	4.3	3.5	3.6	2.8	3.1	2.9	2.8	39.8	44.2	41.5	38.8	24.3	27.0	24.5	26.2
85–89	3.3		3.7	3.4	2.5		2.4	2.6	38.6		40.3	38.6	25.1		25.7	25.8
90 and over	3.9		3.3	2.7	2.4		2.8	2.6	41.2		39.8	39.3	25.0		24.1	24.6

[a]Data for 1941 and 1951A do not include Newfoundland; data for 1951B and 1961 include Newfoundland. Percentages learning French among the English-mother-tongue group are based on maximum rates; percentages learning English among the French-mother-tongue group are based on minimum rates.

French-mother-tongue women show a tendency toward greater bilingualism in the most recent decade.

Changes in bilingualism among one mother-tongue group will tend to generate compensating changes in the other mother-tongue population. This is particularly the case when economic and/or social segregation do not increase. There is clear evidence that the English-mother-tongue group is under increasing pressure to acquire French. On the other hand, at least for French-mother-tongue males, the opposite trend is evident. However, these compensating shifts should not obscure the rather obvious conclusion from Table 5 that the French remain under considerably greater pressure to become bilingual than do their countrymen whose native language is English.

It is difficult to account for the inconsistent pattern among French women. Greater participation in the labor force means that more women are exposed to the pressures and opportunities for bilingualism created through employment. These work pressures, however, are not so intense as they once were. The upward shifts in bilingualism between 1951 and 1961 among adult women in the pre- and postchildbearing ages, one might speculate, is the net product of these conflicting tendencies, for it is during these years that perhaps the greatest gains in labor force participation occurs.

Cohorts

The data shown in Table 5 are displayed somewhat differently in Table 6 in order to make the longtitudinal changes clearer. For the nation as a whole the experiences of early childhood before the school years are not a major cause of bilingualism. Bilingualism among those 5 years of age, beginning in 1951, occurs for only 1 percent of the English-mother-tongue children and 5 percent of the French-speaking youngsters. Since this age category combines those just under 5 with the newly born, undoubtedly the rates are higher for the older children in this category. Among the English-mother-tongue children this technical consideration has little effect, since there is a low increment in the succeeding decade. For the French, in view of the considerable increments among those just a little older, undoubtedly the rate of bilingualism among children just before the school ages is understated. These data suggest that the neighborhood and total city context generate considerably more bilingualism among small French-speaking children than among those whose language of socialization is English. Given the population composition of Canada as a whole and the general dominance of English in the nation, this is to be expected.

During the school years there is a far greater rise in bilingualism among the French-mother-tongue children than among those whose native language is English; for example, among those 5–9 years old in 1951 the jump in bilingualism during the succeeding decade is from about 10 percent to 35 percent for both boys and girls with French mother tongue. English-mother-tongue children in the comparable ages increased from 2 to 7 percent bilingual during this period. Equally substantial differences are observed among other cohorts in the school ages.

The higher frequency of bilingualism for the French probably reflects the fact that mandatory English language education is much more widespread in Canada than is mandatory French instruction. Schools providing instruction in the French medium are located through much of Quebec, but French children outside of Quebec often encounter schools in which English is the medium of instruction. The increments in bilingualism among school-age French children are much greater than in the succeeding or preceding ages. At least a good part of this increase is due to the influence of schooling rather than the general milieu.

The sharp increments during the school ages indicate the considerable importance of the educational system for transmitting at least some ability to speak the second official language. If the frequency of bilingualism among those in the high school ages is compared with the peaks achieved through the life span, it is clear that a sizable part of the net gains in bilingualism occur by the time of high-school graduation.

Within each mother-tongue group boys and girls of high school age have similar rates of bilingualism, although English-mother-tongue girls are somewhat more bilingual than the boys. In 1961, for example, the bilingual rates for boys and girls 15–19 years of age with English mother tongue are 6.6 and 7.5 percent, respectively. Beginning with early adulthood, however, after schooling has ended for most, bilingualism is more common among English-mother-tongue men than women. The most reasonable intepretation is based on the pressure to learn French that is generated by occupational needs. Since many women leave the labor force during the early childbearing ages, this kind of pressure would be felt by far more men. Despite the fact that bilingualism is more common among teenage girls, the rates of bilingualism are persistently higher among men in the early adult ages. This process, looked at longitudinally, is very clear. The percent bilingual among males 15–19 is 5.8 in 1951, rising to 10.4 among the same cohort in 1961 when they are 25–29 years of age. Among women in the same ages the rise is from 6.0 to 7.9 percent.

Sex differentials in bilingualism among the French-mother-tongue group after the school years suggest that occupational pressures also play an important role in the acquisition of English. French girls 15–19 in 1951 rise from 33.1 to 38.6 percent bilingual in the ensuing decade; a period

TABLE 6

Bilingualism by Cohorts, Canada: 1951 and 1961

Age in 1951	Percent Bilingual							
	English Mother Tongue				French Mother Tongue			
	Male		Female		Male		Female	
	1951	1961	1951	1961	1951	1961	1951	1961
0– 4	1.0	3.3	1.1	3.8	5.0	17.8	4.9	17.3
5– 9	2.1	6.6	2.1	7.5	9.8	35.0	10.4	34.2
10–14	3.3	9.0	3.5	7.7	17.5	48.9	17.4	40.3
15–19	5.8	10.2	6.0	7.9	35.4	53.7	33.1	38.6
20–24	7.0	10.4	6.1	7.8	49.2	55.6	39.1	38.8
25–29	7.6	11.2	5.7	7.7	55.4	57.0	40.6	40.2
30–34	8.0	9.5	5.7	7.4	57.1	57.5	41.0	40.1
35–39	7.9	9.4	5.6	6.8	57.3	55.7	40.7	39.7
40–44	8.0	9.1	5.3	6.5	57.6	54.6	39.2	37.9
45–49	8.1	8.4	5.2	5.9	58.2	53.7	37.8	29.9
50–54	7.9	8.1	4.9	5.0	58.9	52.6	36.4	33.2
55–59	7.9	6.8	4.4	4.3	56.7	49.1	34.6	31.1
60–64	6.4	5.6	3.8	3.9	53.6	45.0	32.6	29.4
65–69	4.9	4.0	3.2	3.0	51.0	42.6	30.9	28.0
70–74	4.3	3.6	3.1	2.8	46.5	38.8	28.8	26.2

during which French-mother-tongue males of the same age jump from 35.4 to 53.7 percent bilingual.

A conservative estimate can be made of the bilingualism among adult men that is due to occupational pressures. If the difference in bilingualism between men and women of the same age and with the same mother tongue is assumed to reflect the relatively larger number of males in the labor force, then the percentage of the male bilingualism rate due to this excess is a product of their occupational pressures. This involves the crude assumption that the higher rate of bilingualism for adult men is solely a function of their greater participation in the labor force. The estimating procedure is crude because of the residual explanation employed, namely, all differences between the sexes with the same mother tongue and in the same age group are attributed to occupational factors. It is a conservative method in one sense, however, since obviously many women *are* in the labor force. In this regard the causal importance of occupational pressures is underestimated to the degree that women are in the labor force and become bilingual as a consequence of employment.

The results shown in Table 7 suggest that about 30 percent of the bilingualism found among French-mother-tongue men is due to occupational pressures. Or to put it another way, the rate of bilingualism among adult women is about 70 percent of the rate among men in the working ages. Occupational pressures account for a somewhat smaller proportion of the bilingualism among those with English mother tongue, but an estimate of 25 percent is reasonable.

In most age categories there is a slightly greater relative excess among French males than English-mother-tongue males. However, it should be recognized that the *absolute* excess of male bilingualism is much greater in the French-mother-tongue group. The inferred occupational pressures cause about 15 to 20 percent of the French-mother-tongue men to learn English, but leads to only 2 or 3 percent of the English-mother-tongue men acquiring French.

The reader should recognize that these figures apply to all of Canada and that considerable variation might be expected in different parts of the nation. A closer look is taken shortly at specific communities under a variety of compositional situations.

Bilingualism among the population in the older ages provides some unresolvable problems. At all age levels the French are far more bilingual than the English-mother-tongue group. This is easily understood. The net

TABLE 7

Comparison Between Male and Female Bilingualism in the Working Ages, by Mother Tongue: 1951 and 1961

	Percentage Difference: Male Minus Female			
	French Mother Tongue		English Mother Tongue	
Age	1951	1961	1951	1961
20–24	21	18	13	14
25–29	27	28	25	23
30–34	28	30	29	25
35–39	29	29	29	31
40–44	32	30	34	22
45–49	35	29	36	28
50–54	38	31	38	29
55–59	39	44	44	30
60–64	39	37	41	38

unlearning of English by the French-mother-tongue group, however, occurs at an earlier age than does the unlearning of French by those whose native tongue is English. Between 1951 and 1961 net decreases in bilingualism first occur in the cohorts between the ages of 55 and 59 for both men and women with English mother tongue (see Table 6). In all the younger age groups in 1951 there is a net increase in bilingualism between 1951 and 1961. By contrast bilingualism begins to decline at earlier ages among the French-mother-tongue population. Cohorts of women 20 years and older and men 35 years and over in 1951 all have net declines during the next decade. Similar differences between the French and English exist for changes between 1941 and 1951. No ready explanation is offered for the higher rates of net unlearning among the French.

The net unlearning of second languages is marked by a higher rate of decline for men than women. The removal of occupational pressures from a sizable number of men over 65 probably explains the more rapid decline in bilingualism. A smaller proportion of bilingualism among women is due to participation in the labor force, therefore female rates do not drop off as sharply with increasing age.

COHORTS IN FIVE SPECIFIC CITIES

The data for Canada reflect the net balance of linguistic behavior in the diverse parts of this nation. Case studies of specific communities provide a more suitable vehicle for analyzing the various causes of bilingualism under different compositional conditions. Five cities, representing a broad range of community contexts, are selected for these comparisons. The French are a minor group in both Edmonton and Toronto; they are fairly balanced with the British in Sudbury and Ottawa-Hull and are the overwhelming majority in Quebec.

The computations for each age and sex, as before, are based on the minimum-maximum formulas for each mother tongue's bilingualism (Lieberson, 1966). The figures shown in Table 8 provide the minimum and maximum possible percentages for the English- and French-mother-tongue residents. The range in each urban center is fairly narrow. In Edmonton, for example, no more than 3 percent of the male English-mother-tongue group learned French. The ranges are even narrower in 1941 and 1951 for English-mother-tongue women. Likewise the percent bilingual among the French-mother-tongue inhabitants is narrow; in 1961 it ran from the low 90's to 100 per cent for both sexes. In all cities the choice of the maximum figures for the English-mother-tongue group and minimum figures for the French (based on reasons described earlier) has

TABLE 8

Range in Bilingualism by Mother Tongue and Sex, Specific Cities: 1941 to 1961

City and Year	English Mother Tongue: Percent Learning French				French Mother Tongue: Percent Learning English			
	Male		Female		Male		Female	
	Minimum	Maximum	Minimum	Maximum	Minimum	Maximum	Minimum	Maximum
Edmonton								
1941	0	3	0	2	98	100	97	100
1951	0	3	0	2	94	100	94	100
1961	0	3	0	3	92	100	91	100
Ottawa[a]								
1941	3	12	3	9	75	86	67	75
1951	6	12	4	9	73	82	65	72
1961	0	12	1	10	72	94	65	81
Quebec								
1941	69	83	64	70	36	37	20	20
1951	72	84	67	72	36	36	21	22
1961	71	100	64	82	31	32	19	20
Sudbury								
1941	0	6	0	4	85	100	81	100
1951	0	9	0	7	89	100	87	100
1961	0	8	0	7	87	100	86	100
Toronto								
1941	0	2	0	2	98	100	98	100
1951	0	6	0	3	89	100	89	100
1961	0	6	0	4	88	100	88	100

[a]Ottawa-Hull

little effect on the comparisons between these groups. This is because of the narrow range within each group combined with the considerable differences between the French and English in each city.

Comparisons between males and females with the same mother tongue are sticky in some instances. In Quebec the minimum percentage bilingual among French-mother-tongue males is clearly higher than the maximum percentage for their female compatriots, but in other cities, in which the female maximum exceeds the male minimum, it is not self-evident whether males or females are more bilingual. Another difficulty is due to the limitation of the data to the central city rather than the metropolitan area (except the cities of Ottawa and Hull, which are combined). This is due to the limitations of the available data coupled with the need to maximize comparisons over time in order to make the cohorts meaningful.

Edmonton and Toronto

French is a minor language in both of these cities, being the mother tongue of less than 5 percent of the metropolitan population in 1961. The French are far from being even the second largest ethnic group in these centers. Canadians of German and Ukrainian origin in Edmonton are each close to double the number of French Canadians. In Toronto the Italians and Germans are larger in number.

The two cities differ in both their economies and location. Edmonton, capital of the prairie province of Alberta, and a major wholesaling and retailing center, has been expanding rapidly thanks to the oil discoveries and important chemical and meat packing industries. Toronto is also growing rapidly, but it is growing from its position as one of the great national metropolises of all of Canada. Montreal is its only rival as a center for finance, communications, and commerce. Since Montreal is largely a French city culturally, Toronto stands as the capital of English-speaking Canada in all areas except national government. It is also a city that has undergone an enormous transformation in post-World War II years through a cultural growth often associated with the enormous numbers of European immigrants.

In both cities one is struck by the high frequency of bilingualism among the French-mother-tongue residents occurring at very early ages. By contrast less than 1 percent of the English-mother-tongue population can speak French until the teens (see Table 9). An enormous pressure exists for the French to acquire English rather rapidly in both Edmonton and Toronto, but little pressure is exerted in the opposite direction. Bilingualism among Toronto's French-mother-tongue group approaches or exceeds 90 percent in 1961 in nearly all ages and tends to be even higher in Edmonton.

Notwithstanding the high rates of bilingualism current among the French group, the percentages have declined since 1941 in both cities and for each sex. Particularly notable is the sharp decline in bilingualism among preschool children during the last two decades. Among girls under 5 years in Toronto, for example, it was 85 percent in 1941, but 55 and 51 percent, respectively, in 1951 and 1961. Although less spectacular, the rates have gone down since 1941 for other segments of the French group. Those reaching a given age are less bilingual than were earlier cohorts at the same stage in the life cycle; for example, men 25 to 34 in Edmonton were 99 percent bilingual in 1941; those reaching the same age 10 years later were 98 percent bilingual; and the rate for the most recent cohort at this stage in 1961 is 94 percent.

The existence of "compensating" bilingualism would occur if bilingualism among one group declines while simultaneously increasing in the other group. In the case of Toronto and Edmonton this appears to be the case since there is generally a rise in bilingualism among native speakers of English. In most cases, succeeding generations have higher rates of bilingualism; for example, bilingualism among men 25 to 34 years old with English mother tongue increased from 3 percent in 1941 to 4 percent in 1951 and to 6 percent in 1961.

Although the phenomenon of compensating bilingualism is observed in both of these cities and in Canada as a whole, no ready interpretation can be offered for its existence. The particularly sharp drop in the very early ages suggests that parents are more successful in isolating their children from English. But as for the conditions producing this change, it is difficult to offer an explanation at this stage. One is tempted to explore rising nationalism among the French, but this is hardly satisfactory. In particular, the sharpest drop for French-mother-tongue children in Toronto occurred between 1941 and 1951, rather than in the more recent decade. Further, the interpretation of the origins and causes of this rising nationalism is itself open to question.

Sex differences in bilingualism occur for the English but not for the French. Among children with English mother tongue, the girls have slightly higher rates of bilingualism—possibly reflecting generally superior performance in school. But these differentials are reversed beginning with the late teens and on through adulthood. The more frequent acquisition of French among adult men is interpreted as reflecting the somewhat greater pressures generated by the occupational world. Since the differences between men and women with English mother tongue are small by any absolute criteria, this indicates the obvious fact that even the job pressures for the acquisition of French are slight in such overwhelmingly English cities as Toronto and Edmonton.

TABLE 9

Bilingualism in Edmonton and Toronto, by Age, Sex, and Mother Tongue: 1941, 1951, and 1961

Percent Learning the Other Official Language

City and Age	English Mother Tongue						French Mother Tongue					
	Male			Female			Male			Female		
	1941	1951	1961	1941	1951	1961	1941	1951	1961	1941	1951	1961
Edmonton												
0– 4	0.0	0.4	0.2	0.2	0.3	0.2	91.3	56.8	63.0	88.8	63.5	62.9
5– 9	0.3	0.6	0.4	0.4	0.6	0.5	99.1	96.7	95.4	99.0	97.2	90.9
10–14	0.7	0.9	0.6	0.2	1.0	0.8	98.3	99.1	95.2	100.0	98.6	94.5
15–19	2.1	2.2	4.0	2.3	2.5	3.5	100.0	98.4	93.9	99.4	95.9	93.6
20–24	3.0	3.1	4.8	2.1	3.7	4.2	100.0	95.2	96.8	99.6	98.2	94.5
25–34	3.2	4.0	6.1	2.5	2.7	4.5	99.3	98.4	94.3	98.6	97.5	94.1
35–44	4.5	4.6	6.1	2.9	2.9	4.6	99.5	97.7	92.8	98.8	97.3	92.7
45–54	5.0	4.6	5.9	2.8	3.0	3.6	100.0	95.5	94.4	99.0	94.9	94.5
55–64	3.4	5.3	5.1	2.5	3.0	3.7	97.7	97.0	95.6	90.1	94.9	92.4
65–69	2.9	3.5	6.2	2.7	2.7	3.1	96.0	95.7	92.6	87.5	92.7	90.7
70 and over	2.8	4.0	3.8	1.7	2.1	2.4	94.7	95.3	90.1	85.1	84.6	86.1
Toronto												
0– 4	0.1	0.4	0.3	0.1	0.5	0.4	84.3	61.0	50.4	84.8	55.4	51.4
5– 9	0.2	0.5	0.5	0.2	0.6	0.6	85.7	85.7	83.1	98.0	82.1	90.0
10–14	0.5	0.7	1.1	0.6	0.8	1.3	98.3	89.1	87.4	96.0	88.6	90.2
15–19	2.0	3.5	6.8	2.4	3.9	7.4	98.5	94.5	91.5	99.6	93.3	91.0
20–24	2.7	4.9	9.3	2.3	4.0	8.9	100.0	92.5	91.5	98.6	93.0	90.8
25–34	2.7	5.6	10.3	2.1	3.6	7.6	98.4	90.1	92.2	98.1	90.4	91.4
35–44	3.1	5.4	10.4	2.1	3.3	6.9	99.0	87.7	91.3	99.2	91.7	90.9
45–54	3.1	5.0	7.7	1.6	2.9	5.2	98.7	89.1	90.3	99.1	90.7	90.0
55–64	2.0	3.9	6.0	1.4	2.1	3.9	98.1	92.1	87.8	97.2	89.8	85.6
65–69	1.6	2.6	5.1	1.2	1.7	2.5	100.0	87.7	89.6	97.0	90.1	86.8
70 and over	1.6	2.3	3.2	1.0	1.7	1.9	97.8	95.8	84.4	99.1	87.7	77.7

Sex differentials in bilingualism are not particularly marked among the French-mother-tongue residents. The high rate of bilingualism reached at very early ages point toward the conclusion that occupational pressures in these cities are superfluous; that is, bilingualism is extremely widespread among the French long before the ages when employment in the labor force is an issue. To be sure, there may be a complex chain of pressures moving from the labor market to childhood and schooling, but the simplest interpretation is that the dominance of English is so pervasive as to lead to high rates of bilingualism by the time elementary school is reached. The final touches are then added with the pressures in the lower grades of school.

Quebec

With French as the mother tongue and ethnic group of approximately 95 percent of the residents, metropolitan Quebec provides an extreme contrast to Edmonton and Toronto. The oldest city of Canada and capital of the province of Quebec, it has made an industrial and commercial comeback in recent decades, boasts an important port, and enjoys a significant tourist trade.

Despite the demographic dominance of French, bilingualism in Quebec is not merely the reversal of the rates among French and English in Edmonton and Toronto. Bilingualism is far more frequent among the French-mother-tongue residents of Quebec than is the acquisition of French among the English residents of Toronto or Edmonton; for example, bilingualism occurs among 40 percent or more of Quebec's French-mother-tongue men in the adult working ages in 1961 (see Table 10). Well under 10 percent of Edmonton's English-mother-tongue men in the comparable ages can speak French and, at most, barely 10 percent in Toronto. Similar differences are observed between women. All of this provides a good illustration of how population composition influences bilingualism differently for the English- and French-mother-tongue groups (see Chapter 2).

Relatively modest percentages of the French-mother-tongue residents learn English up through the early teens. Schooling—at least in the early grades—and the community milieu do not yield many bilinguals among the French. Both factors operate to create considerably more bilingualism among the English-mother-tongue children in Quebec; during the last two decades more than 30 percent of the English preschool children acquired French, and 80- to 90-odd percent were bilingual by their late teens.

In the working ages bilingualism is generally greater for men than women with the same mother tongue. This suggests that occupational forces create bilingualism among both English and French. What is most inter-

TABLE 10

Bilingualism in Quebec, by Age, Sex, and Mother Tongue: 1941, 1951, and 1961

	Percent Learning the Other Official Language											
	English Mother Tongue						French Mother Tongue					
	Male			Female			Male			Female		
Age	1941	1951	1961	1941	1951	1961	1941	1951	1961	1941	1951	1961
0– 4	27.5	32.3	38.6	22.8	34.8	38.4	1.6	0.7	0.6	1.5	1.0	0.7
5– 9	62.3	63.1	80.2	65.9	70.0	82.2	2.8	1.8	2.3	2.6	1.9	2.4
10–14	85.0	83.6	95.2	79.8	85.1	91.6	5.2	5.0	4.9	5.9	5.3	5.0
15–19	89.6	94.2	99.6	88.4	90.7	100.0	28.3	25.3	23.1	20.7	27.2	24.6
20–24	90.5	97.5	100.0	79.0	81.4	98.4	48.5	46.5	37.5	27.7	33.0	31.8
25–34	93.2	89.1	100.0	71.7	77.3	94.5	54.3	57.0	40.9	29.3	31.1	26.9
35–44	92.8	100.0	100.0	72.0	77.1	95.8	58.1	55.9	48.3	29.0	27.7	25.3
45–54	92.7	98.6	100.0	72.3	74.5	82.6	58.9	57.8	46.1	26.9	26.8	24.4
55–64	80.4	92.2	100.0	68.4	74.3	73.7	54.5	54.4	48.1	23.9	24.4	22.7
65–69	81.7	85.8	100.0	56.0	64.6	80.5	46.7	49.1	46.7	19.7	20.6	19.8
70 and over	72.4	76.0	89.4	61.6	64.4	60.2	41.0	39.9	36.9	16.0	18.4	17.1

esting here is the comparison with the previous two cities. In Edmonton and Toronto other pressures for the acquisition of English were so great that any differences between French men and women due to occupational factors were prevented. On the other hand, in Quebec the occupational pressures are still a minor influence for the English-mother-tongue residents. At least this is the inference one can make from the only slightly higher rates of bilingualism among English-mother-tongue men compared with women.

In Quebec, as elsewhere, succeeding English-mother-tongue cohorts of both sexes are learning French more frequently. The acquisition of English among French-speaking males has been declining, but no clear-cut trend is evident for women. The latter showed a rather mixed pattern between 1941 and 1951; however, bilingualism declined in all but one age category in the 1950's. Just as in the preceding cities, the mechanism of compensating bilingualism operates in Quebec.

Sudbury and Ottawa-Hull

These two cities are the most interesting of all, with the two groups fairly equal in number. Inhabitants of British and French ethnic origin are numerically similar in both metropolitan areas in 1961, although English is the numerically stronger mother tongue—particularly in Sudbury. This reflects, however, the linguistic movements of the remaining ethnic groups rather than a high level of mother tongue shift among the French ethnic residents. Sudbury is northern Ontario's major retail and wholesale center. It is closely linked to the copper and nickel mining industries in the region. About half the male labor force in this metropolitan area in 1961 were employed in either mines or smelters. Ottawa-Hull has a very different economy and is much more closely linked to Quebec province. Ottawa, the national capital, is located on the eastern edge of Ontario. Just across the Ottawa River is the province of Quebec and the sister city of Hull, an overwhelmingly French community.

Bilingualism in both Ottawa-Hull and Sudbury is similar to the patterns found in the predominantly English communities of Toronto and Edmonton. The acquisition of French among the English-mother-tongue group is higher than in the latter cities but not by a great margin (compare Table 11 with Table 9). Around 2 percent of the preschool children are bilingual and less than 10 percent of those in their early teens. The English in Ottawa-Hull are somewhat more likely to learn French than are their compatriots in Sudbury. The adult sex differential also tends to be greater in the former city. Very likely the industrial complex in Sudbury provides less occupational pressure for the acquisition of French than is the case in Ottawa. In 1961, particularly, men and women with English mother tongue in Sudbury differ by only a small margin in their bilingualism. The learning of French among the English in the preschool ages is actually slightly more frequent in Sudbury, but is reversed by the late teens. This does illustrate how pressures to acquire a second language can be greater in one city for certain ages, but less at other ages.

The bilingual pattern in the two cities for the French residents is even more sharply different. Bilingualism is much higher among children in Sudbury than in Ottawa-Hull; for example, over 90 percent of the children 10–14 years old in the former city can speak English also, compared with 55 to 63 percent among those in Ottawa-Hull. Even greater relative differences exist in the younger ages. Clearly the linguistic environment of Sudbury, both before and during the school years, generates more bilingualism among French children than does the environment of Ottawa-Hull. This may be due to the fact that so many of the French are segregated into Hull, Quebec. Nevertheless, the job market in Ottawa, which is greatly influenced by the federal government's requirements, provides a strong incentive to acquire English. Consequently, despite higher bilingualism among the early ages in Sudbury, the rates are almost as great in adult working years for men in Ottawa-Hull. Close to 100 percent of Sudbury's French-mother-tongue men in the ages of normal employment are bilingual, but the rates in Ottawa do hover around 90 percent.

Consistent with this interpretation is the fact that there is more of a male–female gap in the French bilingualism rate in Ottawa compared to the very slight gap in Sudbury among adults. This may be interpreted as reflecting the greater importance of occupational pressures in Ottawa as an impetus to the acquisition of English. Accordingly, French women are less likely to be bilingual in Ottawa-Hull than in Sudbury, the acquisition of English in the latter city occurring to a high degree even without demands from the labor market.

Not only does bilingualism among the English in these "balanced" cities tend to be on a level closer to that found in the predominantly English centers of Toronto and Edmonton, but the same can be said for the bilingual behavior of the French. To be sure, bilingualism is far more frequent among French-mother-tongue children in Edmonton and Toronto. By adulthood, however, Sudbury's and Ottawa's French-mother-tongue residents are nearly as bilingual as their compatriots in the two centers where they are a very small numerical minority. Sudbury's adults, in particular, are every bit as bilingual as those in Toronto and Edmonton, despite the fact that small children in the first city are considerably less likely to know English.

In summary, this analysis of five large cities, which represents a broad range of linguistic and ethnic contact settings, suggests that some of the

TABLE 11

Bilingualism in Sudbury and Ottawa-Hull, by Age, Sex and Mother Tongue: 1941, 1951, and 1961

City and Age	English Mother Tongue Male			English Mother Tongue Female			French Mother Tongue Male			French Mother Tongue Female		
	1941	1951	1961	1941	1951	1961	1941	1951	1961	1941	1951	1961
Sudbury												
0– 4	2.1	2.7	2.6	1.2	2.9	2.5	39.1	49.7	37.9	40.0	51.8	37.3
5– 9	5.0	6.2	6.2	5.2	6.0	6.6	65.5	80.6	86.5	66.6	82.3	85.1
10–14	5.6	6.9	5.6	5.3	8.8	6.2	93.4	96.0	96.7	90.2	95.4	97.2
15–19	7.8	11.6	8.9	7.6	10.8	9.4	97.9	98.0	97.6	96.0	96.7	97.5
20–24	5.3	9.4	10.8	3.9	9.7	9.7	98.4	97.0	97.9	93.4	93.3	95.8
25–34	5.4	10.1	11.1	3.7	8.9	9.4	98.9	96.5	96.8	94.9	95.2	94.8
35–44	7.0	10.3	12.1	5.2	7.5	9.6	98.3	97.0	96.9	91.2	95.5	94.0
45–54	12.0	13.7	9.4	7.4	7.5	8.1	98.5	96.7	96.3	87.1	91.6	93.3
55–64	8.4	10.3	9.4	2.8	6.3	7.1	94.1	96.4	92.3	84.5	84.7	87.3
65–69	6.8	8.7	7.7	0.0	8.9	4.5	97.2	86.9	90.9	71.1	82.0	72.4
70 and over	7.9	6.1	8.9	1.0	3.3	4.3	90.5	88.6	84.0	62.3	75.0	74.3
Ottawa-Hull												
0– 4	1.7	2.7	2.2	1.7	2.6	2.1	26.3	15.9	14.0	25.3	16.2	14.8
5– 9	6.1	5.8	6.2	6.6	7.4	7.1	40.2	34.9	39.6	42.2	35.7	39.3
10–14	8.2	8.9	8.0	8.9	8.4	9.1	56.0	55.2	63.2	54.1	57.6	59.8
15–19	10.5	12.0	11.9	11.8	13.2	14.4	76.9	80.3	83.9	72.0	77.5	78.2
20–24	11.9	12.2	15.7	10.0	10.5	13.2	89.8	90.4	88.2	80.7	81.5	79.1
25–34	13.5	14.3	17.4	9.6	10.3	13.7	92.6	94.3	89.7	81.4	81.5	79.3
35–44	15.0	15.7	17.1	9.7	10.1	12.4	93.6	94.5	91.9	79.1	79.9	80.4
45–54	16.5	16.6	16.8	8.8	9.0	11.3	93.3	94.5	91.3	76.3	78.2	78.6
55–64	13.3	15.2	15.2	8.1	8.3	9.6	91.1	92.1	89.1	72.7	70.4	72.6
65–69	13.5	12.4	14.4	8.3	7.2	8.1	89.4	89.8	86.6	68.5	65.0	67.8
70 and over	11.9	10.5	10.0	5.9	6.4	6.4	82.2	84.7	81.7	63.8	56.0	60.4

factors influencing bilingualism will vary by the community context. It also provides clear-cut evidence that the acquisition of a second official language differs greatly between the English and French mother tongue components of the community. The age- and sex-specific analysis in the last three decades indicate the varying roles played by the community milieu for the small child, the influence of educational factors, and the occupational pressures. It is particularly important to note that cities may differ substantially in the degree of bilingualism occurring in the early ages but then reach roughly similar levels at later ages as new forces are faced in the life cycle. The frequency of bilingualism can be identical among the adults in two cities but the causes can be very different.

The age-specific rates in cities with approximate numerical equality between the British and French, when compared with predominantly British centers, suggest that both the British and French in Sudbury and Ottawa tend to approximate the patterns found in cities where the former are a strong majority. This indicates how the English- and French-mother-tongue groups respond differently to population composition.

OCCUPATIONAL FACTORS

Sex Differences in Bilingualism

Earlier in this chapter it was observed that men tend to be more bilingual than women. This holds for most cities, although under some circumstances women are slightly more bilingual than men. Roughly speaking, it is assumed that men are subject to all the pressures for bilingualism operating among women with the same mother tongue, but they are under the added pressures generated in the labor market. This is an admittedly crude statement. For one, adult women are probably more responsive to the linguistic needs of their neighborhood, shopping, social pressures, and their children. In addition, many women are employed in the labor market during at least some stages of their adult life. Accordingly, the bilingual gap between males and females is only crudely a measure of the occupational pressures existing in each community.

Having observed these sex differences for five cities and Canada as a whole, it is reasonable to ask whether this phenomenon can be studied for a large number of Canadian communities. Such an analysis could provide some systematic understanding of the conditions under which occupational pressures influence bilingualism. Because the appropriate age- and sex-specific data are available for only a small number of cities, it is necessary to use less appropriate data for an expanded number of communities.

Accordingly, the data reported below are based on bilingualism among all males and all females without regard to age. As shown earlier, however, through at least the middle teens the sex differences in bilingualism are slight. If the assumption is made that most of the differences between the sexes in a given community are a product of the differences between adult men and women, these data provide a reasonably satisfactory measure of the added occupational pressures faced by adult men.

Males tend to have higher rates of bilingualism than females in nearly every community. This holds for the French-mother-tongue residents and for those whose native language is English (see Figure 4.1). The solid line in each scatter-diagram represents equality between males and females; points above the line indicate higher bilingualism rates among men; points below the line indicate the opposite.

For both the English and French there is an association between the community's mother-tongue composition and the male–female gap in bilingualism. Differences between the sexes widen as the mother-tongue composition of the city becomes increasingly French. Of particular importance is the nature of the curves. Among the French-mother-tongue group, there is a gradual widening of the sex gap in bilingualism as the cities become increasingly French in mother-tongue composition. The pattern is different for the English-mother-tongue group (bottom panel of Figure 4.1). There is a flat line just above sexual equality in communities where French is the mother tongue of less than half of the residents. After this point, however, the male excess over females in bilingualism becomes rather considerable.

How is one to explain these different patterns? Assuming that sex differences in bilingualism reflect occupational pressures, the impact of the labor market on bilingualism is different for the French and English. In cities in which French is the mother tongue of only a small part of the population French-mother-tongue bilingualism is high among both sexes. The occupational pressures are virtually superfluous in the sense that French is so weak in the community that nearly all native speakers must learn English. Not only are sex differences in bilingualism rather minor (see top panel of Figure 4.1), but in some of these cities there is slightly more bilingualism among women than men. Moving across the abscissa to places in which French is an increasingly important mother tongue, the pressures for learning English declines accordingly. The pressure for learning English in the job market, however, does not decline so rapidly as the other forces generating bilingualism. Accordingly, the net effect is for a widened gap between the sexes in the acquisition of English. This pattern suggests that such factors as schooling opportunities, services, and

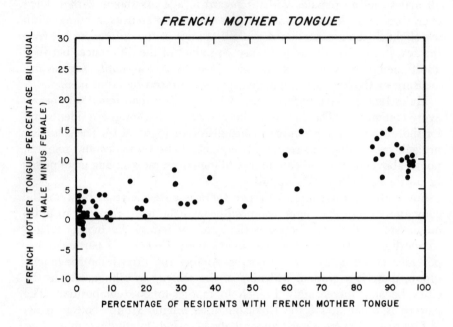

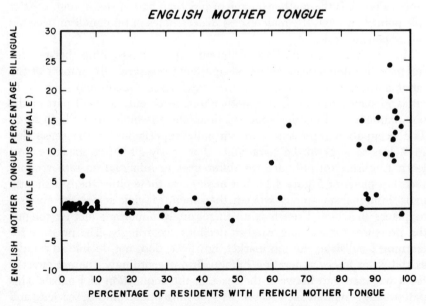

FIGURE 4.1   *City composition and sex differences in bilingualism, 1961.*

the like reflect community mother-tongue composition much more sharply than does general labor force demands. The dominance and impact of English on the work world fluctuates with community composition, but not as sharply as do these other factors.

Along a good part of the abscissa of the bottom panel of Figure 4.1 there is very little difference between the sexes in the bilingualism of the English-mother-tongue residents. When the percentage of the community with French mother tongue is not too large, there is relatively little occupational pressure for the acquisition of French. The net effect is for a fairly flat curve at the lower levels of French-mother-tongue composition due to bilingualism rising about equally for men and women. In communities in which French is the majority mother tongue the pressures for learning this language do rise more rapidly for men than women. This reflects a necessity for the employed population to meet the labor force demands above and beyond the other pressures generating the acquisition of French among native speakers of English.

A notable difference between the two graphs in Figure 4.1 is the position of the French- and English-mother-tongue groups when they are the city's minority language. Bilingualism among French men and women tends to equality when their mother tongue is a small minority language. When English is in an analogous position, the males exceed women by a considerable degree. The English-mother-tongue group does not reach the point at which the pressures for the acquisition of French are so great that the sex difference is eliminated or minimal. Accordingly, occupational pressures are not a superfluous source of bilingualism among English-mother-tongue men. In effect, the English have sufficient institutional support to permit them to live in an overwhelmingly French community without virtually everyone becoming bilingual. This is different for the French in an analogous minority situation. When the French language is numerically unimportant as a community mother tongue, the sex differences virtually disappear because such a sizable percentage of the women must acquire English regardless of their employment.

The two graphs are not completely adequate for some of these inferences since only the relative differences between the sexes are shown. Table 12 gives the actual degree of bilingualism for each sex and mother tongue cross tabulated by community composition. One does indeed observe extremely high rates of French bilingualism in communities where French is the mother tongue of less than 10 percent of the population. The average percentages able to speak English for men and women with French mother tongue are both high and nearly equal, 90 and 89 percent, respectively. Observe how bilingualism tends to drop off for both sexes in cities where French is the mother tongue of a larger component of the population. However, bilingualism among the women does decline more rapidly than among the men.

Bilingualism is very low among the English-mother-tongue population in cities where French is weak (see Table 12). For example, in those places where French is the mother tongue of less than 10 percent of the population, bilingualism occurs among less than 3 percent of either males or females with English mother tongue. One also observes very small sex differences in English bilingualism among all of the communities where French is the mother tongue of less than half the residents. These differences do increase in cities where French is clearly the mother tongue of the majority of the residents.

In passing, Table 12 also provides further evidence of the asymmetrical pressure on bilingualism among the English- and French-mother-tongue segments. In cities in which French is the native language of less than 10 percent of the residents about 90 percent of the French-mother-tongue women and 2 percent of the English-mother-tongue women are able to speak the other official language. But in cities where French is the mother tongue of more than 90 percent of the population, only 64 percent of the English-mother-tongue women are able to speak French whereas 16 percent of the French-mother-tongue women also know English. This absence of demographic symmetry is actually understated since the data in Table 12 are based on the minimum rates of bilingualism among the French, and the maximum among the native English speakers.

TABLE 12

Relation Between Sex Differences in Bilingualism and Mother-Tongue Composition, Selected Canadian Cities: 1961

Percentage of Residents with French Mother Tongue	Number of Cities	Percent Bilingual: By Mother Tongue			
		French Mother Tongue		English Mother Tongue	
		Male	Female	Male	Female
Less than 10	25	90.5	89.2	2.8	2.2
10–20	6	89.5	87.6	5.4	4.7
20–30	3	77.6	72.2	5.7	5.2
30–40	4	81.2	77.3	9.0	8.0
40–50	2	86.2	83.7	12.6	13.2
50–60	1	55.3	43.9	44.0	35.6
60–70	2	60.9	51.1	36.5	28.4
70–80	0	–	–	–	–
80–90	6	37.6	26.1	58.5	51.6
90–100	13	26.4	15.9	76.0	64.3

Phone Book Analysis

The investigator developed an idle curiosity as to what the *Yellow Pages* of telephone directories might be like in cities where both English and French were viable tongues. Are services and products listed under both the English and French language categories? If so, are there separate directories for each language? In the Montreal *Yellow Pages*, one finds that the categories from both languages are employed in the same directory. In other words, one could look up either *avocats* or *lawyers*. However, the listings are not necessarily the same under each category. Some lawyers opt to list only under the English rubric, others only under the French, and some under both categories.

Although curiosity may kill the cat, it does help to feed the graduate student assistant. It soon became apparent that the language listings in the *Yellow Pages* of various cities could provide an index of the various occupational supports and pressures for bilingualism. Although hardly equivalent to the kinds of information that might be obtained from an intensive survey of business activities in each city, *Yellow Pages* provides a measure of each language's role in the various domains of the city's economy. Variations between cities in the language listings might be of value in explaining the rates of bilingualism in the communities.

After pouring through a large number of classified telephone directories, a set of 28 communities was established which had at least some listings under both English and French rubrics. These communities are listed below. The difficulty in expanding the number of communities was due to the very definite favoring of English by listers. Cities with a small proportion of French inhabitants usually do not use French-language rubrics, but the investigator did not encounter one instance in which English listings were omitted entirely from *Yellow Pages*. In effect, this means that the sample of cities are skewed toward those in which French is a numerically important mother tongue.

Bilingual *Yellow Page* Directories Included in the Analysis

Alma, Quebec	Ottawa, Ontario
Asbestos, Quebec	Pembroke, Ontario
Chicoutimi, Quebec	Quebec, Quebec
Cornwall, Ontario	Rimouski, Quebec
Drummondville, Quebec	Rivière-du-Loup, Quebec
Granby, Quebec	Rouyn-Noranda, Quebec
Joliette, Quebec	St. Hyacinthe, Quebec
Jonquière-Kénogami, Quebec	St. Jean, Quebec
La Tuque, Quebec	St. Jerome, Quebec
Magog, Quebec	Sept-Îles, Quebec
Montreal, Quebec	Shawinigan, Quebec

Sherbrooke, Quebec	Trois-Rivières, Quebec
Sorel, Quebec	Valleyfield, Quebec
Thetford Mines, Quebec	Victoriaville, Quebec

A sample of 97 categories was randomly drawn from the Ottawa-Hull *Yellow Pages* (1965 directories are largely used in this section; census data refer to 1961). Some of these categories were in English and others in French, but in all cases the equivalent in the other language was also employed. For each of the 28 cities data were gathered on the percentage of advertisers listing in English only, French only, and both official languages. There is a moderate relationship between the occurrence of dual listings (where the advertiser lists under both language categories) and bilingualism among the residents of each community, $r = .61$, $b = .50$ (where the listing is the independent variable), $a = 12.8$. In general, cities tend to have more bilingual listings if a sizable percentage of the residents speak both official languages; however, the association is not extraordinarily high.

The listings strongly favor English, at least when compared with the mother-tongue composition of each city. Even if advertisers using both languages are ignored, in about half (17) of the cities the percentage of listings in English exclusively is greater than the percentage of the population with English mother tongue. By contrast in only one city does the percentage of listings in French only exceed or equal the percentage of the population with French mother tongue. Naturally the position of both languages would be improved considerably if bilisted advertisers were included, but the point remains that English is treated far more favorably than French when one considers the mother tongue composition of each city.

The frequency of exclusive listings under each tongue is closely linked to the variations between cities in bilingualism among each major mother-tongue group. The first row of Table 13 indicates an extremely high association between listings in English only and the frequency of bilingualism among the French mother tongue population, $r = .97$. Although the correlation between English-mother-tongue bilingualism and listings in French only is lower, the coefficient of correlation is still .84 (row 2).

A distinction can be drawn between "consumer" and "nonconsumer" listings. The former is defined as products and services that are normally purchased or used by and for members of a family unit. "Retail bakers" would be a consumer listing, but "wholesale bakers" would not. This distinction is usually fairly clear-cut but sometimes difficulties are encountered; for example, "typewriters and supplies" would represent retailers oriented to the consumer market as well as business offices. Most listings

TABLE 13

Correlation Analysis Between Yellow Page Listings and Linguistic Characteristics of 28 Cities

| Row | Variables[a] | | r | b_{yx} | a_{yx} |
	Y	X			
1	3	1	0.97	0.77	16.7
2	4	2	0.84	0.78	4.9
3	6	5	0.91	0.94	14.2
4	8	7	0.89	0.82	−11.7
5	9	6	0.87	0.67	− 7.8
6	9	5	0.98	0.78	− 0.2
7	10	8	0.82	0.83	31.4
8	10	7	0.96	0.90	7.5

[a]Variables: 1. Percent of listings in English only. 2. Percent of listings in French only. 3. Percent of French-mother-tongue residents who are bilingual. 4. Percent of English-mother-tongue residents who are bilingual. 5. Percent of consumer listings in English only. 6. Percent of nonconsumer listings in English only. 7. Percent of consumer listings in French only. 8. Percent of nonconsumer listings in French only. 9. Percent of residents speaking English only. 10. Percent of residents speaking French only.

are easily divided into one class or the other. It was necessary to boost the number of nonconsumer categories by adding additional rubrics.

The percentage of consumer listings in English is strongly correlated between cities with the percentage of English listings for nonconsumer items. An analogous relationship also occurs for French (see rows 3 and 4 of Table 13). What is particularly interesting is the relative positions of the two languages in consumer and nonconsumer listings. With the exception of one city, the percentage of listings exclusively in English is greater for nonconsumer items than consumer items. The opposite holds for French, with the percentage of consumer listings only in this language exceeding the percentage of nonconsumer listings in nearly all of the 28 cities. Given the relationship for listings in English only, this finding is not surprising in view of the interdependence of the percentages. Nevertheless these patterns make it clear that nonconsumer activities in Canada favor English to an even greater degree than consumer-oriented businesses.

Comparing the percentage of monolingual residents in each community with the frequency of exclusive listings in each language, it is clear that consumer listings are more closely linked to the linguistic skills of the community; for example, the correlation between the percentage of the residents speaking English only and nonconsumer listings exclusively in this language is .87. Between consumer listings and the percentage speaking English only, however, the correlation is .98. Since a similar pattern exists for French (Table 13, rows 7 and 8), it is clear that the linguistic abilities of the residents are more closely linked to consumer listings than nonconsumer practices.

In all cities the percentage of nonconsumer listings in English only exceeds the percentage of the population speaking English only. On the other hand, the percentage speaking English only tends to be more similar to the frequency of consumer listings in English only (compare the scatter diagrams in Figure 4.2). Among the French, also, the consumer listings exclusively in this tongue are at about the same frequency as the proportion of residents who are French monoglots. Nonconsumer listings are less frequent than the demographic composition would suggest (compare panels in Figure 4.3).

The solid line in each diagram indicates the existence of equality between the two sets of percentages. Observe in the top panel of Figure 4.3 how closely the consumer listings in French hovers around this line. In particular, compare this pattern with the other panel in Figure 4.3 in which the percentage of nonconsumer listings in French only is considerably below the level expected if listing practices merely reflected the communities' linguistic composition.

In summary, the language frequency found in the *Yellow Pages* of various Canadian cities is closely linked to the linguistic skills and composition of the residents. Notwithstanding the high correlations, of greater importance is the fact that listings under the English rubrics are over-represented (and the French categories under-represented) when compared with the mother-tongue composition of the city or the number of English and French monoglots in the community. The strength of English and the weakness of French shows up particularly in the nonconsumer listings; based on the demographic criteria, both tongues are represented in due proportion under the consumer listings.

These results provide further support for the contention that the pressures to acquire English are stronger for the French Canadian in the labor market than for the French housewife. For the English-mother-tongue resident of cities where French is, demographically speaking, at least fairly important, the pressures to acquire French are not as great in the nonconsumer area. This, however, does not necessarily contradict the position taken earlier in this chapter, since the employment pressures are still an added inducement for the acquisition of French. It does suggest that English-mother-tongue workers in administrative positions or noncon-

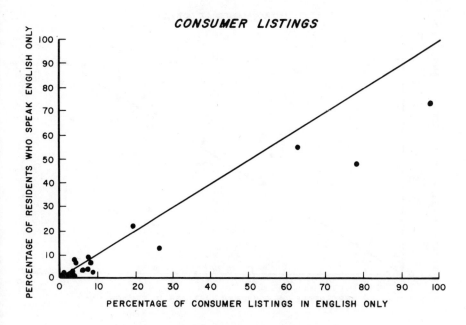

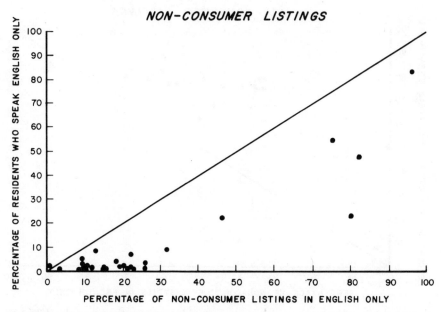

FIGURE 4.2 *Consumer and non-consumer listings in English only, bilingual yellow pages of selected cities, 1965.*

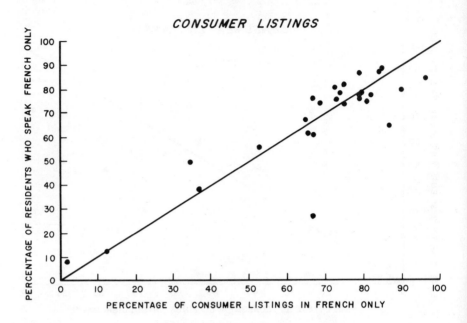

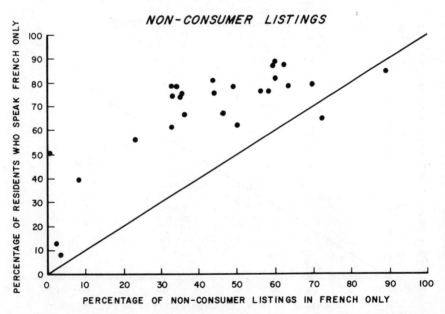

FIGURE 4.3 *Consumer and non-consumer listings in French only, bilingual yellow pages of selected cities, 1965.*

sumer industries are more insulated from the need to speak French than their compatriots who deal directly with consumers. For native French speakers the relative pressures for acquiring English in a given community are in the opposite direction. Attention is given in Chapter 5 to somewhat more subtle dimensions of the labor force pressures for bilingualism in metropolitan Montreal.

Occupational Pressures in Montreal and Ottawa

Two occupational forces operate in opposite directions to create bilingualism in linguistically diverse cities. On the one hand, there is the pressure to meet the customer in his own language. This pressure operates through competition in the market place to generate bilingualism. If only this force were operating, bilingualism among the French and the English would tend to be highest in the same occupations. On the other hand, there is the unilateral pressure toward bilingualism that is generated by the economic dominance of one linguistic group in the business world. This may be expected to produce a high rate of bilingualism among the French in the very same occupational areas in which there is relatively little bilingualism among the British.

The net effect is unclear. There is some reason to expect bilingualism among the two mother-tongue groups to be positively correlated by occupation. On the other hand, there is some reason to expect an inverse relationship by occupation for the two groups. The net effect is a set of rather mild correlations between British and French bilingualism in both the Montreal and Ottawa metropolitan areas in 1961 (see Table 14). Tau is somewhat negative for the male groups in each city and somewhat positive for women. Keeping in mind that these measures of association are based on a small number of broad occupational categories (nine for men and eight for women), there is a tendency for British males to be least bilingual in the occupational areas in which French Canadian men are most bilingual. This can be interpreted as reflecting the net outcome of two contradictory forces. The association between British and French bilingualism among women is also small, but positive. This is probably due to the fact that women occupy less dominant positions and are therefore more likely to deal with the public. Accordingly, the relative importance of these two contradictory forces is somewhat different for men and women in the labor force.

There is definite evidence of a structural pressure towards bilingualism that is generated by the occupational demands. Although Ottawa and Montreal differ in both their industrial makeup and linguistic composition, a fairly strong association exists between the two metropolitan areas in the relative degree of bilingualism generated by the same occupations. Among

TABLE 14

Bilingualism in Occupational Groups, by Sex and Ethnic Origin, Montreal and Ottawa: 1961

| | Tau Correlations | |
Comparison	Male	Female
Montreal		
British versus French	−0.22	0.21
Ottawa		
British versus French	−0.28	0.14
British		
Ottawa versus Montreal	0.33	0.71
French		
Ottawa versus Montreal	0.72	0.79

men of French origin tau is .72 between the degree of bilingualism in each city's occupations. In other words, occupations that require a relatively high frequency of bilingualism for French-Canadian men in Montreal are also the occupations in Ottawa that create the greatest demands for bilingualism among the French. The results are equally high for both French and British women, providing further evidence that there is a persistent tendency for certain occupational pursuits to generate more bilingualism than other occupations.

The one "sour" note is the considerably lower tau between Montreal and Ottawa for British male bilingualism by occupation. This means that occupations in Montreal that have the highest degree of British male bilingualism are only mildly associated with the occupations that have the highest bilingualism among the British in Ottawa. Basically, I am unable to account for the relatively low intercity occupational association for the British men.

Bilingualism in Quebec's Counties

Location and occupation are fused together, of course, when one considers farming as an occupation and rural residence as a locational factor. Analysis of the occurrence of bilingualism among the male residents of each of Quebec's 75 counties in 1961 indicates that these two factors are related to bilingualism. Data are not available on bilingualism among men in the working ages separate from those either younger or older in each county.

An inverse association exists by county between the percentage of males living on farms and the percentage of the men who are bilingual

($r = -.60$, $b = -.49$, and $a = 32.1$, with rural residence the independent variable). Counties with substantial segments of the population located on farms tend to have lower rates of bilingualism than those counties in which relatively small numbers live on farms. The other side of the same coin, almost, is the influence on male bilingualism of the percent employed in manufacturing in each county. A positive association exists between bilingualism and the degree of employment in manufacturing ($r = .47$, $b = .56$, and $a = 7.9$).

These correlations provide further evidence that rural areas are less likely to have bilingualism as contrasted with industrial locales. In this respect, there is some support for the contention that movement off the farms into industrial employment is an impetus for the acquisition of English among the French. If the same two independent variables, rural residence and manufacturing employment, are correlated with the acquisition of English among the French-mother-tongue male population of each county, results in the same direction are obtained as above. The acquisition of English is directly associated with employment in manufacturing ($r = .36$, $b = .53$, and $a = 9.9$) and inversely linked to location on farms ($r = -.49$, $b = -.51$, $a = 33.8$).

RESIDENTIAL SEGREGATION

There is reason to expect some form of interaction between the residential segregation of a group and its linguistic behavior. High segregation causes low bilingualism because it reduces the need for acquiring another language for residentially based activities such as shopping, neighboring, and the like. On the other hand, bilingualism reduces the need for segregation as a mechanism for survival since a group that can communicate with others has much less reason to isolate itself residentially. However, if an ethnic group is so small in number or the pressures for bilingualism are sufficiently strong from other sources such as schooling or the job market, then segregation will not prevent bilingualism or the acquisition of an official language.

Segregation in Thirteen Cities

The index of dissimilarity, described in Chapter 2, is also employed as a measure of segregation. The index ranges from 0 (no segregation) to 100 (maximum segregation). This measure reflects the pattern of isolation between two populations independently of their total numbers in the community. This measure is sometimes referred to as the index of segregation.

Segregation was measured for the 13 cities listed below on the basis of the census tract distributions in 1961. The indexes of segregation between the French and British ethnic groups range from 12 and 13 in Calgary, Regina, and London to more than 50 in the Ottawa and Montreal metropolitan areas. There is a rather strong positive association between the segregation between these two groups and the maintenance of French as the mother tongue within the French ethnic group ($r = .84$). French is less frequently the mother tongue of the French ethnic group in cities with low segregation between the British and French ethnic groups. In effect, the French are not very isolated from the British in cities where many of the former possess an English mother tongue. In communities in which the French retain their native language to a large degree residential isolation between the British and French ethnic groups is considerably higher. Recognizing that ethnic isolation might be maintained even without linguistic differentiation, in Canada it is clear that there is little ethnic isolation when the French mother tongue is given up. In cities in whch the French no longer maintain their ancestors' language, there is relatively little isolation from the British group. The causal order of these two phenomena cannot be determined from *these* data.

Metropolitan Areas in Which Segregation Was Measured, 1961

Calgary	Regina (city)
Hamilton	Sherbrooke (urban area)
London	Sudbury
Montreal	Toronto
Ottawa	Trois-Rivières (urban area)
Quebec	Windsor
	Winnipeg

These results reflect the pattern of isolation between two populations independently of their relative numbers in the community. To consider the combined influence on language behavior of both the groups' spatial distributions and their relative numbers, a slightly modified form of the segregation index proposed by Bell (1954) is employed. The Bell measure, since it is sensitive to population composition as well as the *pattern* of segregation, is appropriate for measuring the combined effect of these two factors on bilingualism among each mother-tongue group. The modified Bell measure describes isolation between any two specified groups in terms of the probability of joint pairing when interaction is restricted to random selections from the subareas of a city. For a more detailed discussion of the modified Bell measure, see Farley and Taeuber (1968) and Lieberson (1969).

Because of the unavailability of the necessary data, segregation is measured for the British and French ethnic groups rather than for the inhabitants with English and French mother tongue, respectively. Isolation of the French ethnic group from the remainder of the city's population (as measured by the modified Bell index) is closely linked to the frequency of bilingualism among the French-mother-tongue residents, the product–moment correlation is −.95. There is alsoo a strong inverse linkage between the isolation of the British ethnic group and the frequency of bilingualism among the English-mother-tongue group, $r = -.89$.

The frequency of bilingualism, as this analysis of 13 cities indicates, is inversely related to the isolation of the ethnic group from the remainder of the population. High isolation, due to a combination of composition and residence pattern, yields relatively low levels of bilingualism. Not only is the correlation high between interaction potential and bilingualism but the regression slopes indicate the proportion of bilingualism rises and falls sharply with segregation. The coefficient of regression for French bilingualism on the Bell index of French isolation is −.78, with $a = .98$. The regression coefficient for English-mother-tongue bilingualism on British segregation is −1.24, with $a = .78$.

Bilingualism by Ward

One can go beyond the thesis that segregation influences bilingualism and examine its implications for the different areas of a city as well as the differential impact of segregation on men and women. Mother-tongue data for the male and female residents of each ward in six different Canadian cities in 1941 permit some exploration into the earlier contentions about male–female differences in the pressures for bilingualism. Unfortunately the number of wards is rather small for most of these cities and the dispersion between wards in mother-tongue composition is not too great.

Neverthless the overall relationship between mother-tongue composition within the ward, bilingualism, and the "city effect" is impressive. Looking across the columns in Table 15, one finds the learning of French among those with some other mother tongue tends to rise in accordance with the French-mother-tongue composition of the ward. This is to be expected if it is argued that the linguistic context of the immediate neighborhood will affect the frequency of bilingualism. In those districts of Montreal in which French is the mother tongue of less than 30 percent of the residents about a quarter of those with a non-French mother tongue are able to speak this language. Observe how the rate changes directly with changes in French-mother-tongue composition, reaching an average of 60 percent bilingual in those areas in which French is the native language of the overwhelming majority of the residents. In general, this pat-

TABLE 15

Acquisition of French by Mother-Tongue Composition of Residential Subareas, Selected Cities: 1941

	Percent Able to Speak French Among Residents With Non-French Mother Tongue					
	Subareas by Percent with French-Mother-Tongue Residents[a]					
City	Less Than 1	1–10	10–30	30–70	70–90	90 and over
Toronto	1.5 (6)	2.2 (3)				
Vancouver	2.0 (13)	1.7 (6)				
Winnipeg	1.1 (28)	1.7 (31)				
Ottawa		7.0 (4)	6.4 (3)	16.3 (3)	33.0 (1)	
Montreal			23.5 (5)	27.9 (9)	46.9 (12)	59.5 (9)
Quebec					66.8 (3)	77.3 (3)

[a]Number of subareas indicated in parentheses.

tern is observed among all six of the cities examined, with slight reversals in the first two columns for Ottawa and a small reversal for Vancouver.

An analogous pattern exists for the learning of English among those with a different mother tongue (see Table 16). Here, of course, the acquisition rate declines as the percentage of the population with French mother tongue increases; for example, the rate of second-language learning for the non-English mother-tongue residents goes from 83 percent in Montreal's wards where French is a relatively weak mother tongue to 43 percent in wards where French is the mother tongue of the overwhelming majority of the residents. Only one exception exists to this pattern, a reversal between two categories in Ottawa.

Tables 15 and 16, in brief, make it clear that bilingualism within a city is connected to residential location for both major linguistic groups. These tables also indicate that the impact of residential isolation on bilingualism varies between cities. Mother-tongue composition of the entire city in 1941 may be used as a crude index of the strength of the nonresidential forces operating on bilingualism in each city. The six cities in the tables above are ordered by the proportion of the residents with French mother tongue. There is little to distinguish Toronto, Vancouver, and Winnipeg from one another; the proportion is very low in all three (about 2 percent of the residents in Winnipeg and even less in the other two cities are native speakers of French). Before an eyebrow is raised about Winnipeg, bear in mind that these data for 1941 refer to the political city and are not available

TABLE 16

Acquisition of English by Mother-Tongue Composition of Residential Subareas, Selected Cities: 1941

Percent Able to Speak ~~French~~ ᴇ*NGLISH* Among Residents
With Non-English Mother Tongue

City	Subareas by Percent with French-Mother-Tongue-Residents[a]					
	Less Than 1	1–10	10–30	30–70	70–90	90 and over
Toronto	97.9 (6)	94.8 (13)				
Vancouver	97.4 (13)	93.3 (6)				
Winnipeg	98.5 (28)	98.2 (31)				
Ottawa		95.1 (4)	88.2 (3)	89.9 (3)	81.3 (1)	
Montreal			83.2 (5)	64.4 (9)	48.2 (12)	43.3 (9)
Quebec					43.3 (3)	20.4 (3)

[a]Number of subareas indicated in parentheses.

for adjacent suburbs such as St. Boniface. The remaining three cities do differ, however, from one another as well as from the preceding three. In 1941 French was the mother tongue of nearly 30 percent of the residents in Ottawa, about two-thirds of those in Montreal, and over 90 percent in Quebec.

Looking down the columns of Table 15, we find at least partial support for the contention that the segregation effect on bilingualism is influenced by the overall mother-tongue composition of the city. Differences between Toronto, Vancouver, and Winnipeg do not display the expected pattern, but this can be discounted because of the minor differences in their mother-tongue composition. The patterns for the remaining cities do show the influence of residential isolation on bilingualism is modified by a "city effect." In all of the possble comparisons between Ottawa, Montreal, and Quebec the degree of bilingualism follows the anticipated pattern. In wards in which 70 to 90 percent of the residents are native speakers of French, for example, the acquisition of French among the remaining residents varies from about a third in Ottawa to 47 percent in Montreal and 67 percent in Quebec.

In regard to the learning of English by those with some other mother tongue, the last three cities are also consistently ordered (Table 16). Holding mother-tongue composition of the subarea constant, the percent learning English is greater in Ottawa than in Montreal and higher in Montreal than in Quebec. Comparisons involving the remaining three cities are not so consistent, but the reader is again reminded that variation in French-mother-tongue composition is small.

These results clearly indicate that the influence on bilingualism of residential isolation is modified by the operation of other forces in the city. There are community-wide pressures that affect second-language acquisition regardless of where one lives in the city.

Sex Differences in the Linguistic Response to Segregation

Earlier, the view was taken that men in the labor force are subject to pressures for the acquisition of a second language above and beyond those faced by women at home. This suggests that the influence of segregation on bilingualism will be different for the sexes. Since men are subject to more pressures that are not linked to residential location, one might anticipate that their rates of bilingualism will be relatively less influenced by residential location.

There is a close association between variations in mother-tongue composition and bilingualism in the wards of Quebec, Montreal, and Ottawa. For both sexes in Quebec, for example, r is —.97 between French-mother-tongue composition and the percentage learning English among those with some other mother tongue. On the other hand, r is .77 between French-mother-tongue composition and the acquisition of French as a second language. Although the correlations for each sex are similar in virtually all cases, it is important to note the differences in the coefficients of regression between males and females with the same mother tongue. In Montreal, for example, the slopes for women are higher than for men. For the ability to speak English as a second language, b is —.65 and —.47 for women and men, respectively; for those learning French, it is .57 and .49.

The net effect of these differences are shown in Figures 4 and 5 where the regression lines are plotted. One observes in some cities that bilingualism rates rise or fall more sharply for women than men when plotted against the composition of the wards. Male bilingualism is influenced by the composition of the areas in which they reside, but the rates for women are even more sensitive to this factor. Montreal is clearly the best illustration of this phenomenon; in Ottawa the results are in the expected direction, but the differences in regression coefficients are minor. Quebec works very nicely for the acquisition of French as a second language, where b is .44 for men and 1.00 for women (see Figure 4.4), but the male regression slope exceeds the female slope (see Figure 4.5) for the learning of English (—1.92 versus —1.71).

The support for the hypothesized difference between men and women, in short, is not conclusive. They are excellent for Montreal, inconsistent for

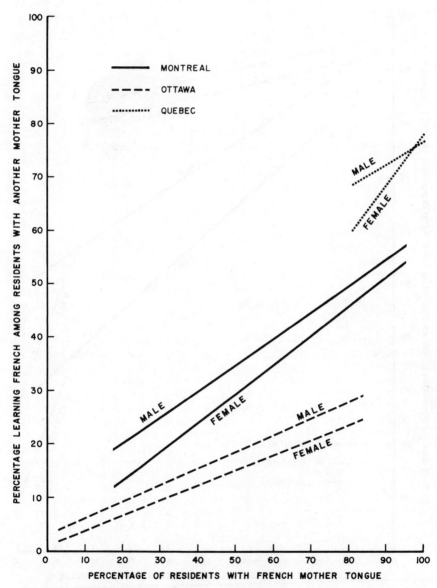

FIGURE 4.4 *Regression lines for the acquisition of French, by sex and mother tongue composition of wards, 1941.*

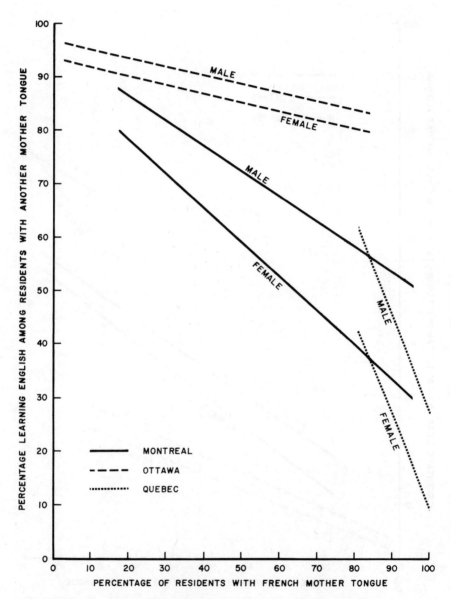

FIGURE 4.5 *Regression lines for the acquisition of English, by sex and mother tongue composition of wards, 1941.*

Quebec, and only minimally in the predicted direction for Ottawa. The reader is reminded of the particularly small number of spatial subdivisions in Ottawa and Quebec. Further exploration with more cities and better data is necessary before one can pin down the thesis presented above.

5

Occupational Demands

The linguistic demands of the work-world are among the most important forces influencing the acquisition of a second language. Since virtually all able-bodied men and an increasing number of women seek jobs, the advantage one language enjoys over another in this sphere can have a profound impact on the degree of bilingualism in each mother-tongue group. Not only may language play a role in obtaining employment, but certain linguistic skills may be a vital prerequisite for advancement and higher income. Unfortunately the interaction between the linguistic demands of employers and co-workers, the kind of service or product involved, the location of the place of business, and the linguistic preferences of customers or clients involve far too many subtleties to permit a broad-gauged intercity comparison of Canadian communities. Instead, Montreal is used as a case study of the interplay between occupational demands and bilingualism.

The influence of occupational demands on bilingualism are complex. First, the importance of communication in any language will vary greatly between jobs. A laborer could get along far more easily than could a sales clerk without speaking to his co-workers or by learning a very minimal number of words. Even jobs demanding a certain level of communication can be subdivided on the basis of whether they are oriented toward co-workers or toward such outsiders as customers, clients, or the general public. A sales clerk will have a far greater need for communication with her customers than with her co-workers. A secretary, by contrast, will be fairly useless unless she can communicate with her co-workers. Occupations can also be subdivided in terms of the linguistic composition of co-workers and customers. A grocery located in the midst of a solidly French neighborhood will have very minimal demands for English-speaking clerks, whereas groceries located in an English-speaking suburb will have little need for a French-speaking employee. Occupations may themselves differ if there are any services or activities oriented particularly to one language world as opposed to the other (see Hughes, 1943, pp. 65–67, 82–83).

Occupations can be viewed as differing in the frequency of "inside" and "outside" interaction, that is, of interaction with fellow employees versus nonemployees. Occupations that involve frequent interaction with the "outside" will create a need for bilingualism when the outsiders are linguistically diverse. "Outsider" interaction will lead to bilingualism for only one of the mother-tongue segments if the outsiders tend to favor one of the languages. Likewise, among jobs that are "insider" oriented, concentration of linguistic compatriots will minimize the need for bilingualism. Ideally, occupations could be classified according to the following four criteria:

1. Linguistic composition of co-workers.
2. Importance of communication with co-workers.
3. Linguistic composition of customers and relevant outsiders.
4. Importance of communication with customers and outsiders.

LABOR FORCE PARTICIPATION AND BILINGUALISM

Participation in Montreal's labor force is hardly the only factor contributing to bilingualism in a city where a second language is taught in the schools, where both groups are numerically important, and both tongues are viable forces in the community. On the other hand, there is little doubt that occupational demands play an important role in generating bilingualism in Montreal. The ability to speak a second language is more common among those working than not. About 45 percent of English-mother-tongue men in the work force are bilingual, compared with 35 percent of those who are at home. Among French males, the respective percentages bilingual are 73 and 56. (In this chapter, unless otherwise noted, the data refer to the metropolitan population 15 years of age and older in 1961). Women in the labor force are likewise more bilingual than those who are not. These data may understate the degree of bilingualism due to occupational pressures since second-language learning among school children more than 15 years of age may reflect the linguistic needs anticipated for employment.

The pressures leading to greater bilingualism among the employed are based on an interaction of other factors with occupational needs. Although work does appear to increase the need for a second language, it still affects the French more than the English. Thus, although 45 percent of the men in the labor force with an English mother tongue are bilingual, nearly 75 percent of those with a French mother tongue are bilingual. Likewise only a third of working English-mother-tongue women can speak French, whereas 60 percent of employed French women know English. Those with French mother tongue who are not in the labor force are still more bilingual than workers of the same sex with English mother tongue. The pressures favoring English are also illustrated by the languages acquired among those whose mother tongue was neither official language. The ratio between the number learning English only to the number acquiring only French is about 4 to 1.

The linkage between education and bilingualism shows that different patterns exist for Montreal's two basic groups. There is virtually no association between educational achievement and bilingualism among those of British origin, whereas bilingualism rises sharply with education in the French segment of the labor force (see Table 1). The discrepancies are striking indeed—French-Canadian men without any schooling are as likely to be bilingual as men of British origin who have attended a university. Nearly all French-Canadian men who have attended a university are bilingual, whereas less than half the British men with similar education know French. Other ethnic groups also have a positive correlation between educational attainment and bilingualism, although their levels of bilingualism are not so high as among the French. Achievement of higher socioeconomic status among the French appears to require a knowledge of English, whereas status and ability to speak French are unrelated for the British.

The kind of occupation held influences the degree of bilingualism, but not in the same way for British and French. Unfortunately, the available data do not permit examination of specific jobs, rather only of about 10 occupational categories, most of which can be subdivided into "wage earners" and self-employed." The heterogeneity of the occupational categories used cannot be stressed too greatly. Included among the professionals, for example, are physicians, dentists, and lawyers—people who must orient themselves to their clientele. On the other hand, the category encompasses various engineers, many being basically oriented toward fellow workers with little contact with the public. In addition, technicians are grouped with professionals. Differences between ethnic groups in

TABLE 1

Percent of Males in the Labor Force Who Are Bilingual, by Education

		Years of School Completed			
Ethnic Group	None	Elementary, 1+ Years	High School, 1–2 Years	High School, 3–5 Years	University, 1+ Years
British	41	44	39	38	42
French	43	58	79	89	94
Other	19	35	53	52	61

their concentration within the detailed occupations of a broad category can affect their degree of bilingualism. The relevant data available from unpublished census tabulations are shown in Table 2, which gives the percentage of each ethnic group who are bilingual tabulated by their occupation.

Regardless of occupation, the frequency of bilingualism does not differ very much among wage earners in the British ethnic group. The highest percentage is in sales (50) and the lowest is among professionals (33). By contrast the French range from 49 percent bilingual among laborers to 94 percent among those who are managers. In 10 of the 11 occupational categories bilingualism is higher among British self-employed males than among wage earners. Assuming that employers generally have more outside contact than employees, this offers further evidence that outside contacts provide pressure for bilingualism. Nevertheless, the French are still more bilingual than the British in all occupational categories, with one slight exception (self-employed in transportation and communication).

Should there be a correlation between the degree French workers in an occupation are bilingual and the frequency of bilingualism among British men in the same occupations? There are occupations where pressure for bilingualism among one group is accompanied by an absence of a similar pressure in the other group; for example, it would be difficult for a French monoglot to pursue an occupation oriented heavily toward American tourists, but the same position will permit an English Canadian to remain ignorant of French. On the other hand, there are jobs which put pressure on both English- and French-mother-tongue workers to become bilingual, for example, telephone operators or policemen. The net effect of this diversity is a weak connection between the degree of bilingualism among the French and British in 18 occupations ($r = -.22$).

Because of the heterogeneity within the occupational categories, only an impressionistic interpretation can be offered here for the variations in bilingualism between ethnic groups. Men employed as laborers in the two groups are relatively similar in their degree of bilingualism. This is an occupation which requires minimal interaction with either customers or co-workers. The net effect is to reduce the degree of bilingualism among the French in this occupation to a level far below that for the labor force as a whole (49 versus 73 percent). With the British amounting to only 7 percent of laborers in Montreal, compared with 18 percent of the total male work force, the pressures for bilingualism among the British are perhaps slightly greater than in occupations where English plays a more dominant role. Thus 43 percent of the British employed as laborers are bilingual, some 3 percent more than all British men in the labor force.

The pattern for laborers is repeated by other "blue-collar" workers such

TABLE 2

Percent of Males Bilingual by Occupation, Employment Status, and Ethnic Origin

Occupation	Wage or Salary Earner		Self-Employed	
	British	French	British	French
Managerial	40	94	51	82
Professional and technical	33	90	60	96
Clerical	38	85	78	85
Sales	50	86	49	83
Service and recreation	35	72	56	73
Transport and communication	44	72	76	75
Farmers and stockraisers	*	*	100	46
Other primary	42	51	*	51
Craftsmen	41	64	47	71
Laborers	43	49	50	57
Total	40	72	54	81

*No males.

as wage-earning craftsmen and those engaged in nonfarm primary occupations. Again, there is a relatively low degree of bilingualism among the French ethnic group and a smaller British–French gap in bilingualism. What is noteworthy here is not the slightly higher frequency of bilingualism among the British in these occupations compared with those employed in other activities, but that these occupations are marked by considerably less bilingualism among the French compared to their overall rate.

Sales employees among both the British and French groups are more apt to be bilingual than other wage earners. This no doubt reflects the need to communicate with a wide variety of customers and the advantages derived from speaking the customer's native tongue. However, the gap between the two groups in their degree of bilingualism is, if anything, slightly greater than for all wage earners. French-Canadian men employed as managers, professionals and technicians, and clerks—all largely white-collar "office" jobs—are characterized by an extremely high frequency of bilingualism. All but 4 percent of self-employed professionals and 6 percent of those hired as managers are bilingual. Employment in these occupations as a wage earner does not yield a high degree of bilingualism among the British. Indeed, clerks and professionals are below the average for all British wage earners. Bilingualism does rise considerably among the British who are self-employed in these categories, probably reflecting a greater orientation toward clients and outside markets.

The bilingual pattern among women in Montreal is fairly similar, recognizing that the actual jobs covered by these broad occupational divisions are not the same for both men and women. French women are more apt to be bilingual than British women in nearly all occupations. The pressure for bilingualism is particularly great among French women in white-collar office positions such as clercial (80 percent) and managerial wage earners (86 percent). Occupations listed under "transportation and communication" are strikingly high in the degree of bilingualism among both British and French wage earners, 57 and 90 percent, respectively. However, women in this category are largely employed as telephone operators—an occupation with a need for bilingualism among both English- and French-speaking employees.

As is the case for men, there is no particularly strong association between the frequency of bilingualism among women in the two ethnic groups. The correlation between bilingualism among British and French women by occupation is rather low, $r = .14$. When compared with their ethnic group average, in some occupations the proportion bilingual is especially low or especially high for both groups. In other occupations, relatively high rates of bilingualism are accompanied by relatively low percentages for women in the other ethnic group.

EMPLOYMENT PRESSURES

Classified advertisements in Montreal's French- and English-language newspapers provide a useful instrument for determining the existence of bilingual pressures at the time of employment. One of the great advantages of "want ads" is that they provide a clear-cut causal sequence since the prerequisites of the job are stated in advance of employment. The cross-sectional associations reported above between occupation and bilingualism may reflect the fact that acquisition of a second language is either a prerequisite, or at least an advantage, in obtaining employment in certain occupations. On the other hand, the associations may reflect the fact that persons in certain occupations are more likely to retain their bilingualism or learn a second tongue after employment. Undoubtedly all of these factors operate, but the goal here is to determine the influence of occupational demands on bilingualism. Accordingly, the April 11 and May 2, 1964 weekend issues of the *Montreal Star* and *La Presse* were studied.

Several assumptions are necessary. First, jobs not indicating any language requirements are assumed to be suitable for applicants who can speak only the language in which the newspaper is published. This seems most reasonable, since there were no advertisements which indicated that the necessary language was the one in which the newspaper was published. A second assumption is somewhat stickier; namely, if the English paper carried an advertisement with a requirement such as "must speak French" or "knowledge of French is required," it was assumed that the applicant had to be bilingual. In point of fact it is possible that the employer required someone who spoke only French and for other reasons chose to advertise in the English paper. It seems unlikely, however, that such advertisements would be common. Analogous assumptions were made about want ads in the French paper. Therefore any mention of the language other than the one in which the paper was published was taken to indicate a job in which the respondent had to know both English and French. In many instances the advertisement was less ambiguous and simply stated that bilingualism was necessary.

There is a severe occupational bias in using newspaper classified advertisements, since there are many types of job which are not advertised at all or infrequently at best. Use of want ads rules out the self-employed, many professionals, jobs obtained through employment agencies, personal contact, and the like. Jobs that have high turnover are more likely to be represented than those with low turnover.

Using the job description in the advertisement, each position is placed in a standard occupational classification based on the *Occupational Classification Manual, Census of Canada, 1961*. Several French manuals were also used to maximize the comparability in the classification of want ads written in different languages. Of particular value were *Classification condensée des occupations: pour les chiffreurs de la section A, recensement du Canada, 1961* and a "Bilingual Summary Index of Occupational Divisions, Groups and Classes, 1961 Census" provided through the courtesy of the Dominion Bureau of Statistics. Nevertheless, many occupations are not described in the advertisements with sufficient detail to make a good classification. Use was made of residual categories in each broad occupational division when a more detailed effort appeared unjustified. Want ads were not weighted by the number of positions indicated in the advertisement. Rather, each specific occupation appearing in a given ad was given a weight of one. A total of 1509 ads were gathered from the *Star* and 1433 from *La Presse* for the two weekends examined.

The frequency of bilingual requirements differ by language. In the English-language paper, 19 percent of the male ads and 17 percent of those for females indicate that knowledge of French is necessary. By contrast 25 percent of male and 23 percent of female ads in *La Presse* require a knowledge of English. Thus the pressure for bilingualism at the time of employment is greater for French-speaking Montrealers.

Differences in the linguistic pressures operating on English- and French-speaking Montrealers are actually greater than the figures above suggest. Some of these differences are hidden by the kinds of occupations advertised in the two papers. Using for the most part a three-digit classification of occupations, the index of dissimilarity between advertisements for men in the *Star* and *Presse* is 30 and a similar index is recorded for women's want ads. If the types of occupations advertised in the two papers were identical in frequency, an index of 0 would be obtained; if complete dissimilarity existed in the kinds of jobs advertised in the two papers, then the index would be 100. Indexes of 30 mean that there is a fairly sizable difference between the newspapers in the occupations listed.

These differences in the occupations advertised in the two papers tend to conceal a stronger pressure for bilingualism in the French newspaper for specific jobs. Using Westergaard's standardization procedure, the expected percent of ads that would be bilingual in the *Star* is 29 if the bilingual rates for the same occupation in *La Presse* were to apply (Table 3). By contrast, if the bilingual rates for each occupation in the *Star* were to occur for jobs listed in *La Presse,* then only 20 percent of the want ads for men in the French paper would require bilinguals. In other words, although only 19 percent of the jobs listed for men in the English paper actually require bilinguals, the percentage would be considerably higher, 29, if the bilingual rates for the same jobs in *La Presse* operated in the *Star*. Were jobs advertised for men in *La Presse* to require bilingualism no more often than the same jobs listed in the English paper, then the frequency of bilingual demands for the French would be 20 instead of 25 percent.

TABLE 3

Newspaper Advertisements Requiring Bilingualism, 1964

Newspaper	Percent Bilingual			
	Male		Female	
	Actual	Expected[a]	Actual	Expected[a]
Montreal Star	19	29	17	38
La Presse	25	20	24[b]	12

[a]Based on occupation specific rates in other newspaper for the same sex.

[b]Differs slightly from earlier figure reported because of adjustment due to absence of rates in the *Star* for some occupations.

Differences between the two papers in the kinds of occupations advertised also understate the greater pressure for bilingualism among French-speaking women. If the bilingual rates for jobs in *La Presse* also occurred in the *Star*, then twice as many of the want ads for women in the English-language paper would require a knowledge of French as actually do (38 versus 17 percent). On the other hand, if women's want ads in *La Presse* had the same frequency of bilingual requirements as the same jobs advertised in the *Star*, then only 12 percent of the French newspaper's want ads would require bilinguals instead of 24 percent.

In summary, there is greater pressure for bilingualism in the French newspaper's job advertisements than in the English paper. Advertisements for the same occupations in the *Star* are less likely to ask for bilinguals than in *La Presse*. Although the occupations for men listed in the two papers are somewhat different, the net effect is that advertisements in *La Presse* require more bilingualism. *La Presse* lists types of jobs for women which require less bilingualism than those found in the *Star*, but this is more than compensated for by the need for bilingualism being greater for French-speaking women. The net effect places greater second-language learning pressure on French-speaking women seeking employment.

One way to consider the differences in the types of jobs offered in the two papers is to examine the income associated with them in the 1961 Census for metropolitan Montreal. For both sexes, the occupations advertised in the English paper tend to be better paying than those in *La Presse*, and likewise positions requiring bilinguals tend to have higher earnings than those for whom monoglots would be suitable. Advertisements in the *Montreal Star* are for jobs which pay several hundred dollars more on the average than those in *La Presse* (Table 4). The differences between newspapers are somewhat greater for monolingual positions than those which require bilinguals. It is worth noting that bilingual jobs in both papers tend to be better paying than those which do not require a second tongue (about 10 percent better for men; 20 percent for women in the *Star*; and nearly 50 percent better for women in *La Presse*).

TABLE 4

Weighted Mean Annual Income of Occupations Advertised, by Newspaper, Sex, and Language Requirements, 1964

Sex	Monolingual		Bilingual		All Advertisements		
	Montreal Star	La Presse	Montreal Star	La Presse	Montreal Star	La Presse	Both Newspapers
Males	$3906	$3599	$4284	$4067	$3977	$3716	$3849
Females	1939	1565	2368	2281	2010	1731	1875

English speakers enjoy an advantage over the French in the kinds of jobs offered, even when the jobs are bilingual; for example, bilingual ads for men in the *Star* pay $4284, compared with $4067 for advertisements in *La Presse* for bilingual men. Despite this advantage, there are obvious rewards for bilingualism among English speakers just as there are for bilingual French Canadians. However, the pressure is not as great since fewer advertisements require bilingualism in the *Star*. Moreover, better jobs tend to be advertised in the *Star* than in the *Presse*. The reader should note carefully that the incomes associated with the jobs in the 1961 Census are used here as a measure of the desirability of the kinds of occupations offered in the two papers and between those which require bilinguals as contrasted with monoglots. Later in this chapter the actual income differences for employed Montrealers classified by language, occupation, education, and sex are considered. The use of income data here, however, enables us to consider the actual differences between jobs offered in the two newspapers.

Broad Occupational Differences

The linguistic pressures vary greatly, both between occupational categories and across mother-tongue lines. Relatively few men who are laborers, craftsmen, or in transportation, communication, and service occupations have to be bilingual (Table 5). By contrast the pressure for bilingualism among those in the "white-collar" world is much greater. Around 40 percent of the ads for managers require men who can speak both tongues (slightly more in *La Presse* and slightly less in the *Montreal Star*). It is noteworthy that the pressure for bilingualism is greater in the French newspaper for nearly all the broad occupational categories, although some percentages are based on very small numbers. With the exception of sales occupations, where the difference is nil, and of those in occupations we could not classify, the requirements for employment are more likely to specify knowledge of English as a second tongue than vice versa. Particularly striking are the occupations associated with office work; 60 percent of the French language ads for clerks require a knowledge of English, whereas only half as many of the ads in the *Star* require a knowledge of French. Along with professional and technical occupations, these are the most lopsided with respect to demands for more bilingualism from French- than English-speaking men seeking employment.

Among women the pressure for bilingualism is always greater in the French ads than in the English newspaper. As before, there is great variation between jobs in the degree bilingualism is required; for example, less than 10 percent of the service jobs require knowledge of both tongues, whereas around a third of female sales positions require bilinguals. The sharpest discrepancies between the two newspapers are for clerical work-

TABLE 5

Number of Newspaper Advertisements and Percent Bilingual, by Broad Occupational Categories, 1964

Occupational Division	Percent Bilingual				Number of Advertisements			
	Male		Female		Male		Female	
	Montreal Star	La Presse	Montreal Star	La Presse	Montreal Star	La Presse	Montreal Star	La Presse
Managerial	37	43	10	100	41	49	10	1
Professional and technical	11	30	13	33	150	56	56	21
Clerical	29	62	30	75	107	42	269	137
Sales	37	37	29	35	149	218	55	51
Service and recreation	10	16	4	8	118	96	238	284
Transport and communcation	13	14	22	33	46	70	9	3
Farmers and stockraisers	0	0	*	*	6	1	*	*
Other primary	*	*	*	*	*	*	*	*
Craftsmen	7	10	0	0	166	211	53	144
Laborers	0	10	0	0	11	21	6	15
Unclassified	40	11	0	25	10	9	9	4
Total	19	25	17	23	804	773	705	660

*No advertisements.

ers and for professional and technical positions. Fully three-fourths of women's clerical ads in *La Presse* require bilingualism, whereas only 30 percent of the same jobs in the *Montreal Star* specify a knowledge of French.

Different kinds of occupations tend to be advertised in the two newspapers. The number of ads appearing in the *Star* is slightly greater than in the French paper, but differences by occupational divisions are striking; for example, the number of advertisements for professional and technical positions in *La Presse* is little more than a third of the number of similar ads in the *Montreal Star* (Table 5). There are more than twice as many listings for male clerical positions in the latter paper. On the other hand, opportunities for male sales and service workers, craftsmen, and laborers are more frequently found in *La Presse*. The slightly larger number of managerial advertisements in the columns of *La Presse* is somewhat surprising and deviates from the general pattern that emerges of favoring English in the white-collar pursuits.

Likewise women's want ads for white collar positions tend to be placed in the *Star*. Clerical positions advertised in *La Presse* amount to little more than half the number found in the English newspaper (269 versus 137). More than two-thirds of the want ads for women in professional and technical pursuits are found in the English paper. By contrast advertisements for female service workers and the crafts are found more often in *La Presse*.

Detailed Occupational Differences

Those specific occupations for which a relatively large number of ads were run provide an opportunity to get a better notion of the linguistic pressures operating as well as the tendencies to favor one newspaper over another. There were 35 requests for engineers in the *Montreal Star* compared with 8 in *La Presse* (Table 6). The percentage requesting bilinguals, although based on small numbers, is likewise unfavorable to the French. Bookkeepers and cashiers, and shipping and receiving clerks are other male pursuits that are disproportionately concentrated in the English newspaper. Moreover, the advertisements in *La Presse* are more likely to require bilingualism than those in the *Montreal Star*. Secretarial and clerical functions for women strongly favor English. The *Star* has twice the number of ads for stenographers, clerk typists, and "other" clerical workers. Again, ads for these occupations in *La Presse* are accompanied by a much more frequent use of bilingualism as a precondition for employment. Consider that 94 percent of the listings for stenographers in *La Presse* require a knowledge of English whereas only 37 percent of ads for this position in the *Montreal Star* have a bilingual prerequisite. Inspection of Table 6 discloses sizable differences for other women's office work.

Commercial travelers are fairly evenly distributed between the papers and balanced in the proportion of ads requiring bilinguals. This occupation tends to involve "outside" interaction with customers from both linguistic segments. The patterns for sales clerks are not too clear for men and women. The pressure for bilingualism, however, appears somewhat greater in *La Presse*.

Among occupations connected with restaurants cooks occupy an "inside" position, dealing almost entirely with fellow workers and having no interaction with the public. It is easy to see why there is little pressure for bilingualism in such listings. On the other hand, waiters are in a very different situation, with those working in the downtown restaurants, popular places, and the like almost certain to encounter customers from both linguistic segments. On the other hand, there are many restaurants in or near residential areas that draw their clientele primarily from a locality that often contains a predominance of one language group. Nevertheless, the results for waitresses in Table 6 are surprising and cannot be readily explained. Although it is possible that some occupations are so obviously bilingual that no mention of this fact is necessary in the want ads, it is unlikely since the author has encountered waiters and waitresses during visits to Montreal who were obviously monolingual. It may be that there are some who can simply record the order in either tongue, but who are required to do little more in their second language.

The frequency of bilingual requirements for maids and hairdressers requires little explanation. The interaction of maids is restricted to their employers and hence they need know only the language used in the house. Interaction for those employed in the crafts occupations specified in Table 6 is for the most part limited to those working in the place of employment and, moreover, these positions would often require little conversation anyway.

Bilingualism is called for in a fair number of driver-salesmen listings in both newspapers, with the pressure being greater on the English. In many instances driver-salesmen have routes including customers speaking both languages. The infrequent mention of bilingualism in ads for taxi drivers is rather surprising, but the advantage for bilingualism may largely be reflected in the tips obtained, rather than affecting the driver's ability to take the rider to whatever destination is requested. The latter would require a very minimal knowledge of numbers in the two languages and an ability to know the other tongue's pronunciation of streets and names of popular public places. Since the employer does not normally share in the tips, the hiring of monolingual taxi drivers would not be a terribly signifi-

TABLE 6

Percent Bilingual and Number of Advertisements, by Detailed Occupational Categories, 1964[a]

Occupation and Sex	Montreal Star		La Presse	
	Percent	Number	Percent	Number
Male				
Management	37	41	43	49
Engineer	11	35	38	8
Teacher	16	25	45	11
Draftsman	11	28	0	6
Bookkeeper, cashier	33	24	71	7
Shipping and receiving clerk	10	31	40	5
Other clerical	61	23	69	13
Commercial traveler	50	52	43	49
Sales clerk	48	21	55	44
Nonspecific sales	28	43	28	81
Cook	4	27	0	30
Janitor	19	37	36	14
Driver-salesman	36	14	25	24
Taxi driver	0	22	9	23
Tailor, furrier, etc.	0	26	6	33
Metalworking	3	31	4	23
Mechanic, repairman	10	29	2	55
Laborer	0	11	10	21
Female				
Office equipment operator	9	23	27	11
Stenographer	37	62	94	31
Teacher	15	39	33	9
Clerk typist	39	66	85	34
Bookkeeper, cashier	14	44	46	13
Waitress	23	31	17	60
Other clerical	41	49	82	17
Maid	1	148	8	156
Sales clerk	36	33	57	28
Hairdresser, barber	0	21	0	2
Launderer, dry-cleaner	11	9	4	24
Spinner, weaver	0	7	0	22
Nonspecific clerical	20	15	71	28
Tailor, furrier, etc.	0	35	0	89

[a]Occupations included are those containing 20 or more listings in at least one of the newspapers for a given sex. "Nonspecific" sales and clerks are residual categories for occupations which could not be classified in further detail. "Other clerical" refers to Occupational Code No. 249.

cant condition from his perspective. Laborers fit nicely, with twice as many listings in *La Presse* coupled with an infrequent use of bilingualism as a condition for employment. Some of the other positions are not easily explained; in particular, teachers and draftsmen are somewhat surprising.

Granted that the detailed occupations shown in Table 6 have been discussed in an unsystematic ad hoc fashion, they fit into a general pattern, namely a strong bias in the white-collar positions favoring English—both in the linguistic demands and the newspaper used for advertising positions. Blue-collar positions which do not entail frequent "outside" contacts usually are more likely to be listed in *La Presse* and require bilingualism less often. Advertisements for positions dealing with the public in an unspecialized way mention bilingualism as a prerequisite in a fair proportion of the cases.

Trends Between 1939 and 1964

Want ads in 1939 were examined for the same newspapers and then compared with 1964. In all respects the use of bilingualism as a precondition for employment was less frequent in 1939. For both men and women 13 percent of the positions advertised in *La Presse* in 1939 required bilinguals. This is little more than half the percentage of bilingual want ads appearing in the same paper in 1964. The shift is nowhere as great in the *Star's* ads for men, 19 percent in 1964 versus 15 percent in 1939, but is rather considerable for women (17 versus 9 percent). In 1939 want ads for men actually required bilingualism slightly more often in the *Montreal Star* than in *La Presse*. The greater pressure for bilingualism among French-speaking women, however, also existed in 1939. The bilingualism rates in the French newspaper are slightly lower for men in 1939 than in the English advertisements even after the standardization procedures described earlier are used. By contrast the frequency of bilingual want ads for women in *La Presse* is still much higher even when the occupational differences between the two papers in the ads offered are taken into account.

As in 1964, occupations requiring bilingualism tend to pay better than those for which monoglots are acceptable. Likewise, want ads for monolinguals in the *Star* are for higher income positions than those listed in *La Presse*, although the difference is slight; for example, monolingual men in the two papers differ $12.00 in average yearly earnings (based on the cross tabulation between occupation and income for Montreal in 1941). Table 7 indicates the average earnings associated with jobs advertised in the two newspapers.

It turns out that 1939 is hardly a desirable year for comparison with

TABLE 7

Weighted Mean Annual Income of Occupations Advertised, by Newspaper, Sex, and Language Requirements, 1939

| Sex | Monolingual | | Bilingual | | All Advertisements | | |
	Montreal Star	La Presse	Montreal Star	La Presse	Montreal Star	La Presse	Both Newspapers
Males	$1198	$1186	$1406	$1314	$1229	$1202	$1214
Females	399	393	561	537	413	411	412

1964 since the economic depression of the 1930's had not ended by 1939. Hence, there were relatively few want ads, even though all four weekend editions during the period between April 8 and 29 were used. Of particular significance is the fact that the kind of positions offered during a period of high unemployment may not be too suitable for comparison. However, there is little doubt that the demands for bilingualism have basically increased in the quarter century since 1939. If the 1964 frequency of bilingual prerequisites for employment in each occupational division are applied to the occupations advertised in 1939, 24 and 30 percent of male want ads in the *Star* and *Presse*, respectively, would have required bilinguals in 1939. These are far greater than the bilingual percentages actually encountered in 1939 (see Table 8) and clearly indicate a basic rise in the demands for knowledge of a second language among both French- and English-speaking Montrealers. Increases are observed for women as well, although not of the same magnitude. In the following section further evidence is presented that suggests bilingualism has become an increasingly important prerequisite for employment.

TABLE 8

Newspaper Advertisements Requiring Bilingualism, 1939 Versus Rates in 1964

| Newspaper | Percent Bilingual | | | |
| | Male | | Female | |
	Actual	Expected[a]	Actual	Expected[a]
Montreal Star	15	24	9	12
La Presse	13	30	13	15

[a]Based on application of rates in 1964 for the same newspaper to occupations listed in 1939.

LANGUAGE AND THE CUSTOMER

The bilingual *Yellow Pages* published by the telephone company provides a ready means for gauging the role of each language in the various commercial, industrial, and social domains of Montreal. A description of this source was provided in Chapter 4 and little more need be said other than noting that *Yellow Pages* is hardly the equivalent to the information which might be obtained from an intensive and costly survey of business activities in the city. To paraphrase the telephone company slogan, we shall "let our fingers do the interviewing."

Listings in the directory suggest rather strong social segregation between the two major linguistic components of Montreal. There are 202 Roman Catholic churches and related institutions listed in *Yellow Pages* (the September 1964 issue is used throughout this section). Nearly 90 percent are listed under the French "Églises" exclusively, close to 10 percent are under the English rubric only, and a handful are listed under both the English and French terms. This clearly indicates the ethnic and linguistic divisions existing within the church, for although French Canadians are the dominant group within the Catholic religion of Montreal nearly 20 percent of the metropolitan area's Catholics in 1961 were not French.

The lack of social integration between the two language groups is also displayed by some other listings as well. Rooming houses tend to involve fairly close contact between the residents, and aversion between ethnic groups is not uncommon. Witness the reluctance in the United States to make many open occupancy laws apply to small rooming houses. There is virtually no overlap among the 593 rooming houses listed in the English or French rubrics of *Yellow Pages*. Only 3 percent are under both listings, 70 percent are under "Chambres á Louer," and about a quarter are under the English listing exclusively. Apartment houses reflect a less intensive form of interaction and, accordingly, 13 percent are listed under both languages, but the degree of linguistic isolation is still noteworthy. There are many more apartment house listings under English than French. Probably only more expensive apartment houses list, and this reflects the general socioeconomic positions of the two ethnic groups.

A sharp discrepancy exists between the frequency of bilingual listings among "billiard halls" and "bowling." Bowling alleys tend to be rather large commercial ventures and, although most establishments probably draw customers from one part of the city, it is still a fairly widespread area. Consequently about three-quarters of the bowling establishments are listed under both languages. By contrast 85 percent of the billiard halls are under only one language (54 percent English, 31 percent French). It is noteworthy that billiard halls are more sociable units, since there is

TABLE 9

Language Rubrics Used by Selected Activities in Montreal's Yellow Pages, 1964

| | Percent of Listings | | | |
Category	English Only	French Only	Both Languages	(Number)[a]
Roman Catholic churches	9	88	3	(202)
Rooming houses	27	70	3	(593)
Apartments	50	37	13	(241)
Bowling	16	7	77	(103)
Billiard halls	54	31	15	(89)
Night clubs	22	36	42	(94)

[a]Organizations listed under both languages are counted only once.

interaction among the players at different tables, challenges, and the establishment is more likely to serve as a meeting place and "hangout" (see Polsky, 1964). Bowling involves interaction that is restricted to players in the same party or league. Hence the activities surrounding bowling are more compatible with a linguistically diverse set of customers than are billiard halls. Also billiard halls probably draw their clientele from a smaller area of the city than bowling units; hence the former's customers are more likely to be linguistically homogeneous.

Nightclubs are rather surprising, since 40 percent are listed under both languages. Although such clubs tend to draw from a large part of the city and are concentrated in certain areas of Montreal, one would expect that the use of comedians as well as singers would lead more of them to be suitable for the speakers of only one of the two official languages.

Retail Establishments

The frequency of double listings ranges widely between the retail services examined in *Yellow Pages* (see Table 10). Retail grocers are easiest to explain; less than 10 percent are bilisted, about a quarter are solely under English, and two-thirds exclusively under "Epiciers-En Détail." Since grocers are ubiquitous and depend on a relatively small trade area, the high residential segregation in Montreal affords little reason for most units to list under both languages since many deal primarily with one group. The percentages of the metropolitan population 15 years of age and older with English and French mother tongues, 23.5 and 63.1, respectively, tend to be fairly close to the percentages of grocers under each listing.

Tire dealers no doubt have larger trade areas and the fact that about half are listed under both categories is not surprising. What is noteworthy is the fact that nearly all the remaining dealers are found only under the English rubric, with less than 5 percent of all tire dealers listed under French exclusively. Granted that the socioeconomic differences between the ethnic groups are such that English-speaking Montrealers are probably more likely to own automobiles than the French, it is unlikely to be sufficient to explain such a striking discrepancy. A matter of conjecture here is that the French word for tires, "pneus," may have been partially replaced by the English word. Hence dealers can advertise exclusively in the English rubric without suffering too badly. Supporting this are several small inserts under the English listing which are entirely in French. It does appear that generally a number of English words for technical and mechanical subjects have become common in French usage. This is particularly striking in the case of automobile parts.

French fares better in some of the other retail trades examined, although not so well as might be expected on the basis of Montreal's linguistic composition. If the second languages spoken by the population are considered, English is almost on a par with French in Montreal. Among those 15 and over, 21 percent speak English only, 28 percent speak French only, and 49 percent are bilingual. Of course this ignores the tendency for bilinguals to favor their mother tongue, a factor which would boost the desirability for listing under French. French does very well among beauty salons

TABLE 10

Language Rubrics Used by Selected Retail and Wholesale Establishments in Montreal's Yellow Pages, 1964

| | Percent of Listings | | | |
Category	English Only	French Only	Both Languages	(Number)[a]
Retail grocers	23	68	9	(1832)
Tire dealers	46	3	51	(116)
Beauty salons	18	46	35	(1084)
Retail bakers	55	19	26	(117)
Pastry shops	28	42	31	(304)
Cleaners and dyers	33	31	36	(546)
Retail shoes	26	20	54	(454)
Wholesale grocers	28	10	62	(39)
Wholesale bakers	16	16	68	(38)

[a]Organizations listed under both languages are counted only once.

and pastry shops; English is probably overrepresented among shoe stores, cleaners and dyers, and very much so under retail bakers. However, we should not lose sight of the fact that both languages are fairly well served on the retail level in Montreal. Combining the bilingual stores with those listing under English or French alone, 50 percent or more of the retail establishments are found under both languages. This only exception is groceries.

It is of interest to follow several of these retail services back a step to their suppliers. In the case of wholesale grocers 62 percent are listed under both languages. Likewise 68 percent of wholesale bakers are bilisted. In both cases the percentages are considerably higher than among the retailers. The wholesaler is less restricted in the area of the city he deals with and therefore must attempt to gain customers among retailers of both linguistic groups.

Industry

Generally, as we turn from services to industrial activities which do not deal directly with the family consumer or small retailer, the orientation toward French declines. Consider various facets of the shoe industry in Montreal (Table 11). About two-thirds of shoe manufacturers list under both languages, with the remaining third nearly all under English listings exclusively. Granted the high percentage of shoe manufacturers with double listings, one should not ignore the almost complete absence of those only under French. Taking a step (no pun intended) backward in the supply chain, there are no suppliers of shoe manufacturers' machinery, findings, laces, lasts, or patterns who list under the French rubric exclusively and only one under the French equivalent of "shoe manufacturers' supplies." Combining all of these categories, 70 percent of companies in Montreal serving the shoe manufacturers are listed only under English and nearly all of the remainder are bilisted. The 30 percent with double listings should be compared with 66 percent among manufacturers of shoes and 54 percent among retailers. The high level of double listings among manufacturers is due to the fact that they are also oriented towards shoe retailers. Table 11 does indicate, however, the very weak position of French in the services oriented towards manufacturers.

The textile and garment industry is important in Montreal. Among the 250 textile wholesalers and manufacturers listed, fully two-thirds are found only in the English category, another 30 percent are bilisted, and only 4 percent appear exclusively under the French rubric. Unfortunately *Yellow Pages* lists wholesalers and manufacturers together. In ancillary services, however, such as textile dyers and finishers, mill equipment and supplies, printers, transfers, and brokers, there are no exclusively French listings and only 21 percent of the 62 listings are in both tongues. Again, the predominance of English increases in the activities furthest removed from retail markets.

Various industrial activities which would be representative of the positions of the two languages are listed in Table 12. One is struck by the poor showing of French almost without exception. It appears that in some industries French is fairly well represented only by virtue of a large number of double listings; for example, 64 of the 112 steel companies are listed under "Acier" (7 + 57), but still this compares with 105 (48 + 57) that are listed under the English category. French is not only a poor second to English in terms of the number of exclusive listings in some industries, but fares very poorly even when double listings are taken into account; for example, only 8 out of 58 machine tool companies are listed in the French rubric and only 32 out of 121 companies in plastic products are found under the French category. Incidentally, according to the pattern observed earlier in shoes and textiles, it is of interest to note that foundry equipment and supplies have no French listings at all. Again we see that suppliers of goods and services that are further removed from consumer markets are less likely to use French listings. In Montreal generally the percentage of double listings increases from retail to wholesale but then drops radically in the manufacturing end. In summary, nearly all companies in the industries examined are listed under English. In a fair number of industries a substantial number are also listed in French, but in many industries the companies are listed only in English. Further, the listing of industrial companies exclusively in French is infrequent.

TABLE 11

Language Rubrics Used by the Shoe Industry in Montreal's Yellow Pages, 1964

	Number of Listings			
Shoe:	English Only	French Only	Both Languages	Total[a]
Manufacturers	34	3	73	110
Manufacturers' machinery	5	0	2	7
Findings	26	0	10	36
Lace manufacturers	3	0	2	5
Lasts	1	0	3	4
Patterns	3	0	3	6
Manufacturers' supplies	19	1	4	24

[a]Organizations listed under both languages are counted only once.

TABLE 12

Language Rubrics Used by Selected Heavy Industries in Montreal's Yellow Pages, 1964

| | Number of Listings | | | |
Category	English Only	French Only	Both Languages	Total[a]
Steel	48	7	57	112
Machine tools	50	3	5	58
Plastic products	89	4	28	121
Steel foundries	13	0	4	17
Iron foundries	14	2	12	28
Brass, bronze, aluminum, and copper foundries	11	0	14	25
Foundry equipment and supplies	16	0	0	16
Chemicals	92	6	68	166
Screws	16	0	7	23

[a]Organizations listed under both languages are counted only once.

Offices

Yellow Pages provides further evidence that white-collar activities are dominated by the English language. Nearly 80 percent of office buildings listed in the directory are found exclusively in English, about 15 percent are double listings, and only 5 percent are solely under the French rubric. The vast majority of office buildings are located in the western part of downtown, an area that tends to be a stronghold of English in the central business district. The powerful position of English is also reflected in listings for "Office Furniture and Equipment," in which about half the companies are bilisted and nearly all the remainder are only under the English rubric. There are 64 retailers of "Office Supplies" listed in English, of which 10 are also found under "Bureaux-Fournitures." Only one is listed exclusively in French.

There are 217 listings under the English category "Hotels—Out of Town." Under the French rubric there are only eight, five of which are also listed in the English heading. Hence of the 220 separate out-of-town hotels listed in *Yellow Pages* more than 95 percent are under the English category exclusively, about 1 percent are under only the French category, and 2 percent have double listings. There are 70 listings for hotels in the United States, all but one of which are under the English rubric exclusively. There are 33 hotels listed for Canadian cities outside Quebec and 31 of these are only under English. The out-of-town hotel listings reflect the lack of direct integration of Montreal's French Canadians into the social and economic life outside of the province as well as the extent to which participation hinges upon knowledge of the English language.

Trends

Using a classified telephone directory for 1939, changes for some services can be examined over a 25-year span. The percentage of companies listing in English only has declined for all categories examined and the percentage listing in French only has increased in the majority of cases (see Table 13). Without exception the proportion of companies with double listings has also increased. In some instances these changes are minor and are due to the fact that no companies were listed in French in 1939. This was the case for "textiles—wholesale and manufacturers," "hotels—out of town,"

TABLE 13

Comparison Between Yellow Page Listings in Montreal, 1939 and 1964

Category	Percent of Listings						(Number)[d]
	English Only		French Only		Both Languages		
	1939	1964	1939	1964	1939	1964	1939
Rooming houses	100	27	*	70	*	3	(220)
Apartments	85	50	14	37	1	13	(159)
Bowling	92	16	*	7	8	77	(26)
Billiard halls	100	54	*	31	*	15	(27)
Grocers[a]	39	23	60	67	1	10	(1626)
Tire dealers	81	46	4	3	15	51	(79)
Beauty salons	39	18	48	46	13	35	(716)
Bakers[a]	49	46	33	18	18	36	(101)
Pastry shops	14	28	79	42	7	31	(14)
Cleaners and dyers	64	33	15	31	21	36	(164)
Textiles[b]	100	66	*	4	*	30	(38)
Office buildings	100	79	*	5	*	16	(39)
Office equipment[c]	88	45	*	5	12	50	(33)
Hotels—out of town	100	96	*	1	*	2	(57)

*No listings.

[a]No distinction made between wholesale and retail in 1939; hence both categories were combined for 1964.

[b]Comparable to "Textiles—wholesale and mfrs." in 1964.

[c]"Office Equipment" in 1939; "Office Furniture and Equipment" in 1964.

[d]Organizations listing under both languages are counted only once.

"office buildings," and "billiard halls." Judging by the changes in office buildings and office equipment listings, French is receiving far more recognition in white-collar activities than it did in pre-World War II Montreal. The postion occupied by each tongue is not at an equilibrium, but appears to be changing. English is still dominant, however, particularly when the mother tongue and ethnic composition of Montreal is taken into account.

In some instances the shifts are enormous. All but two of the 26 bowling establishments listed in 1939 are exclusively in the English rubric. Perhaps as a reflection of the greater prosperity of the French Canadians in Montreal or of greater mobility due to automobiles, a far greater proportion of the enterprises are listed under both the English and French rubrics in 1964. This occurs even among such locally based services as cleaners, grocers, and bakers.

Shown in Table 14 are the percentages of establishments listed under each language in the two periods. They were obtained by adding the percentage bilisted to the percentage listing exclusively under each tongue. Hence they total to more than 100 percent if any establishments are bilisted. The percentage of enterprises listed in English has declined in many instances, risen in a few such as bakers and pastry shops. By contrast, with the exception of pastry shops, in all cases the percentage of enterprises listing in French has increased. Some activities tend to make an appeal to both language groups. Fifty percent or more of the companies in the following categories are in both English and French rubrics: cleaners and dyers, office equipment, beauty salons, tire dealers, apartments, bowling alleys, bakers, and pastry shops. In 1939 only beauty salons and bakers would have met these criteria.

The reader should interpret these results carefully. These figures indicate the degree services of a given type are offered to both language groups, they do not necessarily indicate the extent to which individual enterprises pursue both groups of customers. The latter was indicated in Table 13 by the percentage of enterprises which are listed under both tongues. Among rooming houses, for example, about half the listings were in French and the other half in English in 1939. As inspection of Table 13 should make clear, this does not reflect any particular effort among many rooming houses to obtain customers from both groups. Less than 1 percent were bilisted.

This growth of double listings between 1939 and 1964 means there is increased pressure for bilingualism among those engaged in the occupations involved. This is consistent with the earlier finding that bilingualism is more frequently used as a job qualification in want ads.

TABLE 14

Percent of Montreal Yellow Page Listings in Each Language, 1939 and 1964[a]

| | Percent of Enterprises Listed | | | |
| | English | | French | |
Category	1939	1964	1939	1964
Rooming houses	55	30	46	73
Apartments	86	63	14	50
Bowling	100	93	8	84
Billiard halls	100	69	*	46
Grocers	40	33	61	77
Tire dealers	96	97	19	54
Beauty salons	52	54	61	82
Bakers	67	82	51	54
Pastry shops	21	58	86	72
Cleaners and dyers	85	69	36	67
Textiles	100	96	*	34
Office buildings	100	95	*	21
Office equipment	100	95	12	55
Hotels—out of town	100	99	*	4

[a]See footnotes to Table 13.

PHYSICIANS

Physicians and lawyers, two of the classical professions, have both undergone the same shift toward dual listings in *Yellow Pages.* Less than 5 percent of all the physicians and about 20 percent of the lawyers were listed under both languages in 1939. By 1964 30 percent of the physicians and 60 percent of the lawyers chose double listings. In both periods the remaining members of the two professions were split fairly evenly between English and French. Physicians in 1964 and lawyers in both periods choosing to list under only one language were slightly more likely to elect French than English, but the differences are slight. Considering the linguistic composition of Montreal, members of both professions are more likely to solicit English-speaking clients or at least be oriented in their direction. It is not clear why lawyers are more likely to have dual listings than physicians. However, one can speculate on what is probably a greater degree of ethnic, linguistic, and religious segregation in the medical profession than in the legal world. There is the split along hospital affiliations as well as the religious practices that influences certain areas of medicine such as obstetrics (see Solomon, 1961; Hall, 1948, 1940).

Although there is the same tendency for the ethnic origin of a lawyer to influence the kind of practice developed, nevertheless segregation is less complete since all lawyers must deal with the same legal institutions. Advocates must be prepared to understand testimony given in either English or French. Hence, more lawyers will very likely be bilingual and thus able to pursue clients from both linguistic groups. (I am indebted to Professor Jack Ladinsky for some of the points made in these two paragraphs.)

In an effort to understand some of the less obvious influences on listing practices, physicians were examined in some detail for both 1939 and 1964. Their office locations were placed into three categories; those in the western part of the central business district; those in the eastern section of the central business district; and those located outside of the downtown area. The appendix at the end of this chapter indicates the census tracts included in each of the areas delineated.

Physicians segregate within the central business district along linguistic lines that correspond to the residential patterns of Montreal. Areas located east of downtown tend to be heavily French whereas relatively more of the English speakers are located in the western part of the city. In turn, less than five percent of physicians in the eastern part of downtown are listed under English exclusively and a similar percentage in downtown west are listed only under French. By contrast about 60 percent of physicians in the eastern segment are listed under "médecins and chirurgiens" exclusively and a similar percentage located in western downtown are listed only under the English category. To a certain degree patients drawn to downtown physicians are attracted to two different markets depending on the language they speak.

The relationship is complex between medical practice and directory listing. Obviously, a physician with a sizable clientele among patients of a given language group may be expected to list his name in the appropriate language; one attracting patients from both groups would be expected to list under both "physicians and surgeons" and "médecins and chirurgiens." Physicians whose clientele are drawn from a narrow segment of the city would be more likely to have a linguistically homogeneous group of patients compared with those whose patients come from a broader areal base. In this connection, slightly more than half of all physicians who are specialists have dual listings compared with 20 percent of nonspecialists. Likewise, although the differences are not great, 34 percent of doctors with offices downtown are bilisted, compared with 29 percent of those located elsewhere in the city. There is a sharp difference between the English and French oriented segments of downtown. In each case about a third of the physicians have dual listings; however, two-thirds of the western physicians are under the English rubric exclusively. Nearly as large a percentage are under the French listing only in the eastern sector of the central business district.

There appear to be two downtowns for medical practice in Montreal. In one part the orientation is much more toward English and in the other toward French. Physicians listed only under English are more likely to be downtown than doctors who list solely under the French rubric. About 45 percent of all the doctors located outside the central business districts list exclusively in French, compared with a quarter who list only in English. The net effect, if the bilisted are included, is that three-fourths of non-downtown physicians list under French, compared with half in English. In the western section of downtown less than 5 percent list only in French; in the eastern section of downtown less than 5 percent list only in English. Both dual listings of physicians and medical specialization were far less common in 1939. The handful of specialists sampled, however, were all bilisted and downtown doctors were also more likely to choose double listings.

Specialists are more likely to take double listings than nonspecialists located in the same area (Table 16). Half the non-downtown specialists are listed under both linguistic rubrics, whereas 20 percent of those with general practices in the same area have dual listings. Similar or greater differences occur in the two downtown districts. ("Specialists" are defined as those doctors who indicate some specialty after their name in the telephone directory.) Medical specialization depends more on physicians' referrals than does a general practice and hence it is easier for a specialist to obtain patients from both linguistic groups. Moreover, there is a wider population base necessary to support specialists and this probably makes it more necessary for specialists to obtain patients from both linguistic segments (Lieberson, 1958).

TABLE 15

Physicians' Listings in Montreal Yellow Pages, 1964

| | Percent Distributions | | | | | |
| | | | Downtown | | | Not |
Listing	Specialists	Nonspecialists	East	West	All	Downtown
English only	28.8	35.4	4.0	63.0	49.1	26.1
French only	18.6	44.6	60.0	3.7	17.0	45.2
Both	52.6	19.9	36.0	33.3	34.0	28.7

The strong attraction of western downtown for physicians listed under English and eastern downtown for French-listed physicians remains unaltered after differences between specialists and nonspecialists are taken into account. About three-quarters of nonspecialists in western downtown are listed only under English and the same proportion of eastern downtown physicians list only the French rubric. This holds true for 1939, when 85 percent of nonspecialists in western downtown were listed only in English and 89 percent of those in the eastern part were exclusively in French. (The small number of specialists and dual listings in that year precludes a more extensive tabulation for 1939.)

Office location per se does not have much effect on the likelihood of a dual listing, with the exception of the small number of specialists located in the eastern downtown district. In fact, among nonspecialists, those located away from downtown are more likely to have two listings than those in either central business district (20.5 percent versus 18.6 and 17.6 percent).

Among specialists and nonspecialists alike, "English only" doctors are most likely to be downtown, "French only" physicians least likely, and those with dual listings occupy an intermediate position. If by limitations of language ability or intentional choice, a physician restricts himself to an English-speaking practice, he must draw patients from a very wide spatial area. Hence these specialists need a central location such as that provided downtown. By contrast a specialist who deals solely in French is less restricted to downtown since he has a greater number of patients in the city to draw from. This broader areal market makes it more possible for a specialist listing only under French to locate outside of the central busi-

TABLE 16

Percent of Physicians with Dual Listings, by Office Location and Practice, 1964

Location and Practice	Percent with Dual Listings
Downtown, East:	
Specialists	75.0
Nonspecialists	17.6
Downtown, West:	
Specialists	50.0
Nonspecialists	18.6
Not Downtown:	
Specialists	51.2
Nonspecialists	20.5

ness district. A bilisted specialist, although needing a large population to draw from in the same way as other specialists, can practice anywhere. It is easy to see why nonspecialists listing only in French can more readily locate away from downtown than "English only's" who need to draw on a larger spatial area because fewer of Montreal's population are native speakers of English than French.

We should not overlook the fact that a rather large number of physicians in 1964 were listed under only one rubric. This indicates the existence of occupational segregation or dualism such that important segments of the medical profession are oriented toward providing the services needed by only one part of Montreal's population.

Changes Between 1939 and 1964

A special examination was made of changes between 1939 and 1964 of physicians who were listed in the *Yellow Pages* in both periods. Two noteworthy shifts occurred; they were more likely to have dual listings and to indicate a specialty in 1964. About 30 percent of physicians who were listed exclusively under either French or English in 1939 were listed under both language rubrics in 1964. The great majority of the small number of bilisted physicians in 1939 who were still practicing also retained their double listings. The trend toward specialization is also apparent, with about 28 percent of nonspecialists in 1939 listing specialties 25 years later. Bear in mind that "specialization" refers to self-declared restriction of practice, not necessarily successful completion of a residency or examinations.

Longitudinal evidence to support the earlier contention that a broader-based clientele as well as the referral system tend to encourage bilingual practices is found in the analysis of the degree of bilisting among physicians who shifted from general practice to a specialty during this period. Of those doctors listed under English only in 1939 and who later restricted their practice to a specialty, 70 percent had dual listings in 1964 (Table 17). Of those physicians who declare no specialty in either period, only 15 percent have shifted from an exclusive English listing to a dual listing. Almost the same results are obtained for physicians who were nonspecialists in 1939 and listed themselves only under the French language rubric. Only 12 percent of those remaining as nonspecialists had dual listings in 1964, whereas 68 percent of those restricting their practices were bilisted in 1964.

In summary, this consideration of physicians provides further support for the proposition that services oriented toward a consumer market in Montreal are likely to have increased pressure for bilingualism when they increase the size of the area from which they draw their clientele or cus-

TABLE 17

Listing and Practice of Physicians in 1964 Who Were Both Nonspecialists and Singly Listed in 1939

Nonspecialists in 1939	Percent with Dual Listing, by Practice in 1964	
with Single Listing	Nonspecialist	Specialist
English only	15	70
French only	12	68

tomers. In the case of medicine increased specialization leads to increased attention on the part of physicians to the potential clientele available from both linguistic groups. The greater frequency of dual listings among medical specialists than general practitioners is evidence for this. In 1964 the medical profession was divided into about equal thirds among doctors listing only in English, only in French, and those listing in both languages. Between the dual-listing practices of some physicians and the practice of monolisted physicians locating in a segregated downtown area medical practice in Montreal provides further evidence that consumer-oriented services do not put the population-at-large under pressure to become bilingual, although they do affect those employed in the economic activity being followed. The shift toward specialization between 1939 and 1964 also indicates how changes in the structure of an occupation can alter the linguistic demands on the incumbents.

INCOME

One of the most important linguistic pressures generated by the work world hinges on the income differences between the linguistic segments. The average income for both men and women in Montreal's work force is much greater for English monoglots than for those speaking only French. The mean income for English monoglot men in the metropolitan area in 1961 was 71 percent higher than for those speaking French only ($5536 versus $3246). Women speaking only English earn 37 percent more than those who know only the French official language (Table 18). For each sex English monolinguals earn the highest incomes, although the bilingual women are exceeded by only a slight margin. Bilinguals also earn more than the average for their sex, but by a smaller margin. People speaking only French earn less than the average, although considerably more than those who speak neither official language. The results for bilinguals are rather surprising, since one would expect them to enjoy advantages over monolingual speakers of either English or French. More about this later.

There are some important determinants of income that covary with language. The French ethnic group have less education and are in poorer paying jobs than the British. Although education and occupation are clearly important determinants of income, the latter is of a somewhat different order in the sense that French concentration in the less desirable jobs may itself reflect linguistic disadvantages. Inspection of the graph between education and income for the different official language groups shows that English monoglots tend to earn more than others with the same level of education (Figure 5.1). Bilingual men are a fairly close second, actually exceeding speakers of English with only an elementary school education by 17 dollars. The French monoglots' earnings, however, are considerably lower than the English speakers on all educational levels. The absolute gap actually rises with education from a low of $660 among those with an elementary school education to a high of $3130 between English and French monoglots with some University education. The differences in income between the linguistic segments of the working male population of Montreal are not to be explained simply in terms of their levels of educational attainment.

Income differences among women tell the same story. Except for those with no schooling, women who speak English earn more than those speaking only French. Bilingual women are close to English monoglots in most educational levels, actually exceeding the latter in the very lowest and highest categories of attainment. Women unable to speak either official language earn the least in all but one educational category. The exception, those with a University education, is based on only 31 women who report an inability to speak either official language.

TABLE 18

Total Income by Official Language and Sex, Montreal Metropolitan Area, 1961[a]

Official Language	Average (Mean) Income	
	Men	Women
English only	$5536	$2561
French only	3246	1867
Bilingual	4954	2515
Neither tongue	2195	1290
All workers	4720	2328

[a]Based on persons reporting income.

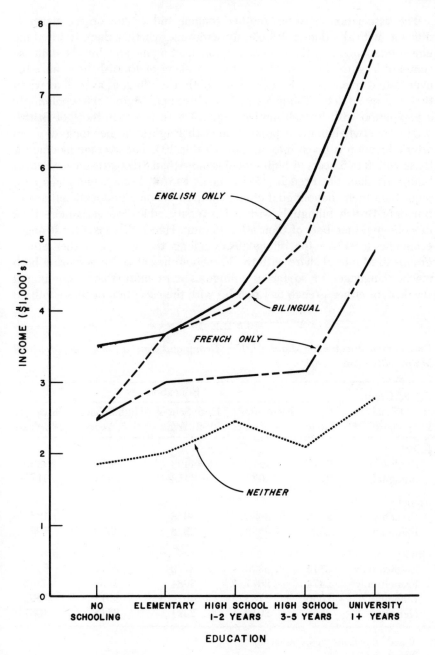

FIGURE 5.1 *Income by education and official language, males in Montreal Metropolitan area, 1961.*

The association between mother tongue and ethnic origin makes it difficult, with the data available, to determine whether there is an ethnic effect independent of the mother-tongue effect on income, but the data are compatible with the view that native speakers of English have an edge over native speakers of French, when both are bilingual as well as when they are monoglots. Bilinguals of French ethnic origin (overwhelmingly a population with French mother tongue) earn less than those of British origin (overwhelmingly a population with English mother tongue) even after education is taken into account (Table 19). The average income for those with 3 to 5 years of high school is more than $1200 greater for British bilinguals than the French ($5818 versus $4576). French bilinguals earn more than their monolingual ethnic compatriots on all educational levels, but only British bilinguals with a University education earn more than monolingual members of their ethnic group. Hence there is a far stronger economic incentive for bilingualism among the French. Other ethnic groups in Montreal share with the French an incentive for acquiring both official languages in so far as bilinguals earn more than monolingual speakers of either French or English (with the exception of those with no

TABLE 19

Employment Income for Men by Ethnic Group and Official Language, Montreal Metropolitan Area, 1961[a]

Ethnic Group and Official Languages	Education				
	None	Elementary 1+ Years	High School 1–2 Years	High School 3–5 Years	University 1+ Years
British:					
English only	$3323[b]	$4077	$4498	$6074	$8830
Bilingual	2773[c]	4077	4413	5818	9116
French:					
French only	2510	3036	3048	3131	4879
Bilingual	2529	3608	3958	4576	7068
Other:					
English only	3515	3396	3779	4917	6351
French only	2474	2677	3084	3125	4506
Bilingual	2346	3783	4514	5917	7691
Neither	1857	2016	2391	2115	1687[d]

[a]Based on persons reporting income.
[b]Based on 65 cases.
[c]Based on 45 cases.
[d]Based on 64 cases.

schooling where the income level of English monoglots may be suspect). Again, however, those among the other ethnic groups who speak English only earn more than French monoglots. Granted that greater income is possible for bilinguals, English is a more desirable first language for those whose native tongue is neither official language. Furthermore, the increment in income associated with bilingualism is much greater among those already speaking French than for those who are English monoglots.

Standardization for Occupation and Education

The optimal procedure for determining the effect of language and ethnic origin on income requires that both occupation and education be taken into account simultaneously. Using the occupation-by-education distribution of all men in the labor force, the income patterns for various ethnolinguistic segments were used to determine the effect of language and ethnic group on income independent of occupation and education. The standardized results are shown in Table 20; for example, application of the occupation-education specific rates for British men speaking English only would yield an average income in the total male labor force of $5124. Direct standardization in this case may be interpreted in the following manner: If all men in the Montreal labor force earned the same amount of money as British monolingual speakers who held their occupation and had the same level of education, then the average income for the male labor force in 1961 would have been $5124. Using the average incomes for French bilingual men in each education- and occupation-specific category as the norm for all employed men in metropolitan Montreal, then the average income for men in the city would have been $4385 in 1961.

Bilingualism is an important advantage among French-Canadian men; the standardized income is close to $1000 greater than for their monoglot compatriots. An even larger gap exists for other ethnic groups between French monolinguals and bilinguals, $3260 versus $4535. The British monolingual earns nearly $1700 more than the French Canadian who knows

TABLE 20

Effect of Ethnic Origin and Official Language on Male Income After Standardizing for Occupation and Education, 1961

Ethnic Origin	Official Language			
	English Only	French Only	Bilingual	Neither
British	$5124		$5041	
French		$3448	4385	
Other	4185	3260	4535	$2682

only French. Keep in mind that these figures are after occupational and educational differences between ethnolinguistic groups are taken into account. As might be expected, those unable to speak either official language are most disadvantaged of all. Although the data are not presented here, comparisons for specific other ethnic groups in Montreal disclose that in all instances the bilingual members earn more than English monolinguals. Thus it is only among the British ethnic group that the advantages of bilingualism disappear. Indeed the standardized British monolinguals are slightly greater than their bilingual compatriots ($5124 versus $5041).

The average incomes for different occupational groups after education is taken into account are shown in Table 21. French-Canadian bilinguals earn more in all occupational categories than do their monolingual compatriots. On the other hand, in seven of the ten occupational categories, British bilinguals still earn less than English monoglots. For Montreal's other ethnic groups, however, bilinguals earn more than English monoglots, with the exception of laborers. In turn, speakers of English only earn more than those speaking French only. Finally, in all but two categories, those speaking neither official language occupy the lowest position in income after educational attainment is taken into account.

Although the data are not shown, women in the labor force have a similar pattern. Among the British ethnic group, those who speak English only earn slightly more than bilinguals. On the other hand, bilinguals in the French ethnic group earn more than their compatriots who are French monolinguals. Among those with other ethnic origins income rises from those speaking neither tongue to French only, English only, with bilinguals highest of all.

One can only speculate why British men and women who are bilingual earn slightly less than their monolingual compatriots. Surely, we would not want to argue that acquisition of French will reduce the income of British ethnics in Montreal. It may well be that the best paying positions, those highest in an organization's hierarchy, are those for which knowledge of French is the least necessary. Evidence has been presented which indicates that as one turns to customers and consumers French increases in importance. Hence the pressures for bilingualism among the British are greater for those lower in organizations than those above them. As a consequence British bilinguals earn less than monolinguals not because acquisition of French creates a handicap, which it obviously does not, but possibly because those lower in position within a given occupational and educational level are more likely to need a knowledge of French. In this connection top managers, technicians, and the like who are brought into Montreal from the United States, Great Britain, and other parts of Canada are less likely to know French but have very high income.

The earlier analysis of want ads suggested that job opportunities requir-

TABLE 21

Effect of Ethnic Origin and Official Language on Male Income for Occupations After Standardizing for Education, 1961

Occupation	Ethnic Group and Official Language							
	British		French		Other			
	English Only	Biling.	French Only	Biling.	English Only	French Only	Biling.	Neither
Managerial	$9570	$9171	$5361	$7100	$8293	$5293	$8511	$7606
Professional and technical	7529	7953	4818	6658	5894	4081	6679	1870
Clerical	3724	3637	2755	3501	3180	2288	3311	2314
Sales	5461	5359	3065	4605	4480	3528	5381	1563
Service and recreation	3396	3333	2550	3399	2565	2467	3097	1875
Transport and communication	4374	3948	2892	3599	3159	2871	3488	2235
Farmers and stockraisers								
Other primary[a]	2771	2818	2204	2601	2688	1861	3031	1439
Craftsmen	4293	4273	3260	3807	3476	3023	3684	2310
Laborers	2794	2627	2399	2590	2582	2413	2581	1942

[a]Excluding farmers and stockraisers.

ing bilingualism in the *Star* are somewhat more desirable than those for which English alone is sufficient—at least as measured by the income associated with the two types. It may well be that this apparent contradiction can be explained as a reflection of the advantage in bilingualism for native English speakers in obtaining certain kinds of employment, but that this advantage diminishes as they move up the hierarchy afterward. Unfortunately, one can do little more than speculate at this point since there are a number of technical considerations which themselves could explain the apparent inconsistency. The newspaper analysis is basically an ecological correlation with census income data, there is great selectivity in the jobs offered in the advertisements, and our analysis here is based on only the British ethnic population of Montreal. In connection with the last point keep in mind that for other ethnic groups beside the French, bilingualism is associated with a distinct income advantage over monolingualism.

Some inferences about the nature of the occupational pressure for bilingualism can be drawn from the variations in income advantage which French-Canadian bilinguals enjoy over monolingual French Canadians. with the same job. Among men with an elementary school education, for example, bilingual laborers earn $152 more than monolinguals, whereas the income of bilingual technical workers exceeds French monoglots by more than a thousand dollars. If French Canadians become bilingual in part because of the ensuing income advantage, there should be a strong correlation between the percentage of French Canadians in an occupation who are bilingual and the income advantage that bilinguals enjoy. Such is precisely the case, as the Spearman rank order correlations in Table 22 indicate. In the illustration cited above, for example, only 42 percent of the laborers with a grade school education are bilingual whereas 75 percent of the technicians with the same schooling are able to speak both official languages. Considering that these comparisons are between men with the same level of educational attainment, there is strong evidence that bilingualism among French Canadians tends to be a response to the presence of income advantages. When the gain in income is minor, there is a relatively low percentage of French Canadians in the occupation who can also speak English.

By contrast there is essentially no association in Table 22 between the percentage of British men who are bilingual and the magnitude of the income difference between bilinguals and English monolinguals. Thus there is further evidence for a rather persistent theme: a relative absence of strong economic pressure among the British to learn French, but the presence of a distinct gain for French Canadians who acquire English as a second language.

TABLE 22

Correlation Between Income Advantage of Bilinguals and Frequency of Bilingualism, Male, 1961[a]

Education	French Ethnic Group: Bilinguals versus French Only	British Ethnic Group: Bilinguals versus English Only
None	−.10	−.80
Elementary, 1+ years	.87	.08
High School, 1–2 years	.90	.02
High School, 3–5 years	.88	−.15
University, 1+ years	.50	.22

[a]Spearman correlations based on nine occupational categories except among British with no schooling ($N = 4$) and French with no schooling ($N = 5$).

APPENDIX

BOUNDARIES OF THE CENTRAL BUSINESS DISTRICT OF MONTREAL

Boundaries for the two downtown areas were based on a map in the 1964 *Yellow Pages* which delineates districts in Montreal used in the classified headings. By use of several street directories for Montreal made available by the Dominion Bureau of Statistics, *Liste Des Rues, Montreal, Partie I* and *II*, each medical office location was placed into Enumeration Districts (and E.A.'s if the Enumeration District was partially in one or both downtown areas) and then classified accordingly. For purposes of analysis the census tract boundaries were followed even if this meant including small areas outside the two downtown subareas delineated in *Yellow Pages*. Shown below are the census tracts, based on the 1961 tract scheme, included in each of the central business districts delineated in *Yellow Pages*:

Downtown, West	Downtown, East
51 (includes only Enumeration Areas 1–3 of District 468)	29–50
54–62	51 (includes only Enumeration Areas 66–68 and 112–114 of District 472)
69–72	52–53
118–121	137–139
	154

6

The Next Generation:
Impact of Bilingualism
on Language Maintenance

The central focus now shifts from the causes of bilingualism to concern about the mother tongue transferred to the children of bilinguals. Language continuity is almost inevitable among the monolingual segment of each mother-tongue population since such parents will have no choice but to raise their offspring in the same first language. Accordingly, there is no further difficulty in interpreting mother-tongue maintenance among the children of monolingual parents. By contrast, because there is a choice, the mother tongue acquired by the children of bilingual parents is not predetermined.

This option means that knowledge of the causes of bilingualism are not necessarily sufficient for determining whether the mother tongue or another language will be transferred to the offspring of bilinguals. Second-language learning is a necessary prerequisite for intergenerational shift, but is not a sufficient condition. Obviously mother-tongue continuity between bilingual parents and their children cannot be explained wholly by the same factors which initially led to the acquisition of a second language; the forces determining mother-tongue shift need not be the same in form or operation as those leading to bilingualism.

The basic dependent variable in this chapter is the magnitude of inter-generational shift in mother tongue among the children of bilingual parents. Bilingualism is now taken as a "given"; the basic issue is the choice made by bilinguals in the language transferred to their new offspring. Is the child's first language the same as the first language of both parents or is it a language that was acquired by one or both parents at a later age?

Linguistic maintenance may be viewed as a series of branching processes beginning at birth and ending with parenthood and the new generation (Figure 6.1). The parental generation is represented by solid lines

176

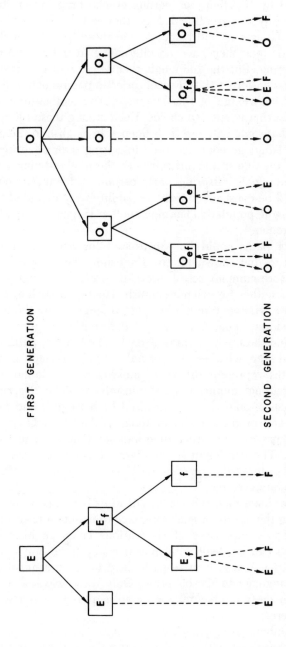

FIRST GENERATION

SECOND GENERATION

NOTE: MOTHER TONGUE IS REPRESENTED BY A CAPITAL LETTER; ACQUIRED LANGUAGES BY A SUBSCRIPT.
E, e = ENGLISH; F, f = FRENCH; O, o = OTHER TONGUE.

FIGURE 6.1   *Branching process affecting mother tongue maintenance between generations.*

and their offspring by dashes. Starting with native speakers of English, designated by "E," there are certain crucial branches or "turning points" along the way to parenthood. First they will be divided into those who learn French as a second language and those who do not. The latter may be ignored since they have no alternative in the tongue transmitted to their offspring. But the bilinguals themselves will be further subdivided into those who forget their French prior to parenthood and those who retain their knowledge of this language. The mother tongue of only the latter's offspring is open to choice. Even among these bilinguals it is conceivable that some will lose their fluency in English to the point that only the other language could be used in raising their offspring. Finally, one arrives at the age of parenthood with the mother-tongue outcome of all but the bilinguals' offspring fairly certain. A far more complicated diagram could be constructed if the possibility were included of the English-mother-tongue population learning another language instead of, or in addition to, French.

A set of paths could be constructed for native speakers of French analogous to that shown for the English-mother-tongue population. But an even more complex set of alternatives exist for those whose first language was neither French nor English. The first branching would be three ways: those who acquire neither official language by the time they reach parenthood and hence must pass on their native tongue; those who learn English; and those who acquire French. The last two paths can be further subdivided into whether the second official language is also acquired. These paths represent different combinations of language options for intergenerational mother-tongue transmission. The offspring of an O_{ef} parent, that is, one who has acquired both English and French, can be raised in any of three different tongues. An O_e or O_f parent faces the option of passing on either their mother tongue or one of the official languages. The combinations in Figure 1 would be even greater if the possibility of forgetting one's native tongue or one of the official languages was taken into account.

What we have then is a set of paths involving many turning points, all influencing the ability of each language to maintain itself in the next generation. The complexities of the various language histories leading to parenthood can be dealt with only partially here, but it is important to recognize that many of these paths lead to the transmission of only one possible language to the offspring. Only those exposed to the choice of passing on one's mother tongue or an acquired language are of crucial interest here.

The numbers occupying various points along these paths cannot be readily determined with the data currently available, but the net consequences may be examined. Shown in the first three columns of Table 1 is the mother-tongue distribution among small children in Canada for the last three decades. Columns 4 through 6 indicate the distribution that would be expected on the basis of the mother-tongue composition of the adult population after differences in fertility are taken into account. Observe that English makes a net gain in each decade, largely at the expense of "other" mother tongues, with French more or less holding its own. Among every thousand children under five in 1961, there were 76 more with an English mother tongue than among their fathers (.614 — .538 = .076). By contrast there were only 85 per thousand with an "other" mother tongue, little more than half the number expected if all fathers with such tongues had passed them on to their children (.147). The French also lost ground in 1961, but not too much. Of all fathers .316 were native French speakers, whereas .301 of the children had a French mother tongue.

Demographic processes do not account for the intergenerational shifts found in Table 1 because fertility was taken into account, the population resides in Canada, and differentials in mortality among the mother-tongue populations are unlikely to be that severe. Rather, these numbers represent the net impact of a wide array of linguistic processes and social forces which took place over the decades between the time the future parents themselves first learned to speak and the acquisition of speech by their offspring.

At least two distinctive approaches are possible for dealing with mother-tongue transmission between generations. One could attempt to explain why bilingual families with the same combination of mother tongue and acquired languages differ in the language used to raise their offspring. One could determine why the mother-tongue transmission rates for bilingual parents differ between communities. In both instances the emphasis

TABLE 1

Actual and Standardized Mother-Tongue Composition of Children Under Five Years of Age, Canada (Excluding Newfoundland): 1941, 1951, and 1961

| | Proportion with Each Mother Tongue | | | | | |
| | Actual | | | "Expected" | | |
Year	English (1)	French (2)	Other (3)	English (4)	French (5)	Other (6)
1941	.518	.364	.119	.489	.364	.148
1951	.602	.336	.062	.541	.344	.114
1961	.614	.301	.085	.538	.316	.147

is on the continuity–shift option in mother tongues between bilingual parents and their offspring. However, the explanatory emphasis in the first problem is on the characteristics of families whereas in the second it is on the characteristics of communities. There is nothing to be gained from a long discourse on the relationships between these two levels of analysis; nor is there any merit in ranking one approach over the other since both can be fruitful. For both intellectual and practical reasons, emphasis here is on the community level. Data are not available for analysis by family units and the community level is consistent with the general ecological framework used throughout this volume.

As an illustration of the type of problem to be studied, consider the variations found between provinces in the ability of languages to maintain their positions between generations. English gained and "other" mother tongues lost ground in all parts of Canada in 1961 (compare columns 1 and 4, and columns 3 and 6 of Table 2). French also declined in all provinces except Quebec (columns 2 and 5). What is striking, however, is the great variation across the nation in the strength of the various languages. The number of French-speaking children in Quebec is virtually equal to the number expected on the basis of the mother tongues of their fathers, but in British Columbia there is only a third of the number that might be expected if the French-mother-tongue population had all passed on this tongue (column 8). Likewise speakers of "other" mother tongues are much more likely to pass on their native languages in Prince Edward Island, the Northwest Territory, and Quebec than in Saskatchewan, Alberta, or Nova Scotia (column 9).

These results, which indicate considerable variation in linguistic retention, even on a simple provincial level, suggest the approach that will be taken as well as the kind of problem to be pursued; namely, what characteristics help explain differences between provinces and cities in their linguistic retention rates among bilinguals? Second, what are the trends in these retention rates over time and how are they to be explained? In both cases the main thrust is to determine the forces influencing areal variation in the language transmitted by bilinguals to their children.

Analysis of the linguistic transfer between generations in various parts of the nation over a span of several decades must be based on the data available in censuses. The ideal source would give a cross tabulation between the linguistic characteristics of parents and their children, coupled with various social characteristics that one might hypothesize as relevant. There is nothing even approaching such information available for Canada on the scale necessary for this study. As a consequence it has been necessary to make numerous assumptions and estimates to infer the rates of intergenerational mother-tongue shift. Rather than overburden the text

TABLE 2

Actual and Standardized Mother-Tongue Composition Children Under Five Years of Age, by Province: 1961

| Province | Proportion with Each Mother Tongue | | | | | | Actual as a Percentage of "Expected" | | |
| | Actual | | | "Expected" | | | | | |
	English (1)	French (2)	Other (3)	English (4)	French (5)	Other (6)	English (7)	French (8)	Other (9)
Prince Edward Island	.925	.062	.013	.900	.086	.015	103	72	87
Nova Scotia	.953	.034	.013	.918	.057	.026	104	60	50
New Brunswick	.608	.375	.017	.590	.394	.016	103	95	106
Quebec	.118	.840	.043	.109	.841	.050	108	100	86
Ontario	.832	.065	.103	.743	.084	.173	112	77	60
Manitoba	.745	.059	.196	.598	.082	.320	125	72	61
Saskatchewan	.851	.027	.123	.644	.045	.311	132	60	40
Alberta	.856	.022	.122	.701	.036	.262	122	61	47
British Columbia	.895	.006	.098	.771	.020	.209	116	30	47
Yukon	.898	.015	.086	.728	.039	.234	123	38	37
Northwest Territories	.395	.016	.588	.320	.036	.644	123	44	91

with a series of cautions and technical notes, these adjustments are described in an appendix to this chapter.

In short, the basic measure for the dependent variable is called a "retention ratio." For the children of bilingual fathers this ratio provides an estimate of the proportion who have the same mother tongue as their parent. The complement of the retention ratio is the proportion of children whose bilingual parents have passed on a different mother tongue. The complement describes the magnitude of "intergenerational shift" in mother tongue among bilingual parents whose children are exposed to the risk of a different mother tongue.

Bilingualism and Retention Ratios

An inverse association exists between the degree of bilingualism among the French-mother-tongue population and the retention of French by their children (Figure 6.2). The F_e's are more likely to transfer French in cities where most native French speakers are monolingual than in those places where most native French speakers also know English. But inspection of the scatter diagram in Figure 6.2 shows enormous variation in the retention ratios of cities where 90 percent or more of the native French speakers are bilingual. Because this finding is based on a relatively small number of cities, an even cruder procedure was employed for estimating retention among the children of F_e's in order to increase the number of cities that could be studied. The results, shown in Figure 6.3, are quite consistent.

Keep in mind that the two variables, percent bilingual and retention ratios, are not spuriously correlated with one another. The denominator of the retention ratio is the total number of F_e fathers and the numerator is the estimated proportion of *their* children whose mother tongue is French. Thus cities with a given level of bilingualism among their adult native French population are free to vary from 100 percent to zero in the degree of shifting or nonshifting among their children. The latter, the degree of nonshifting, is the retention ratio.

The absence of a strong association between bilingualism and retention in these cities, subject to confirmation by better and more direct measurements, is not altogether surprising from the perspective indicated above. For it suggests that the forces influencing the French-mother-tongue population to learn English are by no means identical to those that determine whether English will be passed on by bilingual parents to their offspring. In this regard variations between cities in the frequency English is learned are largely independent of what tongue the *bilingual segment* passes on.

By contrast there is a much closer association between intergenerational shift among the bilingual segment and the propensity of those whose first

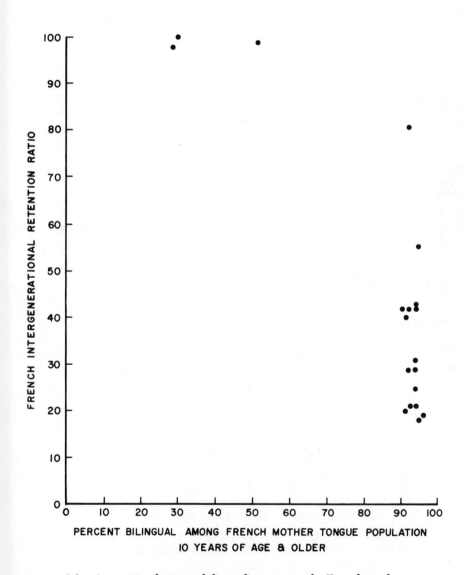

FIGURE 6.2 *Association between bilingualism among the French mother tongue population and intergenerational retention of French, selected cities, 1961.*

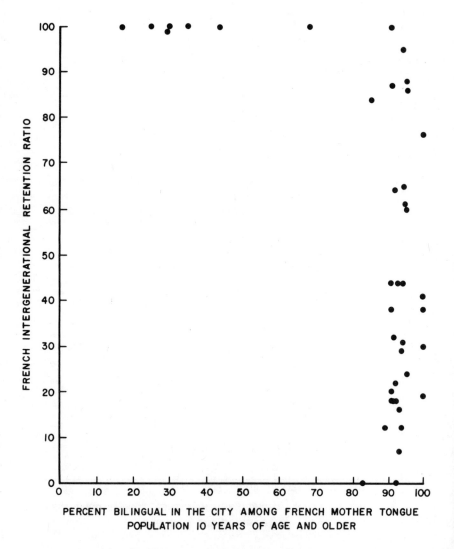

FIGURE 6.3   *Association between bilingualism and intergenerational retention of French, expanded number of lesser cities, 1961.*

language is neither English nor French to learn an official language (Figure 6.4). The rank order correlation, tau, is .70. This suggests that the forces leading the French to become bilingual has a different effect on future generations than do the factors leading to bilingualism among the "other"-mother-tongue groups. It is impossible to examine the retention ratios for the English-mother-tongue population since they nearly always exceed the preceding generation and therefore the net estimate of shifting is meaningless. (For a more detailed discussion see the appendix to this chapter.)

Further evidence that French and the "other" mother tongues differ is obtained when the French retention ratio is compared with the retention ratio for the offspring of "other"-mother-tongue parents. The analysis is restricted to those cities in which the percent bilingual among the French-mother-tongue population is high, 90 percent or more. Intergenerational shift for "other"-mother-tongue bilinguals is somewhat lower in those cities with high French retention ratios; for example, the average loss among children of other-mother-tongue parents exposed to risk is 49 percent in "high" French retention cities and 61 percent in "low" French retention cities. Nevertheless the correlation is positive and low between French and other-mother-tongue retention in these cities; tau is .25. This suggests that the maintenance of French and the immigrant-group languages is largely a function of either different specific factors or else the same factors have different levels of impact.

Composition and Retention

French intergenerational retention is also influenced by the mother-tongue composition of the city. As Figure 6.5 indicates, French is transmitted by nearly all French bilinguals in cities where their native language is the largest mother tongue. On the other hand, there is wide variation in the maintenance of French among cities where it is the mother tongue of 10 percent or less of the population. These wide variations in French intergenerational maintenance cannot be explained simply in terms of composition, although it is clear that cities in which French is the dominant mother tongue are also places where virtually no loss of French occurs.

Lesser Cities

Rather than attempt to explain variations in French language transmission among all cities, part of the analysis focuses only on those in which French is the mother tongue of 10 percent or less of the population. These places are called the "lesser" cities and refer only to the small percentage of the residents with French mother tongue. Thus Toronto is a lesser city

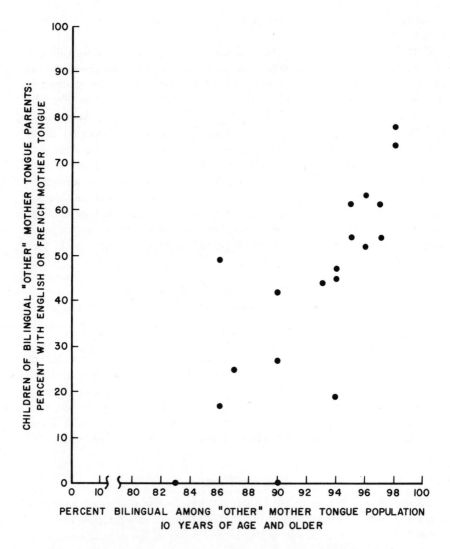

FIGURE 6.4   *Association between bilingualism among the "other" mother tongue population and their children's rate of mother tongue shift, selected cities, 1961.*

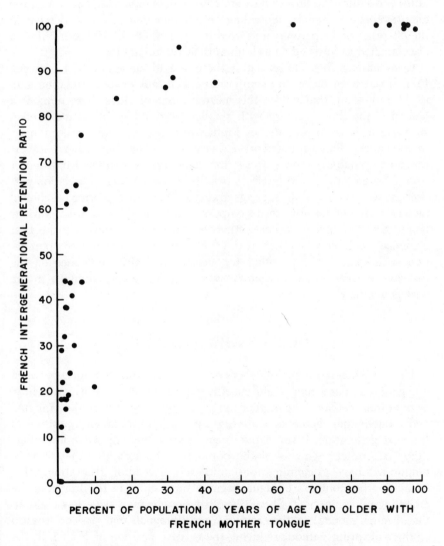

FIGURE 6.5 *Association between French mother tongue composition and French retention ratio, expanded number of cities, 1961.*

by this criterion, despite its large total population. The low rate of shifting in cities in which French is the numerically dominant native language appears to be adequately explained by the influence of composition.

Because of the measurement error resulting from the necessarily crude estimates of intergenerational shift, causal analysis of French retention will be restricted largely to rank order correlations or dichotomies. In the latter procedure the lesser cities are classified as either high or low in the maintenance of French, depending on whether more than 30 percent of the offspring of F_e parents are raised in French. Of the 29 lesser cities 15 are classified as low and 14 as high in their retention rates.

Even among these lesser cities there is still an association between French retention ratios and composition. The rank order correlation, tau, is .44, indicating that within this narrow range of cities there remains a tendency for those centers with smaller percentages of native French speakers to have lower rates of French intergenerational mother-tongue maintenance. This is noteworthy because among the "other"-mother-tongue population, those whose first language is neither English nor French, there appears to be no association between their population percentage and the rate of language transfer. Because of various technical factors, it is not feasible to decompose native speakers of these various languages into specific other-mother-tongue groups. However, the best evidence available suggests that the sheer proportion of the city's population with some "other" mother tongue has very little influence on the decision of their bilingual components to maintain the language in the next generation.

DEMOGRAPHIC FACTORS

There are demographic influences on mother-tongue continuity between one generation and their children. Any differentials in fertility, mortality, or migration between the mother-tongue groups, or between the bilingual and monolingual segments of each group, affect a language's position in the next generation. If the native speakers of a language have lower fertility than other segments of the population, for example, their mother tongue will have a declining position in each succeeding generation. Likewise a mother tongue's bilingual segment may differ in fertility from the monolingual component. Should English monolinguals have less children than French monoglots, then some French bilinguals may pass on English to their offspring without reducing the relative position of French in the next generation. But since these demographic factors were described in an earlier chapter, elaboration is not necessary at this time other than to note their influence when inferring intergenerational shift among bilinguals. Of direct relevance here is the way demographic factors influence not only the net impact of various intergenerational processes, but may themselves have a direct effect on intergenerational shift.

Mother-Tongue Maintenance within a Life Span

It is possible for a bilingual's knowledge of his mother tongue to decline to the point where he has become a monoglot by the time his children are born. Fishman and his associates (1966, p. 421) argue that within the bilingual speaker's life span a new tongue may replace the mother tongue to the point that the latter language is forgotten or is nearly useless. Under such circumstances the bilingual becomes a monolingual, there is intergenerational change due to this intragenerational shift, but none of these phenomena would be recorded under the methods used here. If intragenerational changes of this sort occur for numerous native speakers of a given language, then the tongue will decline in the next generation even if all the remaining native speakers pass the mother tongue on to their offspring. Clearly, Fishman has noted an extremely important mechanism for language shift which, if operating extensively in Canada, would seriously undermine this analysis.

Fortunately, the best available evidence indicates that mother tongue loss within the lifespan is not an important factor in Canada. The mother-tongue distribution of various age groupings were compared with the responses given by the same group 10 years later (Lieberson, 1966, p. 274). Since the current Canadian definition of "mother tongue" includes the proviso that the respondent still understand the language, minimal linguistic ability is measured as well. The results suggest a fairly high degree of retention among the native speakers of both official languages. In all but one cohort, however, there was a decline between 1951 and 1961 in the percentage reporting some other mother tongue.

It is therefore unlikely that persons first raised in English or in French fail to maintain their skills in Canada. Apparently it is a more realistic possibility for those with some other native tongue. With the considerable movement to Canada from countries where neither English nor French is used, very likely some migrants lose mastery of their mother tongue at some point during their stay in Canada. The sharpest losses for the other-mother-tongue cohorts appear in the younger age groups (see Table 3 in Lieberson, 1966), suggesting that small children migrating to Canada are particularly likely to lose their mother tongue after they acquire English or French.

These findings provide further support for approaching linguistic continuity as a problem that hinges primarily on intergenerational transfer rather than intragenerational changes. It must be recognized, however, that the latter does play a role in undermining the strength of at least some of the nonofficial mother tongues.

Rural–urban Differences

The literature generally suggests that rural residents retain their mother tongues in multilingual situations for a longer period than do urban dwellers (see the studies cited by Fishman, 1966, p. 443). This greater tenacity is interpreted as reflecting the homogeneous ethnic enclaves in isolated rural settlements. However, frequently these statistical examinations have been concerned with rural–urban differences between comparable generations in the knowledge or usage of their ancestors' tongues, with little or no effort made to distinguish between the causes of these differences. The mother-tongue distribution of a given generation is not normally viewed as the net product of the two factors distinguished here, namely, the degree of second-language learning in the preceding generation coupled with intergenerational shift among the children of bilinguals. Although results such as those reported by Haugen (1953, p. 291) and by Useem and Useem (1945, p. 383) are perfectly appropriate for inferring the net differences between rural and urban residents in mother-tongue retention, they are not adequate for telling us whether location influences shift among those exposed to the risk. For it is possible that rural and urban areas differ only in the frequency of bilingualism, but not at all in the language transmitted among those who are bilingual.

The 1961 Canadian census defines urban as "all cities, towns, and villages of 1000 population and over, whether incorporated or unincorporated as well as the urbanized fringes of all such centers if the agglomeration was 10,000 or over" (Dominion Bureau of Statistics, 1964, Bulletin 3.2-5). Rural is subdivided into those on farms of minimal size and sales, called "rural farm," and those living in rural localities but not on farms, called "rural nonfarm." The vast majority of the rural farm residents are engaged in agriculture whereas only a small proportion of the latter are employed in this industry. The broad definition of urban is not altogether suitable for comparing the intergenerational shifting rates along an urban–rural scale.

The minimum rate of intergenerational shift to English among the children of bilingual French-mother-tongue fathers is shown in row 1 of Table 3. Although rural areas have the lowest shift, the rates are fairly similar and not very high in any of the locales. (The appendix to this chapter describes the method used to calculate these measures and the assumptions made.) Thus between 87 and 98 percent of the children of French bilinguals retain their fathers' mother tongue. Among "other"-

mother-tongue fathers who can speak English and/or French as well, urban and farm areas have almost identical switching rates. As row 2 of Table 3 indicates, nearly half such bilingual parents pass on an acquired tongue rather than their native language (48 and 46 percent in urban and farm areas, respectively). This is a high rate in the sense that it spells a rapid decline in other languages once English or French is learned. No ready interpretation is available for the somewhat higher maintenance of other mother tongues among rural nonfarm residents.

Rural–urban differences are not substantial determinants of the mother tongue that bilinguals pass on to their offspring. There is, however, somewhat greater resistance to mother-tongue shift among French bilinguals living on farms. It must be kept in mind that these results do not contradict previous studies that were concerned with the net differences in mother-tongue retention. Nor can one infer, on the basis of these results, that mother-tongue tenacity differs only silghtly between rural and urban areas in Canada. For the overall pattern is a reflection of the occurrence of bilingualism in these locales as well as the behavior of those who are able to speak a second language. Although twice as many urban as rural French Canadians are bilingual, there is almost no difference in the retention ratio of rural versus urban bilinguals.

These results throw some light on Fishman's challenge (1966, pp. 443–444) of the widely held proposition that urban dwellers are more inclined to shift. This generalization, he contends, is derived from only a particular kind of language contact setting. Granted that the present analysis is limited to the Canadian scene in 1961, the fact that the French- and "other"-mother-tongue groups differ in their response to the rural–urban factor tends to support Fishman. For the French may be viewed as a subordinate "indigenous" group whereas most of those with "other" mother tongues are subordinate "migrant" groups (Lieberson, 1961).

TABLE 3

Rural-Urban Differences in Mother-Tongue Maintenance, Canada (Excluding Newfoundland): 1961

Characteristic	Urban	Rural Farm	Rural Nonfarm
Minimum percentage shift to English among the children of French-mother-tongue bilingual fathers	12	2	13
Percentage shifting to an official language among the children of "other"-mother-tongue bilingual fathers	48	46	35

Moreover Fishman suggests that language revivals tend to originate in an urban setting rather than rural areas. Using the analytical approach of the present study, the shift back to an earlier mother tongue can be viewed as distinctive from the question of the intergenerational shift to English among the children of native French speakers. For the question of language revival pertains to the behavior of, say, French Canadians who are native speakers of English. The relevant matters would be the degree to which they acquire French and, further, the transmission of French as the native tongue of their offspring. In the context of the French ethnic group in Canada language revival deals with the movement from English to French, whereas mother-tongue maintenance pertains to the lack of movement from French to English. Fishman is quite correct in challenging the proposition that rural settings are more conservative with respect to mother-tongue maintenance not only on empirical grounds, but also because there are two analytically separate phenomena to be considered.

Absolute Size

The French retention ratio in the lesser cities is related to the absolute number of French-mother-tongue residents (tau is .36). However, this association is partially explained by the joint association between absolute numbers and the percent with French mother tongue. Thus the partial tau between French retention ratios and the absolute number of French speakers is only .17 after the percentage with French mother tongue is taken into account. For cities in which French is the mother tongue of less than 10 percent of the residents variations in the sheer number of native French speakers has a small influence on the chances that French will be maintained as the mother tongue of the next generation. This effect is probably due to the fact that many institutions which can support the continuance of French themselves require certain minimal population bases in order to exist. Therefore those cities in which the French-mother-tongue group is somewhat larger in absolute number have a slight advantage in retaining this tongue in the next generation. In cities of different sizes but with comparable percentages of native French speakers, mother-tongue maintenance will tend to be favored in those centers with larger absolute numbers of French speakers.

Age of Bilingualism

The age of second-language learning is an extremely important influence on the level of skills acquired in the tongue. Although no concensus exists about the optimal age for learning languages, it is safe to say that fluency and comfort in using a tongue will generally be less if it is first learned in adulthood or in the late teens. Fluency in a second tongue might be expected to influence the chances that it will replace the bilingual's native language in the next generation. Accordingly, the age at which native French speakers learn English should influence the likelihood of an intergenerational shift, since fluent speakers of the latter tongue are, on the average, more likely to have acquired this language at an early age.

It is possible to estimate the ages of bilingualism by tracing cohorts of the French-mother-tongue population in a limited number of cities over a 20-year span between 1941 and 1961, examining the acquisition of English at three different points in time. In nearly all of the lesser cities (in which French is the mother tongue of less than 10 percent of the population) an overwhelming majority of French-mother-tongue children also know English at an early age. By contrast in six cities in which French is a major mother tongue a much smaller percentage of the children are bilingual (column 1 of Table 4). An average of 89 percent learn English in the former cities whereas from 1 to 40 percent learn English in the six major French centers, with a median of only 4 percent.

By 1951, when the cohorts are 10–14 years of age, the proportion able to speak English has increased in both sets of cities. Virtually all French-mother-tongue children at this age in the lesser cities are also able to speak English and the median is 12 percent in the major cities (column 2). The gap between the two sets of cities in their median percentages remains unchanged for this cohort (85 in both 1941 and 1951). Tracing the linguistic abilities of the same cohort to 1961 when they are 20–24 years old, slightly more than 50 percent of those with French mother tongue also speak English in the major cities (column 3). Since the median for lesser cities can hardly get much higher by adulthood than it was in the early teens (in fact it dropped slightly), the gap between the two sets of cities has receded greatly to the point where the difference in medians is only 37 percent in the early adult years. Virtually all the native French speakers in Sudbury also know English by the early adult ages, but the figures are also high for Montreal (over 50 percent) and Ottawa-Hull (around 80 percent). Even in Trois-Rivières, where only 1 percent of the French-mother-tongue cohort knew English in 1941 and 3 percent in 1951, a third of the cohort could speak this second language at the time of early adulthood. An almost exact inverse relationship exists among the six major cities between the percentage of the population with French mother tongue and the extent of bilingualism among those 20–24 years of age.

These findings have several important implications. First the composition of a city influences not only the chances of a native French speaker

TABLE 4

Minimum Percent of the French-Mother-Tongue Population Able to Speak English, Major and Lesser French Cities by Age Cohorts: 1941, 1951, and 1961

City	Year and Age								
	1941	1951	1961	1941	1951	1961	1941	1951	1961
	0–4	10–14	20–24	15–24	25–34	35–44	45–54	55–64	65+
	(1)	(2)	(3)	(4)	(5)	(6)	(7)	(8)	(9)
Major French Cities									
Montreal-Outremont-Verdun	4	14	56	58	66	61	62	54	42
Ottawa-Hull	26	56	83	80	88	86	84	81	72
Quebec	2	5	37	30	43	36	42	38	27
Sherbrooke	4	11	51	60	55	53	69	56	40
Sudbury	40	96	97	96	96	95	93	91	80
Trois-Rivières	1	3	35	33	43	40	38	32	21
Medians									
Six major French cities	4	12	54	59	60	57	66	55	41
Eighteen lesser French cities	89	97	91	99	97	93	99	97	89
Difference	85	85	37	40	37	36	33	42	48

learning English, but also the timing. The gap between cities with small and large proportions of native French speakers varies according to the ages of the residents. The acquisition of English occurs very early for the vast majority of French-speaking residents in the cities where their tongue is a small minority. Although these lesser centers exceed the major French centers in all parts of the life span, the gap narrows considerably in the young adult ages. Thus these two classes of cities are distinguished not only by the percentage learning English but also by the equally important fact that French bilinguals in the major centers learn English at a later age. In the lesser cities the rates of bilingualism among French children are so high at such early ages that clearly the use of English permeates their milieu. In cities in which the French constitute a large segment of the population, the acquisition of English reflects less of a pressure from the immediate neighborhood and context of childhood. Rather, it reflects the pressures due to schooling and the demands of the labor force.

This analysis of cohorts by age of learning suggests one of the mechanisms through which a city's mother-tongue composition influences the retention ratios among the offspring of French bilinguals. Bilingualism occurs much later in life on the average in those cities in which French is the mother tongue of a large percentage of the residents. The pressures to learn English are far more intense and start much earlier in lesser French cities. The gap between major and lesser cities continues to decline during the middle years (Table 4, columns 4–6) and then increases somewhat in the older ages (Table 4, columns 7–9), but these shifts are minor when compared with changes among the younger ages.

Although major and lesser cities differ in the age of bilingualism, variations between lesser cities in their retention ratios are not explained by the influence of age of bilingualism on intergenerational mother-tongue switching. High and low retention among these lesser cities is not a function of the age at which parents' bilingualism occurred, at least as measured by the cohorts for which data are available. Tracing the three different cohorts—those in 1941 who were under 5, 15 to 24, and 45 to 54 years of age—indicates very little difference in the age of bilingualism between lesser cities with high and low retention (Table 5); for example, acquisition of English among the children under 5 was actually slightly greater in high retention cities (medians of 89 versus 88 percent). Ten years later, in 1951, when this cohort was 10 to 14, a slightly higher degree of bilingualism occurred in those places with low retention ratios, but it is not of the magnitude to explain much of the difference between these cities. The differences are nil in 1961 for this cohort as they are in the various years covered for the two additional cohorts. It is therefore not possible to explain retention ratio variations between lesser centers in

TABLE 5

Median Percent Able to Speak English Among the French-Mother-Tongue Population in High and Low Retention Lesser Cities, by Age Cohorts: 1941, 1951, and 1961

Age and Year		Low Retention Cities	High Retention Cities
0– 4	(1941)	88	89
10–14	(1951)	100	96
20–24	(1961)	92	91
15–24	(1941)	99	99
25–34	(1951)	98	97
35–44	(1961)	94	93
45–54	(1941)	99	99
55–64	(1951)	97	96
65+	(1961)	90	88

terms of the age at which bilingualism first occurred among the parents.

Assuming these results are not a statistical artifact due to differential migration or mortality within the age cohorts of these lesser cities, some interpretation is in order. Since virtually all small children acquire English through one means or another in lesser cities, the option is really whether they will learn English as their native tongue or at an early age as a second language. Nevertheless this does not mean that the differences between high and low French retention need to be viewed as random or inexplicable. First, the supports for French have not been considered. The existence of institutional and other forces which encourage the transmission of French to the offspring may not prevent the acquisition of English, but it could influence whether English is acquired as a mother tongue or as a second language learned relatively early in life.

Second, the possibility still remains that the high and low retention cities differ in either the origin or the strength of the pressure to learn English. The causes of bilingualism are varied and so too are their implications for mother-tongue retention in the next generation. Although there is evidence for differential causes of bilingualism, the proposition that they in turn vary in their impact on mother-tongue retention remains to be examined in this chapter. One can at least entertain the proposition that the causes for learning English in high French retention cities are strong enough to lead to almost certain acquisition of this tongue as a second language, but that these forces are less powerful or from different sources than those operating in cities with low mother-tongue retention among the children of French bilinguals.

Restricting the analysis to the French ethnic population with a mother tongue other than French (in the vast majority of cases it is English), one finds that a somewhat larger proportion of such people learn French as a second language in high retention cities. In other words, cities in which the children of French bilinguals are more likely to retain French as their mother tongue are also places where members of the French ethnic group with some other native language are more likely to learn French as a second language. Among the 18 cities examined by cohorts tau is .29 between the French retention ratio and the percent able to speak French among those members of that ethnic group with some other mother tongue. Although other interpretations are possible, this correlation is compatible with the view that certain institutional features occur in high-retention cities which lead to the maintenance of French as the mother tongue of children whose parents are bilingual.

INSTITUTIONS

It is difficult to visualize an institution remaining completely neutral in its impact on mother-tongue maintenance. In actual practice most institutions tend to favor one language over another, thereby having consequences for mother-tongue maintenance. The military in Canada, for example, tends to favor English, but clearly there is no inherent reason why it could not place a premium on French and put speakers of English at a disadvantage. To be sure, it is possible for an institution to be structured to be linguistically neutral by providing equal and identical opportunities for either mother tongue, a policy used successfully in some South African schools for Europeans, but dropped in recent decades (Malherbe, 1943). However, since it is likely that many if not all institutions will favor one tongue or another in actual practice, generally institutions can be examined in terms of their variation between cities in policies which favor one language over another. Further, if they do vary, then the next question to ask is whether it appears to significantly affect the retention of French between generations.

A second perspective may also be employed. In a given society a specific institution may be viewed as largely favoring one language. With this assumption one can determine whether quantitative variations between different communities in an institution's presence will alter the language socialization practices of bilingual parents; for example, it is commonly held that industrialization favors English over French because it is largely in the hands of English-speaking people from the United States, the United Kingdom, or Canada. As a consequence, one can ask whether differences between communities in the degree of manufacturing activities will influence the retention ratios of their French bilinguals.

Occupational and Industrial Pressures

In an earlier chapter it was noted that occupational pressures influence the acquisition of English among native French speakers. Whether the occupational and industrial pressures generated in each community influence intergenerational shifting is, however, a separate question. Unfortunately, retention ratios could be computed for only a small number of cities with bilingual *Yellow Pages*; for example, none of the "lesser" cities have phone books with French listings. The use of French as an advertising medium in *Yellow Pages* is not necessary in cities in which French has such a weak demographic position and virtually all know English. As far as *Yellow Pages* go, there is apparently no significant support for the use of French in the work world of any of these cities.

There is some association between the retention ratios and the degree of dual listings among the small number of cities for which information is available (keeping in mind that French is the mother tongue of considerably more than 10 percent of the residents in these cities). The tau between the French retention ratio and the percent of nonconsumer listings in English only is $-.33$ for these nine cities. In other words, bilinguals are more likely to transfer French to the next generation in those cities where relatively few businesses use English exclusively. Thus cities in which French is a recognized medium for industrial use are also places where the intergenerational shift for French bilinguals is low.

Turning to the central focus, the lesser cities and their variations in the retention of French, there is some indication that the economic activities in high retention cities differ from those with lower retention ratios. The median percentage of the labor force employed in manufacturing industries in 1961 is greater for the former group of cities (26.5 versus 17.5). Possibly bilingual French parents in the more industrialized centers obtain less of a mastery of English in a factory than in a white-collar setting. Or it may be that the labor market opportunities in industrial cities provide less of a need for the kind of fluency in English that is usually obtained only by native speakers of a tongue. Needless to say, these interpretations are speculative and are based on a type of aggregated association known as "ecological correlations." Nevertheless there is a moderate association between retention ratios in these cities and the degree to which the labor force is employed in manufacturing industries (tau is .22).

Schools

The educational opportunities provided in the French medium are greatest by far in the province of Quebec. None of the 29 lesser cities under study are located in Quebec, a fact hardly surprising in view of the predominance of French Canadians in this province and the criterion used for inclusion among the lesser cities category. However, as noted earlier, the policies toward instruction in tongues other than English vary widely in the remaining provinces. Moreover, because of local options in many provinces, there are often differences between lesser cities located in the same province.

An inquiry was sent to the school boards of each lesser city to learn about the availability of schooling in French for both the public and parochial schools. Information was obtained from all but four of the cities under study. In many instances in which the medium of instruction was French it was available only through the parochial schools and even then not from all Catholic schools. Nevertheless the results do indicate that the availability of some schooling in French can play an important role in influencing mother-tongue retention. Of 13 cities with high retention 8 report that some grade schools use French as the medium of instruction. Among the 12 reporting cities with low retention ratios, only one offered instruction in the French medium in either public or parochial schools. This suggests that school policies have some influence on the language used by French bilinguals to socialize their offspring.

Television

There were only 14 French-language television stations around the time of the census (based on data as of March 1, 1962). All but five of these are located in Quebec. Moreover, as might be expected because of the expense involved in television, a rather large population base is necessary. Thus even those television stations located outside Quebec are found in areas with sizable concentrations of French Canadians. Aside from Quebec, there are stations in Moncton, New Brunswick; Sturgeon Falls, Timmins, and Ottawa, Ontario; and Winnipeg, Manitoba. The latter is the only "lesser" city with a French language station (Saint John, New Brunswick is not terribly far from Moncton but the effective radiated power of Moncton's transmitter is rather low). Winnipeg's retention ratio ranks rather high for a lesser city, but it is obviously impossible to draw any inferences based on a single instance. At any rate, there is evidence to support the contention that French speakers can maintain their mother tongue in cities that do not offer linguistic support through television. To put it another way, high and low retention among the lesser cities is not explained by the presence or absence of television since only one such city has a station.

Although these results indicate that French bilinguals in lesser cities can retain French despite the absence of French-language television, it does not follow that the presence of a station will not influence the rate of intergenerational shifting. The data do not permit testing the latter proposition and it is perfectly possible that language continuity would be increased—to say nothing of French television's possible effect on the need for native French speakers to acquire English. The necessary data are also not available to consider whether the presence of French language telecasts affects the quality of spoken French.

As for radio, there is little reason to doubt that French Canadians in virtually any part of Canada can listen to French broadcasts if they are willing to purchase a sufficiently powerful receiver. As a consequence, no attempt is made to explore the influence of this communication medium on mother-tongue retention. Undoubtedly radio would be more relevant for earlier periods in Canada as well as in many parts of the world where television is currently not widespread.

Marriage

The family is a key institution for understanding mother-tongue maintenance between generations, for it is within the family that most children learn their first language. Since it is almost certain that offspring will be raised in a language that is used and understood by both parents, the linguistic abilities of a bilingual's mate will have a considerable impact on the language used to socialize their offspring. If the spouse is a monoglot, for example, the children will be raised in the tongue common to both parents, whether this be the bilingual's first or second language. The degree of bilingualism among each sex can, in this regard, influence the mother tongue passed on to the offspring.

Data are not available for determining the frequency of various linguistic combinations among the mates of bilinguals in specific Canadian cities. However, there is good reason to believe important demographic forces operate to mold the kinds of linguistic combinations that will occur in the marital process. It is generally recognized that the frequency of endogamous marriages is influenced by the composition of a community such that a given group's rate of out-marriages tends to go up in cities where they comprise a small proportion of the population, (e.g., see Heer, 1966). The ethnic origins of children in various provinces provide crude evidence suggesting that this process also occurs in Canada. Considering only British- or French-origin parents, in the early 1940's in Quebec less than 2 percent of the children born to French fathers had British mothers, whereas more than half the children in British Columbia with French fathers had British mothers. The rates of intermarriage, as crudely measured by data on births, generally varied inversely with the group's percentage of the total population (tau is −.83 for nine provinces).

Assuming this process operates among Canadian cities with respect to language, the percentage of bilingual French Canadians who are wed to English monoglots is affected by the mother-tongue composition of the city. Suppose, in Cities A and B, that French is the mother tongue of 5 and 50 percent of the residents, respectively. Suppose that 20 percent of those with French mother tongue are bilingual in each city. Further assume that the remainder of the population in both places are all English monoglots (respectively, 95 and 50 percent). One can see how the linguistic composition will make it more likely that marriages in city A will lead to the transfer of English to their offspring. Table 6 below describes the linguistic combinations expected in each city if French bilinguals were to select their mates randomly.

In city A, in which only 5 percent of the total population are native speakers of French, nearly all bilingual men will be married to English-speaking monoglots. Assuming that the children are raised in a tongue known by both parents, a shift to English is very likely for the offspring of 95 percent of the men exposed to risk, possible for 4 percent, and improbable for only the 1 percent whose mates speak only French. In city B, in which half the population are native French speakers, random mating would pair only half the bilingual men with women who speak English only. The remaining half are in marriages in which the retention of French is either possible (40 percent) or assured (10 percent). Since French is more likely to be acquired by native English speakers in city B, the influence of composition is actually understated in the hypothetical figures shown above. Although there is every reason to expect in-group marriages

TABLE 6

Linguistic Distribution among Wives of Bilingual Men With French Mother Tongue

Official Language of Wife	Likelihood of Intergenerational Language Shift	Percent Distribution	
		City A	City B
English only	Probable	95	50
English and French	Possible	4	40
French only	Improbable	1	10
Total		100	100

to exceed the expectations generated under the assumption of random mating, nevertheless Chart 1 provides an illustration of how compositional features influence the likelihood that bilinguals will marry an English monoglot.

Several additional compositional features would also lead one to expect greater intergenerational shifting in cities in which the French comprise a small segment of the population. For one, the percentage learning French among those with some other tongue (English included) will reflect the composition of the community, but, since this tends to be low in most cities, even more important is the fact that bilingualism among the French-mother-tongue group varies inversely with the position of the language in the city. This means that relatively few of the bilinguals will have spouses who can speak only French even when they marry within the ethnic group. As a consequence, in cities in which the vast majority of French Canadians can also speak English French is the assured language of socialization in very few marriages.

Population composition also influences the linguistic characteristics of a bilingual's perspective mates in a very significant way. Among the population with French mother tongue in each of 12 major cities examined in 1961, males were more likely to know English than were females (based on the population 15 to 44 years old). On the average 66 percent of the men were able to speak English whereas only 55 percent of the women knew this language. Among these cities there is an inverse relationship between the percentage of French-mother-tongue men who are bilingual and the absolute gap between the sexes in bilingualism (tau is $-.35$). In Moncton, for example, at least 98 percent of the French-mother-tongue males can also speak English, and at least 95 percent of the women are also bilingual. But in Granby, by contrast, only 48 percent of the males and 31 percent of the females are bilingual for certain, a gap of 17 percentage points.

The lower frequency of bilingualism in the major centers, even if it were identical for the two sexes, means that the proportion of bilingual men who are married to bilingual French-Canadian women is reduced. In the average major city in which 66 percent of the French-mother-tongue men are bilingual only 66 percent of these would be married to women who could also use English if the women were equally bilingual (assuming no out-marriages). Since bilingualism is actually lower for women, an average of 55 percent, it means that little more than half of the endogamous bilingual men would have wives who could use English in raising their children. Under the hypothetical condition of only in-group marriages the absolute frequency of bilingualism as well as the relative differences between the sexes influence the mother tongue transferred by bilinguals to their children.

There is a fairly strong inverse association in these major cities between the intergenerational retention rates and the magnitude of the difference between the sexes in their degree of bilingualism (tau is −.62). Major cities with high French retention ratios possess certain demographic features which reduce the chances that a bilingual will have a mate who will either require or even facilitate the transmission of English to their offspring. Exogamous marriages, it is speculated, are less likely in cities in which the French comprise a large segment of the population. Within the group French women are less likely to be bilingual than the men, thereby eliminating for many bilinguals any strong chance that they will transmit English to their offspring.

Not only are men and women with French mother tongue in the lesser cities both more likely to know English but the differences between the sexes are virtually nil (93 percent among men and 92 percent among women on the average in the 29 lesser centers). Moreover in about a third of the lesser cities women are either equally or more bilingual than men. By contrast men are more bilingual than French mother-tongue women in all of the major centers. Under these conditions, in which most of the French mother-tongue population of both sexes is bilingual, the potential for transmitting English as the mother tongue of the offspring is very high. Added to this is the probability that exogamous marriages are more frequent for the French-Canadian population in these lesser centers. English-speaking offspring are almost assured in such marriages because very few nonnative speakers of French are able to speak this language. Thus the potential for transmitting English as the mother tongue is great in all of the lesser cities.

Differences between the sexes do not influence the retention ratios in the lesser cities. There is virtually no difference between those classified as high and low in retention. For lesser cities with high retention men and women 15 to 44 years of age are, respectively, 94 and 92 percent bilingual. The means are 93 and 91 percent bilingual for men and women in low retention cities. Thus males and females differ only slightly in their frequency of bilingualism and, moreover, not in a way which can account for variations in the retention ratios among the smaller French cities.

The demographic influences on marriage in major French cities do not affect retention in places where French is the mother tongue of only a small component of the population. There is reason to believe, however, that high and low retention lesser cities do differ in their marital patterns. Since French Canadians are a predominantly Catholic ethnic group, it is of interest to note that the French constitute a larger segment of the Catholic population in high retention cities than in low ones (the means are 20 and 12, respectively). The correlation (tau) is .43 between the retention ratios and the percentage of Catholics who are French Canadians in the 29 lesser cities. If a large segment of the Catholic population is not French Canadian and therefore probably does not know French, then French Canadians who marry within the Catholic fold will tend to have mates who do not favor French. In cities in which the French are a more important segment of the Catholic population religious endogamy will mate a larger proportion of the French Canadians with others who also know French. This may explain the tendency for cities in which the French are a larger percentage of the Catholic population also to be communities with lower rates of intergenerational shifting to English.

To be sure this association could be a spurious one, reflecting the operation of very different forces. For one, the position of the French language within the Church no doubt varies by the ethnic composition of Catholics in each community. The Church in those cities where a relatively large segment of Catholics are French is probably more supportive of the French language; for example, the association observed earlier between French educational opportunities and the retention of French was due in no small way to the availability of French language instruction in the parochial schools in many of the high retention cities.

There is crude evidence suggesting that religious intermarriage for French Canadians is more frequent in the low retention cities. Simply calculating the proportion of French Canadians who are Catholic in each of the lesser cities, the average is somewhat higher in high retention cities (76 percent versus 69 percent in low retention places).

Among those with a mother tongue other than French only a very small percentage learn to speak French in the lesser cities; ranging from a high of 3.4 in Toronto to a low of 1.1 in Moose Jaw, Saskatchewan. This is more or less to be expected, in view of the fact that French is the native tongue of less than 10 percent of the population in these places. Nevertheless the ability of others to speak French has a slight influence on the French intergenerational retention ratios. The mean percent of non-French able to speak this language is 2.4 for high retention cities and 1.8 for low retention centers, with a tau of .38 with the French retention ratios. To be sure, the differences are small, but this relationship is compatible with the view that French Canadian out-marriages in cities where some others can speak French will reduce the number of French bilinguals with mates who are English monoglots. It should be kept in mind that even if a small proportion of people learn French as a second language they can constitute an important number of mates for French Canadians in cities in which the latter are a relatively small group.

In summary, marriage is an institution of considerable importance for mother-tongue maintenance among bilinguals and is itself influenced by the community's population composition. In-group marriages in lesser cities, for example, will often pair mates who are both exposed to the risk of intergenerational switching. Because the pressures to learn a second language are less uniformly applied to both men and women in major French cities, the French-Canadian mates of bilinguals are more likely to be French monoglots who will not be prone to rear their offspring in a tongue that is foreign to them. In these cities the pressures generated by the labor market are a necessary prerequisite for bilingualism and therefore adult women are less influenced by this factor. Other pressures generate bilingualism in the smaller cities such as those derived from early childhood contacts with an overwhelmingly English-speaking environment. These pressures do not differentially affect men and women. Nevertheless it is possible to distinguish between high and low retention cities in terms of other demographic features which influence the linguistic characteristics of bilingual mates.

Political Factors

To what extent does the general political milieu influence the retention of French? As indicated in chapter 3, Quebec is distinctly more supportive of French than the remaining provinces of Canada. Because none of the lesser cities are located in this province, however, it is not possible to examine the implications of Quebec's policies on the maintenance of French among the offspring of bilinguals.

It is possible to consider political variations between the remaining provinces and their influence on French language maintenance. Aside from Quebec, Ontario and New Brunswick are generally more supportive of French demands than the remaining provinces. The 230,000 French Canadians in New Brunswick make up 40 percent of the province's population in 1961. Although comprising little more than 10 percent of the residents of Ontario, French Canadians number 650,000 in this province and tend to be concentrated in certain counties. Based on these demographic features as well as the institutional supports offered in their educational systems, language retention in the lesser cities of these two provinces can be compared with the remaining provinces. This provides a measure of the impact that the general political milieu may have on retention among the bilingual population.

The median retention in the 16 lesser cities of Ontario and New Brunswick (only one is located in the latter province) is 41 percent of the children of bilingual French-mother-tongue parents. Among the 13 cities located in the remaining provinces (three each in Alberta, Saskatchewan, British Columbia; two in Nova Scotia; and one each in Newfoundland

TABLE 7

Median Retention Ratios among Lesser Cities, by Province: 1961

	Lesser Cities		
Province	All	Small	Large
Ontario and			
New Brunswick	41	29	44
All others	20	12	30

and Manitoba), the median retention rate is considerably lower, 20 percent. Subdividing the lesser cities into those with less or more than 1500 native speakers of French over 10 years of age, the results still indicate that communities in Ontario have higher rates of retention than those located elsewhere (Table 7).

One interpretation of these results is that the milieu in which a city is located will have a bearing on the maintenance of a language. Another view is that the findings merely reflect the greater support for French-language instruction in Ontario and New Brunswick which, in turn, reflects the stronger position of the French population in these provinces. Table 8 indicates the median retention ratios in the two sets of provinces cross-tabulated by the presence of at least some elementary school instruction in the French medium. Although the retention ratios for lesser cities in Ontario are higher than the remaining provinces, the differences are rather small after the presence or absence of French medium instruction is taken into account. Keeping in mind the small numbers in the cells, these results suggest that the "provincial effect," independent of its influence on the schooling available to French Canadians, is relatively unimportant. Rather the bulk of the differences in retention ratios between the provinces outside of Quebec are due to the greater French educational opportunities available in Ontario and New Brunswick.

TABLE 8

French Retention Ratios in Lesser Cities by Province and Educational System

	Ontario and New Brunswick		All Other Provinces	
French Medium School Support	Median	(Number of Cities)	Median	(Number of Cities)
Present	44	(6)	41	(3)
Absent	25	(10)	19	(6)

A BRIEF REVIEW

Because discussion of language maintenance between generations is continued in the next chapter, only a brief review is necessary at this point. Empirical evidence has been offered to justify the conceptual distinction between the acquisition of second languages and, on the other hand, mother-tongue shift between parents and their children. The operation of demographic and institutional influences on mother-tongue maintenance has been examined. In some cases, particularly marriage, simple compositional features may influence the impact an institution will have on mother-tongue maintenance.

The failure to find that several commonly held demographic and institutional characteristics actually influence language maintenance is hardly to be viewed as a "disappointing" result. To be sure, the data are less than optimal and they are hardly international or comparative in character. Nevertheless the results reported in this chapter represent a relatively distinctive empirical approach to bilingualism and, until contrary empirical evidence is presented, at least suggest that several widely held causal interpretations of linguistic switching between generations are in error.

APPENDIX

THE BASIC DEPENDENT VARIABLE

The basic variable is the language transmitted to their offspring by *bilingual* parents in each mother-tongue group, that is, by parents exposed to the risk of passing along a mother tongue different than their own; for example, among native French speakers who also know English what percentage of them transfer English to their offspring? What percentage French? Since these data are not available, the only alternative is a rather indirect procedure which merits some explanation.

The first step involves determining the proportion of fathers with each mother tongue who, because they are monolinguals, have no choice in the language used with their children. Employing Canada in 1961 as an illustration, these figures are subtracted from the proportion of children possessing each mother tongue (column 1 minus column 2 in part A of Table 9). The remainder is the number of children with a given mother tongue whose fathers had a choice; for example, 61.4 percent of all Canadian children report English as their mother tongue and 51.3 percent of all fathers are English monolinguals. Hence 10.1 percent of all Canadian children have English mother tongues but their fathers speak one or more other languages ($.614 - .513 = .101$). The percentages of such children are shown in column 3 of part A.

The next step involves determining the language choices of bilingual and multilingual fathers. So far it is known that 7.3 percent of all Canadian children have other mother tongues but that they cannot be accounted for by monolingual fathers. It is estimated that about 13.5 percent of all fathers could speak one or more of Canada's official languages in addition to some other mother tongue. Therefore it follows that 6.2 percent of all Canadian fathers had other mother tongues but transmitted some official language to their children (13.5 − 7.3). This yields an important dependent variable, namely, the percentage of bilingual fathers with some other mother tongue who passed on English or French. In this case, $\dfrac{6.2}{13.5}$, or 46 percent.

The new languages transmitted by these fathers are apportioned under the assumption that those who could speak both English and French were half as likely to pass on their mother tongue as those who could speak only one of the official languages in addition to their mother tongue. The results of these computations are shown in part B of Table 8. In column 1 are the distributions by official language of fathers with some other mother tongue. In column 2 are estimates of how many of these passed on their mother tongue to the next generation. Column 3, which is obtained by subtracting column 2 from column 1, gives the proportion of all Canadian fathers who did not pass on their other mother tongue to their children. Observe that only one figure in this last column causes any further difficulty. The 5.5 percent who did not pass their mother tongue on must have transmitted English since this was their only choice. Had there been any fathers who spoke French only remaining they would have caused no problem either since their only choice would have been French. The only difficulty lies among those fathers who were able to speak both official languages in addition to some other mother tongue. It is unclear how many of them passed on each official language.

Returning to the English- and French-mother-tongue children, .101 and .099, respectively, of Canadian children had these mother tongues but could not be accounted for in terms of the contributions made by monolingual parents. This was obtained from column 3 of part A. It is now possible to account for some of these. Learning from part B that 5.5 percent of all parents had passed on English even though they had some "other" mother tongue, it follows that .046 of English-mother-tongue children remain to be linked with fathers (.101 − .055 = .046). Since none of the fathers with other mother tongues who also spoke French are estimated to pass on the official language, it is still necessary to account for .099 of all children who have French mother tongues.

These computations provide the figures necessary for a balance sheet, shown in part C, which is used for computing the dependent variables. First, there are 2.5 and 11.3 percent of all fathers who are native English and French speakers, respectively, but know both official languages. In addition, 0.7 percent know both official languages as well as have some other mother tongue which they did not transfer to their children. On the other side of the ledger, 4.6 percent of the new generation have English mother tongues and 9.9 percent have French mother tongues that cannot be accounted for thus far. On the basis of these

TABLE 9

Procedure for Estimating Cross-Tabulation Between Fathers and Offspring, by Mother Tongue and Official Language, Canada (Excluding Newfoundland): 1961

A. Children Accounted for by Monolingual and Bilingual Fathers

Mother Tongue	Children Under 5 (1)	Monolingual Fathers (2)	Children of Bilingual Fathers (Col. 1 − Col. 2) (3)
English	.614	.513	.101
French	.301	.202	.099
Other	.085	.012	.073
Total	1.000	.724	.276

B. Accounting of Children with "Other" Mother Tongue

Fathers' Official Language	Fathers with "Other" Mother Tongue (1)	Children with "Other" Mother Tongue (2)	Children Whose Fathers Have Passed on an Official Language (Col. 1 − Col. 2) (3)
None	.012	.012	—
English	.124	.069	.055
French	.001	.001	.000
English and French	.010	.003	.007

C. Balance Sheet for Children with English or French Mother Tongue Whose Fathers Speak Both Languages

Mother Tongue of Fathers Able to Speak Both Official Languages Who Pass on English or French		Mother Tongue of Children	
Mother Tongue	Proportions	Proportions	Mother Tongue
English	.025	.046	English
French	.113	.099	French
Other	.007		
Total	.145	.145	

figures it is possible to compute several measures of linguistic transfer among French- and English-mother-tongue bilinguals. Bilingual is here defined as an ability to speak both official languages. These are shown above with illustrations drawn from Table 9.

Mother-tongue distribution of children with bilingual fathers:

English	32 percent (.046/.145)
French	68 percent (.099/.145)

Mother-tongue distribution of bilingual fathers who have passed on an official language:

English	17 percent (.025/.145)
French	78 percent (.113/.145)
Other	5 percent (.007/.145)

By comparing these two distributions, both of which are derived from part C, it becomes very clear that more French-mother-tongue parents have English-speaking children than vice versa. Thus only 17 percent of the bilingual parents have English mother tongues, but 32 percent of the children of bilingual parents do. On the other hand, 78 percent of the bilingual fathers are native speakers of French, compared with only 68 percent of the children of bilingual parents.

It is also possible to construct certain minimal transfer percentages. Assuming that bilingual fathers with some other mother-tongue shift in the direction where the deficit among the children are, two key variables can be computed:

> The minimum percentage of bilingual English mother-tongue fathers who have French-speaking offspring

and

> the minimum percentage of bilingual French mother-tongue fathers who have English-speaking offspring.

Comparing the two percent distributions shown above, it is clear that the minimum shift among English-mother-tongue fathers is zero, for, in the case of a mother tongue whose proportion among the children, .32, is greater than among the bilingual fathers, .17, the minimum shift is zero (given the assumption about bilingual fathers whose mother tongue is some other language). On the other hand, since the proportion of bilingual fathers with French mother tongue, .78, is greater than the proportion of children with a French mother tongue that are unaccounted for, .68, it follows that at least some of the French-mother-tongue fathers have transmitted English to their offspring. To be more precise, the differences between the two proportions, when divided by the proportion of French-mother-tongue fathers who are bilingual, yields the minimum percentage of these men who have shifted. Thus $\frac{.78 - .68}{.78} = 12.8$ percent. We can conclude that in Canada in 1961 at least 13 percent of bilingual French-mother-tongue fathers had children whose native tongue was English.

The emphasis given to the fact that these are *minimum* percentages shifting is derived from the possibility of greater gross shifting among both groups. Thus, although it has been concluded that the minimum shift among the offspring of native English bilingual fathers is zero, it is likely that some of these men raised their children as native speakers of French. Given the net differences shown above, it would mean that even more of the French-mother-tongue fathers who were bilingual had passed on English to their children. Thus these minimum percentages indicate the frequency of shifting if it is assumed that as far as possible the bilingual fathers pass on their native tongues to their children.

Cross Tabulation Between Mother Tongue and Bilingualism

These computations are possible for only those cities for which one can estimate the cross tabulation between mother tongue and official language. To my knowledge the Canadian census has never published such cross tabulations. However, the marginal totals (which are known) can be employed under certain assumptions to estimate these associations. Looking at the cross tabulations desired in the table below, note that some combinations of official language and mother tongue are rather unlikely; for example, one would not expect to find someone with English mother tongue who can speak only the French official language. "X" is placed in those cells with mother tongue–official language combinations that are unlikely or infrequent at best. These cells are assumed to be zero in each community. The capital letters indicate the marginal figures available from published census reports.

One consequence of these assumptions is that people unable to speak either official language are classified only among those with some "other" mother tongue, that is, neither English nor French. This makes the entire "D" population, those unable to speak either official language, a subpart of the other-mother-tongue group. In all cities for which this procedure was applied G is greater than D. As expected, this means that some of the other-mother-tongue population can also speak English and/or French. At this point it is necessary to distribute the population with other mother tongues not accounted for (G − D) into the remaining cells of the bottom row. The 1931 census of Canada provides the official language cross tabulations among the other-mother-tongue population for a limited number of cities. The other-mother-tongue population able to speak some official language (G − D) in 1961 was distributed into the three official language categories, English only, French only, English and French, on the same proportional basis as in 1931. The proportion of those with other mother tongues unable to speak an official language was free to vary between 1931 and 1961 on the basis of the actual numbers in each period, being a function of $\frac{D}{G}$ in each census, but the (G − D) population was distributed between the first three columns in 1961 on the basis of their relative frequency in 1931.

With this accomplished, the remaining cells can be easily filled. For example, the number of English-mother-tongue speakers able to speak English only, E_o, is equal to $A - O_e$, the number of F_o speakers is equal to $B - O_f$, the number of English mother tongue bilinguals, E_f, is equal to $E - E_o$, and French mother tongue bilinguals, F_e is obtained from $F - F_o$. As a consequence all of the cells can be estimated with these assumptions.

It was also necessary to take fertility differences between ethnic groups into

TABLE 10

Cross Tabulation Between Mother Tongue and Official Language Based on Marginals

Mother Tongue	Official Language				Total
	English Only	French Only	Bilingual	Neither	
English		X		X	E
French	X			X	F
Other				D	G
Total	A	B	C	D	

account. This was accomplished in crude fashion by weighting the fathers' linguistic distribution for each ethnic group by the number of small children of the same ethnic origin. Since Canadian census procedure traces ethnic origin through the father's side in cases of mixed marriages, this was a more desirable procedure for taking fertility differentials into account. It must be noted that data limitations prevent standardization for fertility differences along linguistic lines within each ethnic group.

The necessary official language distributions in 1931 are available for only 19 of the larger communities after combining cities that are part of the same metropolitan area. Since some of these communities are major French centers, it was necessary to expand the number of places with estimated cross tabulations between mother tongue and official language in order to pursue the analysis of "lesser" cities. Because the research focus was primarily on the French intergenerational retention ratio, it was possible to use another procedure which could be applied to an expanded number of cities, 29. The 10 additional urban places are units consisting of one or more cities with at least 30,000 population in 1961. Cities were combined if they were part of the same metropolitan or urban area.

Formulas are available which determine the maximum and minimum numbers with a given mother tongue able to speak each or both official language (Lieberson, 1966, pp. 264–266). In many cases the range is rather small between the minimum and maximum estimates. Moreover, comparison of this procedure with unpublished data for several Canadian cities in 1961 indicates that the lower estimates of French-mother-tongue bilingualism were generally more accurate. By using these formulas it was possible to estimate the official language distribution among the male French-mother-tongue component of each ethnic group. After using fertility controls similar to those described above, this permits an estimate of the net retention of French among the children of French-mother-tongue bilinguals. Among the majority of the cities for which the earlier estimating procedure was possible there is a close fit between the results obtained under the two procedures.

7

Further Analysis of French-Mother-Tongue Retention

The focus remains on the forces influencing the mother tongue transferred by bilinguals to their children. A somewhat more dynamic approach is taken, involving the use of retention ratios based on several points in time. An effort is also made to develop some models of the forces determining mother-tongue shift. The reader should keep in mind that the inclusion of certain causal factors in this chapter, as opposed to the preceding one, is based only on the availability of data over time or the development of a more abstract interpretation of the results. The processes are far too complex and the data much too scanty to permit any ordering of the various ecological influences on language maintenance.

SEGREGATION

There is good reason to expect language shift in urban centers to be influenced by the residential patterns of bilinguals. If French bilinguals reside near French monolinguals, the latter will support the bilinguals' maintenance of French in the next generation. On the other hand, there will be less chance of French intergenerational continuity if French bilinguals are highly segregated from French monoglots, but have a spatial distribution similar to English monolinguals.

French bilinguals located in English areas of a city will probably have greater facility and skills in English since their bilingualism will be required for communication in the neighborhood. Compare this situation with that faced by a bilingual located in a French district; English may be required at work, but this pressure declines when he leaves the job for home. Moreover, residential patterns will also influence the desirability for bilinguals raising their children in English as opposed to French.

Clearly, French will be more of a handicap to children living in pre-dominantly English-speaking areas compared to those located in pre-dominantly French parts of the city. In brief, the residential patterns of bilinguals compared to the English and French monoglot distributions will influence the quality of second-language skills, the domains in which they are applied, and the utility each tongue will hold for children.

In Montreal the residential patterns are important influences on the small degree of intergenerational shift found among bilinguals from both the English and French mother-tongue groups. In each case the bilinguals are much more segregated from the other mother-tongue group than from their mother-tongue compatriots who are monolingual (Lieberson, 1965b); for example, the F_e population (French mother tongue but also able to speak English) is much less segregated from French monoglots than from English monoglots (19 versus 52), despite the fact that F_e's can communicate with either group. Likewise the bilingual segment of the British ethnic group is much less segregated from the remaining native speakers of English than from French monolinguals.

The influence of the segregation patterns on language maintenance will be greatly affected by the size of the various monolingual and bilingual groups within the city. Keeping in mind that the segregation index used here (the index of dissimilarity) is not affected by the relative numbers in each group, we must consider compositional factors as possibly modifying the significance of a given pattern of segregation. Segregation will have relatively little isolating power for a mother-tongue group that is small in *number* in the city or when its *proportion* of the total population is low. Both of these compositional factors will influence the impact a group's level of segregation will have on isolating it from the remainder of the population. To take an extreme case, if the bilingual component of a minor mother-tongue group in a city has a high level of segregation, this may occur even if most or many of their neighbors are native speakers of some other tongue. Intergenerational shift is hardly prevented by a spatial pattern that leads to a high index of segregation since the bilinguals still reside in areas where the numerically dominant population speak some other tongue. On the other hand, an equally high index of segregation for the bilingual component of a numerically important mother-tongue group will greatly reduce the chances of intergenerational shift.

This implies that the degree of residential segregation between the bilingual population and English or French monoglots, by itself, has only a limited influence on the retention ratio since the groups' composition within each city is not taken into account. Based on 11 cities for which both segregation and retention data are available (Table 1), tau is .31 between the retention of French among the children of bilinguals and

the relative segregation of bilinguals from the two monolingual populations. Shifting tends to be less frequent in those cities where bilinguals
are more segregated from English monoglots than from their French
monolingual compatriots. The reader should keep in mind that the segregation indexes are sensitive to the spatial delineations in each city and
that no attempt is made to take this into account. This difficulty, however,
is partially avoided by the fact that the relative segregation of bilinguals
from English and French monolinguals is examined here rather than the
absolute degree of segregation from a group in each city.

Further evidence exists to suggest that segregation per se does have
some influence on the language transferred by bilinguals. For seven leading cities changes in both retention ratios and segregation were measured
between 1951 and 1961. The retention ratios for French bilinguals declined
in all but one of the cities during this period, remaining the same only in
Quebec. During the same decade the index of segregation between the
bilingual and English monoglot populations in most of these cities also
declined. The small number of cities studied and insufficient variance in
the shifts do not make these data suitable for even rank correlation analysis. The trend, however, is at least supportive of the contention that segre-

TABLE 1

French Retention Ratios and Segregation of Bilinguals, 1961[a]

City	French Retention Ratio	Index of Segregation Between Bilinguals and Speakers of:		Bilingual Segregation from English Only Minus French Only
		English Only	French Only	
Calgary	.21	15	16	− 1
Hamilton	.43	13	26	−13
London	.20	15	31	−16
Montreal	.99	43	25	18
Ottawa	.81	50	42	8
Quebec	1.00	36	30	6
Regina	.18	10	11	− 1
Toronto	.40	17	30	−13
Trois-Rivières	.98	31	16	15
Windsor	.25	26	12	14
Winnipeg	.31	41	19	22

[a]Segregation indexes based on entire metropolitan areas, except for Trois-Rivières
(urban area) and Regina (city proper).

gation does influence the behavior of those exposed to the risk of transferring a new language to their children.

Population Composition, Segregation, and Retention

French is the mother tongue of no more than 10 percent of the population in 17 cities for which segregation data are available in 1961. For such cities a high index of residential segregation between bilinguals and those speaking only English cannot be assumed to represent optimal conditions for the retention of French in the next generation. Such high indexes may occur even if the vast majority speak only English in the areas where bilinguals are located. To consider this effect a slightly modified form of the segregation index proposed by Bell (1954) is employed.

This type of measure was described in an earlier chapter. In this particular case, it indicates the probability that bilinguals have of randomly interacting with English monoglots within the census tracts where bilinguals reside. The percentage of the residents in each census tract speaking English only is determined and then weighted by the number of bilinguals located in the same tract. When summed for the entire urban area and divided by the total number of bilinguals in the city, this measures the proportion of the population speaking English only encountered by the average (mean) bilingual in his tract. Obviously in practice social interaction is neither random nor restricted to one's census tract, but this index does provide a useful summary measure which reflects both the residential patterns and population composition of the community. It should be noted that the modified Bell measure is not simply the functional equivalent of the index of segregation weighted by population composition. Knowledge of the index of dissimilarity and the population composition of a city will not invariably lead to a given value of the measure of interaction used here.

The hypothesis to be tested is that French retention ratios will vary between cities inversely to the degree bilinguals encounter people who speak only English. In all these lesser cities the probability is at least fairly high that a bilingual interacting randomly with his neighbors will encounter an English monoglot; the modified Bell measure ranging between .98 in the St. John's, Newfoundland metropolitan area to .73 in Winnipeg. An inverse association does exist between the retention of French in the next generation and the probability of bilinguals interacting randomly with English monolinguals in their residential neighborhood (tau is —.44). Even among lesser cities, the residential patterns of bilinguals, coupled with compositional factors, does appear to influence the probability of French bilinguals passing on French as the native tongue of their children.

Variations in Linguistic Segregation

Not only will the influence of segregation on language retention differ from city to city, depending on the linguistic composition, but there is reason to expect that the pattern of linguistic segregation will itself vary greatly. Earlier it was observed that French bilinguals in Montreal are far less segregated from French monoglots than from English monoglots. In analogous fashion British bilinguals are far more segregated from French monolinguals than from English monolinguals. The net effect in Montreal is for bilinguals to remain residentially enmeshed with their mother-tongue group despite the potential for communicating in the other official language. The situation is radically different in Edmonton where the overwhelming majority of native French speakers are bilingual. These bilinguals are actually less segregated from British monolinguals than they are from the small number of French monolinguals in the metropolitan area. Contrasts between Montreal and Edmonton suggest that ethnolinguistic segregation may itself vary widely between cities. This, in turn, opens up the possibility of examining the ecological features of each community with the goal of explaining the residential distributions themselves.

The necessary census data are available in unpublished form for three metropolitan areas which represent considerable variation in linguistic composition and maintenance: Montreal, Ottawa, and Edmonton. In Montreal French is the mother tongue of the majority of the population 15 years of age and older (63 percent), whereas only 23 percent are native speakers of English. The numerically dominant mother tongue in Ottawa's metropolitan area is English, but French is still the native language for more than a third of the residents. The ratio of English to French among those 15 and older is therefore about 1.5:1. English enjoys a favorable numerical position in Edmonton by a substantial margin, being the mother tongue of 64 percent whereas only 4 percent are native speakers of French. As might be expected, Montreal is the most favorable of the three settings for French maintenance and provides the greatest threat to English. The opposite holds for Edmonton, where English is not challenged, but French is highly vulnerable. Ottawa occupies an intermediate position. In Edmonton nearly 40 percent of the French ethnic population are native speakers of English and the current retention ratio indicates that this figure will probably increase in the future. By contrast the percentage of the British ethnic group with French as their mother tongue is low in all three cities, although varying in the direction described.

Two technical notes are necessary before discussing the residential patterns shown in Table 2. First, the absolute values of the segregation indexes cannot be compared between cities. Various factors, such as the tract delineations, operate to influence the relative magnitude in each city. It is still appropriate, however, to compare the *patterns* of relative segregation within one city with those in other places. Second, although the mother tongue of bilinguals in each ethnic group is not specified in the data available for measuring segregation, the overwhelming majority of French-Canadian bilinguals in each city are native speakers of French. Likewise, English is the mother tongue of the vast majority of British bilinguals. Consequently it is reasonable to describe these as French- and English-mother-tongue bilinguals, respectively, even if some bilinguals in each ethnic group have a different mother tongue.

Considerable differences exist between the three cities in the residential segregation patterns of their ethnolinguistic segments (Table 2). The spatial patterns of both the British and French bilingual groups in Montreal are conducive to the maintenance of their mother tongues. Each group is less segregated from monolingual compatriots with the same mother tongue than from ethnic rivals who speak the acquired language. The index of segregation between French bilinguals and English monoglots, for example, is 59, whereas the former has an index of only 19 from French monoglots. French-Canadian bilinguals in Ottawa are less closely linked to their French monolingual compatriots; the index between them is 43 compared to an index of 61 between French bilinguals and British monoglots. Finally, in Edmonton, French-Canadian bilinguals are actually less segregated from those British who speak only English than they are from the small number of ethnic compatriots who speak only French (Table 2).

The patterns of French ethnolinguistic segregation vary between these cities in a manner which will influence the relative chances for French mother-tongue retention among the offspring of their bilinguals. This is in sharp contrast with British bilinguals, who are more than twice as segregated from French monoglots than from their English monolingual compatriots in all three cities. Only in Montreal does the analogous pattern hold for the French bilinguals. For even in Ottawa the ratio of French bilingual segregation from, respectively, English and French monolinguals is less than 1.5:1 (61 versus 43). Generalizations based on three cities would be foolhardy, but the data do suggest that the British bilinguals consistently maintain a residential pattern which facilitates the maintenance of their mother tongue, whereas the spatial location of bilingual French Canadians is less consistent in discouraging an intergenerational shift in mother tongues.

There is some reason to believe that these residential patterns are not altogether haphazard. Compared to the linguistic segments within the French group, the monolingual and bilingual components of the British

TABLE 2

Indexes of Segregation Between Ethnolinguistic Segments: Montreal, Ottawa, 1961

Ethnic Group (and Official Language)	Metropolitan Area		
	Edmonton	Montreal	Ottawa
British (bilingual) versus			
British (English only)	21	19	26
French (French only)	47	56	68
French (bilingual) versus			
British (English only)	25	59	61
French (French only)	36	19	43

ethnic group are less likely to be sharply differentiated in other important ways. The occupational composition of French bilingual men differs greatly from French monolinguals in such cities as Montreal and Ottawa (Table 3). By contrast British Canadians with different linguistic skills are much more similar in their occupational distributions in these cities. Bilingual and monoglot British Canadians are differentiated by occupations much more in Edmonton where the small number of British bilinguals tend to have high educational attainment, but here also the two French-Canadian subgroups are even more dissimilar in occupational composition.

TABLE 3

Indexes of Occupational Dissimilarity Among Male Ethnolinguistic Segments, 1961[a]

Ethnolinguistic Components	Edmonton		Montreal		Ottawa	
	Actual	Expected	Actual	Expected	Actual	Expected
British ethnic group: Bilingual versus English monoglots	22	20	7	1	5	6
French ethnic group: Bilingual versus French monoglots	30	7	27	15	32	13

[a]Indexes based on males 15 years of age and older in the metropolitan area's work force. Expected indexes are computed on the basis of the educational composition of each segment combined with the general relationship between education and occupation among males in the metropolitan area.

Because English dominates economic life throughout Canada, the effect of bilingualism on the occupational possibilities of British Canadians is less severe than among the French mother-tongue group. This is seen when the educational levels of the ethnolinguistic groups are taken into account. The indexes of occupational dissimilarity shown in Table 3 indicate the occupational differences between monolingual and bilingual members of each group expected on the basis of the general association between education and occupation in each city. The actual occupational distributions of the two British subgroups are quite similar in both an absolute sense as well as relative to what might be expected on the basis of their educational composition. In Montreal, for example, bilingual and monolingual British men have an actual index of 7, which is not terribly more than what might be expected on the basis of their educational differences. Likewise there is virtually no difference between actual and expected for British subgroups in Edmonton and Ottawa. A rather different pattern emerges among French Canadians. The monolingual and bilingual subgroups are much more differentiated in occupational composition than would be expected solely on the basis of their differences in educational attainment. In Montreal, for example, the index of occupational dissimilarity is 27, whereas it would be only 15 if linguistic ability had no influence.

The French linguistic segments are also more differentiated by income than are the British in Montreal and Ottawa. Bilingual and monolingual British Canadians differ by little more than $25 in Montreal and $250 in Ottawa. Income differentiation is much greater in Edmonton where bilinguals of British origin earn nearly $1800 more than those speaking English only (as noted earlier, the former have considerably higher education). Bilinguals and French monoglots in the French ethnic group, however, are much more sharply differentiated by income: $1300 in Montreal; $800 in Ottawa; and nearly $2400 in Edmonton (all based on 1961 census data). In the latter city, the direction of the difference is rather surprising since the bilinguals earn less than those speaking French only. This may be due to the small number of employed males of French origin who speak French only (96). For French-Canadian women in Edmonton, as well as both males and females in Toronto, bilinguals earn considerably more than their French-speaking compatriots.

Going beyond the fact that residential segregation combined with the community's population composition influences mother-tongue retention in the new generation, it seems reasonable to speculate that variations in segregation have a certain order to them. Linguistic skills differentiate the British less sharply than the French. As a consequence, the bilingual and monolingual segments among the British will tend to be less segregated from one another. By contrast the influence of language is much greater for the French and therefore the two major linguistic segments are more sharply differentiated. This, in turn, promotes greater segregation among the French segments in the very same cities in which, demographically speaking, they are most vulnerable to intergenerational language shift, namely, where English is the numerically dominant language. Hence the cities where bilingualism among the French is greatest also have considerable segregation between the two linguistic components of the group. This is not the case for the economically dominant group. The British bilinguals in Montreal, where the risk of passing on French is most severe, are not greatly segregated by residence from their monolingual compatriots. British monolinguals fare remarkably well and are not greatly differentiated from the bilingual British Canadian in education, occupation, and income.

By way of a concluding generalization the degree of residential segregation not only influences mother-tongue retention among bilinguals, but itself will reflect other sociolinguistic dimensions within the community. If acquisition of a second language is greatly advantageous for native speakers of a given tongue, the monolingual and bilingual components of the group will be sharply differentiated on other important socioeconomic characteristics as well. Under these conditions high segregation can be expected which will undermine intergenerational maintenance of the mother tongue. On the other hand, if acquisition of a second language has fewer ramifications in the socioeconomic sphere for the native speakers of a language, those who do become bilingual will be less segregated from monolinguals with the same mother tongue. In turn, the absence of high segregation will provide residential support for the continuation of the same mother tongue among the children of bilinguals.

TRENDS IN THE RETENTION OF FRENCH

If a society were closed to international migration and had identical mortality and fertility rates among its ethnolinguistic segments, then language maintenance would be determined only by the frequency of bilingualism coupled with the retention ratio. The population exposed to risk is measured by the frequency of bilingualism; the retention ratio indicates what happens to the bilinguals. Although Canada is not a closed society, indeed migration is on an enormous scale, the retention ratio is still one of the crucial long-run determinants of a language's potential for survival. This is particularly the case for the French tongue, which is not helped to any appreciable extent by international migration and whose earlier advantage based on higher fertility is diminishing.

Among the children of French bilinguals French mother-tongue retention has been declining in most Canadian provinces during the past few decades (Table 4). Among the offspring of French bilinguals in Ontario, for example, the maximum percentage with French mother tongue decreased from 95 in 1941 to 79 in 1951 and 71 in 1961. In the nation as a whole, which is heavily weighted by the French-mother-tongue population in Quebec, shifting also increased during this period. Some exceptions are found in specific provinces but overall there is little doubt that a French Canadian who becomes bilingual is increasingly likely to raise his children in English.

A similar decline occurred among most Canadian cities between 1951 and 1961 (it was not possible to estimate the frequency of shifting in 1941). Among the 19 cities examined the retention ratio declined in 14, remained unchanged in 1, and rose in 4.

Cross-sectionally, in both 1951 and 1961, the French retention ratio is correlated with the degree of bilingualism among both the French-mother-tongue population (inversely) and the English-mother-tongue residents of each city (directly). The tau between retention and percentage of the French-mother-tongue population learning English in these 19 cities is —.60 in 1951 and —.54 in 1961. The percentage learning French among the English-mother-tongue group is correlated with retention in both 1951 and 1961 (tau is .44 and .29, respectively). (Based on comparisons with known rates of bilingualism among mother-tongue components in 1961,

TABLE 4

French Retention Ratios by Province: 1941, 1951, and 1961[a]

Province	1941	1951	1961
Prince Edward Island	.87	.66	.67
Nova Scotia	.78	.66	.53
New Brunswick	1.00	.96	.90
Quebec	1.00	1.00	1.00
Ontario	.95	.79	.71
Manitoba	.94	.80	.68
Saskatchewan	.85	.68	.55
Alberta	.84	.67	.56
British Columbia	.44	.32	.22
Yukon	.28	.14	.35
Northwest Territories	N.A.	.17	.43
Canada (excluding Newfoundland)	1.00	.94	.87

[a]Retention ratios based on maximum possible number of French-mother-tongue bilinguals passing on French to their offspring. Lower ratios would be obtained if it were assumed that greater switching existed among bilingual parents in both the English- and French-mother-tongue groups.

TABLE 5

French Retention Ratios by Province: 1941, 1951, and 1961[a]

City	1951	1961
Brantford	.37	.29
Calgary	.31	.21
Edmonton	.50	.42
Halifax	.30	.19
Hamilton	.39	.43
Kitchener	.75	.42
London	.13	.20
Montreal-Verdun	1.00	.99
Ottawa	.84	.81
Quebec	1.00	1.00
Regina	.21	.18
St. John, N.B.	.64	.56
Saskatoon	.33	.42
Toronto	.42	.40
Trois-Rivières	1.00	.98
Vancouver	.23	.21
Victoria	.18	.29
Windsor	.41	.25
Winnipeg	.48	.31

[a]Retention ratios based on maximum possible number of French-mother-tongue bilinguals passing on French to their offspring. Lower ratios would be obtained if it were assumed that greater switching existed among bilingual parents in both the English- and French-mother-tongue groups.

the degree of bilingualism among the French-mother-tongue group is based on minimum estimates and the frequency of bilingualism among the native English speakers is based on estimates of maximum possible bilingualism.) Rather than attempt an elaborate explanation of the causal linkage between bilingualism and retention, it is best to first examine the longitudinal trends between these two phenomena.

Examining the trends in bilingualism over time, some rather surprising results occur. The frequency of bilingualism among the English-mother-tongue population increased between 1951 and 1961 in all but two of the 19 cities. Accompanying this is a decline in all but one city in the estimated proportion of the French-mother-tongue group able to speak English. What is surprising here is not that a decline in bilingualism among one mother-tongue group was complemented by a rise in second-language acquisition among the other group—indeed this is to be expected if the pressures for communication remain constant—rather that this period of declining English language acquisition among the French was during a decade when the French retention ratio also fell. Indeed, there is no association between the changes in the retention ratios and changes in the occurrence of bilingualism among the French-mother-tongue population (tau is −.02). On the other hand, there is a moderate association (tau is −.27) between the decline in the French retention ratio and the increase in the percentage of native English speakers who know French.

Of particular importance here is the fact that shifts in the retention of French over time is not caused by the same set of factors which influence bilingualism among the French-mother-tongue population. Indeed, these findings suggest that changes in the French retention ratio are more closely linked to changes in the acquisition of French among others than to changes in bilingualism among the French group. A span of 10 years, coupled with the crudeness of the indices, is insufficient to mark this as a definitive result, but it does provide further justification for viewing the two central phenomena as independent. Whether one becomes bilingual or not certainly determines the chances of one's children having a different mother tongue, but language continuity among bilinguals is not merely a reflection of the occurrence of bilingualism among the population. In this instance, in fact, there is no correlation at all between the variables.

A DEMOGRAPHIC MODEL OF RETENTION

The language transferred by bilingual French-mother-tongue parents will be influenced profoundly by the linguistic capacities among both their own ethnic group and the remainder of the population. Hardly all the ethnolinguistic demographic variables that might influence retention are included, let alone the many institutional considerations that could be introduced. Nevertheless, a preliminary attempt to order but one part of the total picture is of value. Even at this stage it is important to consider the model's application to retention ratios over time, as far as possible, rather than be content with an explanation of only a single period in time.

Table 6 indicates the factors to be considered:

TABLE 6

Variables in Demographic Model of French-Language Retention in Cities.

Variable
"Communication advantage" within the French ethnic group
"Communication advantage" within the remainder of the city population
Relative importance of the French ethnic group
Mother-tongue composition of the French ethnic group
"Ethnic drawing power"

Communication Advantage

By "communication advantage" is meant the relative numbers with whom one can talk in each of the tongues. Recognizing that bilingual persons give neither English nor French an advantage as a *mandatory* medium of communication, the strength of one language over another is a function of the relative numbers of English and French monoglots. If the number of English minus the number of French monoglots is divided by the total population, the figure obtained reflects the net advantage (or liability) in a child being raised in English. It is possible to determine this index for subparts of a community as well. In its applicaton to the problem at hand, the "communication advantage" has been computed separately for the French ethnic group and for the remainder of each city's population. This allows for comparison of the relative advantages of English vs. French within both the French ethnic group as well as among other residents. For a given group, the index is obtained by the following formula:

$$\frac{E_o - F_o}{\text{total population}} \times 100,$$

where E_o and F_o are the numbers of English and French monoglots, respectively, in the city.

The index reflects three linguistic characteristics of the population: first, the relative numbers of English and French monoglots; second, the number of bilinguals; third, persons unable to speak either official language. Use of the total population under study as a denominator, rather than merely focusing on the relative numbers of English and French monoglots, permits the investigator to consider the significance for communication of an excess in monolinguals of one language. If the overwhelming majority of French Canadians are bilingual, for example, then even a large ratio of English to French speakers among this ethnic group's small monolingual segments would produce only a minor communication advantage for one tongue over another. Because most bilinguals are not equally fluent in each tongue, more elaborate information about the bilingual capacity of the population would lead to a refined measure, but the basic form and intent of the index would remain the same.

Ethnic Composition

Since interaction within an ethnic group will normally be influenced by the ethnic composition of the city, it is necessary to consider this variable in trying to explain linguistic communication in the communty. Assuming that French in-group interaction varies directly with the percentage of the residents who belong to this ethnic group, a simple measure is available based on the French ethnic composition in each community.

If we use rank order correlations, it is not necessary to make either a linear or curvilinear assumption about the association between interaction and composition, but merely that it is monotonic. In applying the index of communication advantage within the French and non-French ethnic segments, it will be useful to take the community's ethnic composition into account since the impact of a given level of communication advantage will reflect the numerical importance of the group.

Mother Tongue

The differential in "communication advantage" between French and English is not the only linguistic consideration, for quality of communication is also an issue. Probably in most instances bilinguals are able to communicate on a broader range of subjects and with greater precision when using their native language. Consequently in a city in which the number of English and French monoglots are approximately equal or in which the difference amounts to a relatively small proportion of the total ethnic population it is reasonable to expect that the relative numbers with French and English mother tongue will play an important role in the frequency French is retained by the children of bilinguals. The number of French and English monoglots in Moncton is approximately equal, but the French ethnic group has 13,000 members who are native speakers of French compared with only about 2000 members who are native English speakers. Other characteristics being equal, one would expect a higher level of French retention than in a city in which English was the numerically larger mother tongue of the French ethnic group. Indeed, even in cities in which there is a small communication advantage for English it is possible for the retention ratio to remain fairly high if French is the overwhelming mother tongue within the group and if this variable does operate in the manner hypothesized.

This suggests that mother-tongue composition within the French ethnic group be considered in this demographic model. However, because of certain contaminating factors, extreme caution is warranted when researchers use this variable in attempting to explain retention. The difficulties, both logical and statistical, are sometimes overlooked, but they are described shortly.

Ethnic Drawing Power

It is not possible to use residential segregation or some other direct measure of ethnic integration in determining the influence of ethnic cohesion on retention. The measure of "ethnic unity" employed here does tap the linguistic strength of the French Canadians in each city. It is based on the frequency that French ethnics, with a mother tongue other than

French, learn French as a second language. When this is compared with the acquisition of French among the remainder of the population with a mother tongue other than French, an index of the relative linguistic drawing power of the French ethnic group is generated. To put it another way, the percentage learning French among those with another mother tongue is computed separately for the French and non-French ethnic groups. The net difference, assuming that the percentage is higher for the French group, indicates the "pull" or drawing power of the French ethnic group.

Special Considerations

There is danger in constructing a model that can "explain" the influence of various demographic characteristics on linguistic retention for a given point in time, but which has no validity for interpreting changes in retention through the years; for example, it seems reasonable to consider the mother-tongue composition of the French ethnic group as a possible determinant of the retention ratio. If French is the mother tongue of nearly the entire French-Canadian group in a city, there will be greater resistance to intergenerational shift than in a community in which, say, half the group are native speakers of English. Yet even if a correlation between retention and mother-tongue composition is found among cities, there would be the danger of attributing more to the relationship than could be justified on either logical or statistical grounds.

If this hypothesized relationship is carried back to the period of initial contact, when essentially all French Canadians were native speakers of French and all others were not, it would be logically impossible to use this factor alone as an explanation of the initial breakdown in mother-tongue continuity, for at this point we would anticipate full retention of French in the next generation. Thus, although the group's mother-tongue composition might appear to be a suitable explanatory factor in dealing with retention ratios at a later stage of contact (when there are native speakers of English among the French Canadians in a community), by itself it would not be a suitable factor for explaining how English made its initial inroads. Some of the explanations of mother-tongue retention suffer from just this kind of shortcoming; namely, while applicable to one particular period of linguistic contact, logically they are not self-sufficient to explain the dynamics of change through the various stages.

A statistical difficulty remains even when the logical difficulties in analyzing the influence of mother-tongue composition on intergenerational retention are resolved. Suppose the influence of a group's mother-tongue composition is viewed as also interacting with its proportion of the total population. It would then be possible, at least on logical grounds, to explain the retention ratio during each phase of contact. In the initial stages of contact, when French was the mother tongue of all French Canadians, some decline might be expected if the community contains a small proportion of French Canadians. In later stages this decline would be accelerated because the group's mother-tongue homogeneity would be broken as well. (For simplicity, assume that French is not the mother tongue of anyone else in the community.)

Even here, where the logical implications are not at issue, there is a statistical problem of redundancy between the variables which may operate. One of the independent variables, the percentage of the French ethnic group with French mother tongue, is closely related to the dependent variable, mother-tongue shift among the children of French bilinguals. The former is more or less a reflection of the past experience of the group with respect to mother-tongue maintenance between generations; the second reflects the current experience of mother-tongue maintenance among the new generation of offspring. Despite the fact that the two variables differ in one important respect, the former reflecting the rates of bilingualism as well as the past retention rates among those exposed, clearly the two variables are likely to be interrelated. As a consequence, even after population composition is taken into account, the danger remains that the two variables are so intertwined that they cannot help but be correlated.

To make the point somewhat more abstractly, suppose the retention ratios differ between Canadian cities, but remain constant over time within each community. Under such circumstances the intercity correlation between current retention ratios and current mother-tongue composition of the French ethnic group would be very high. This would, however, result from the fact that both variables were reflecting the same phenomena. Were the frequency of bilingualism among the French-mother-tongue population also to remain constant within each city, there would be a perfect correlation between the independent and dependent variables.

Two procedures are used to solve this problem. First, one can determine whether the retention ratio among children of French-mother-tongue bilinguals remains constant over time. If the rate of intergenerational switching is steady through the years, there is good reason to suspect any causal interpretation that would imply changing rates. In this case it has already been observed that the retention ratios do change, mainly decline, through the years in both the provinces and the cities studied.

This suggests a second solution to the difficulty noted above; namely, by analyzing changes in the retention ratio to see if they are accompanied by the predicted changes in ethnolinguistic characteristics. If the mother-tongue composition of an ethnic group influences the retention ratio, for example, the ratio should change over time as the mother-tongue composition of cities shifts through the years.

Empirical Findings, 1961

English enjoys a substantial advantage as a communication medium within the French ethnic group in all 29 of the "lesser cities." The index of communication advantage ranges from a low of 24 percent in Winnipeg (including the two suburbs of St. Boniface and St. James) to a high of 82 percent in Peterborough, Ontario. The median advantage of English over French in these cities is nearly 60 percent, meaning that a monolingual French Canadian can communicate with 60 percent more of his ethnic compatriots if he knows English rather than French. As the model suggests, retention of French among the offspring of French-mother-tongue bilinguals is least frequent in cities where English has a relatively high communication advantage. The retention ratio varies inversely with the index of English "communication advantage" among French ethnics in these centers (tau is $-.49$).

As one might expect, the communication advantage of English over French is even greater within the non-French ethnic component of each city's population. The index ranges from 89 to nearly 99 percent, indicating an overwhelming advantage for English in these lesser centers. The association between the index of "communication advantage" among the non-French ethnic groups and French-mother-tongue retention in the city is not terribly high (tau is $-.16$), particularly when compared with the earlier correlation between retention and the communication advantage within the French ethnic group ($-.49$). It may well be that the medium of communication within the French ethnic group is a more important influence of retention than is the communication advantage among the remainder of the population.

The index of communication advantage within the French ethnic group of these cities is only moderately correlated with the index among the remainder of the city's population (tau is $.22$). This suggests that ethnic cohesion creates linguistic pressures within the French group that are to some degree independent of those existing in the remainder of the community. After the communication advantage within the French ethnic group is taken into account, the partial tau between the French retention ratio and the English communication advantage within the non-French ethnic group drops to $-.06$. Once the communication potential of French within the French ethnic group is taken into account the linkage between retention and language skills among the non-French population is eliminated. As a consequence, for the purposes at hand, further consideration will be limited to the communication advantage only among the French group.

Ethnic composition does have an influence on the retention ratio. Keeping in mind that only a narrow range of communities are covered, due to the restriction of the analysis to the "lesser" cities, there is a positive association between retention and the proportion of French ethnics in the community (tau is .39). Also, a negative association exists between French ethnic composition in each city and the index of communication advantage within this group (tau is −.34). This indicates that English has its greatest advantage within the French ethnic group in cities where a very small proportion of the population are French Canadian. The partial tau between ethnic composition and retention after taking communication advantage into account is .27, suggesting that the size of the French ethnic group in a city influences retention even after the negative effect of the English communication advantage is taken into account.

Indeed, both the English communication advantage within the French ethnic group and the relative size of the French ethnic group in the community operate to influence the chances of an intergenerational language shift. Each variable maintains an influence on retention after the other is taken into account, although tau declines in each instance from the zero-order level. (The tau between communication advantage and retention drops from −.49 to −.41 after French ethnic composition is taken into account.) These results indicate that both factors, ethnic composition and communication advantage, exert important independent influences on the retention of French among the children of French bilinguals.

Mother-tongue composition within the French ethnic group is positively associated with retention on the zero-order level. Tau is .39 between retention and the percentage of French ethnics with a French mother tongue. On a purely descriptive basis, this means that cities where French is the mother tongue of a relatively large proportion of the French ethnic group tend also to be communities in which the new generation is more likely to retain French if their parents are bilingual. However, the association between these variables is essentially nil after English "communication advantage" within the French group is taken into account (partial tau is .05).

As noted earlier, there is a close connection between communication advantage and mother-tongue composition of the French ethnic group. For the lesser cities in 1961 tau is −.90 between these two variables. Mother-tongue composition sets certain limits on the range possible for the index of communication advantage. Ignoring mother tongues other than English or French (an insignificant number among the French ethnic group), the maximum communication advantage for an official language is equal to its proportion of the group's mother-tongue composition. The maximum disadvantage is equal to the proportion the other language is of the group's mother-tongue composition. If English is the mother tongue of 70 percent of the French ethnic population and French is the mother tongue of 30 percent, for example, the index of English communication advantage has a possible range of .70 to —.30. The former would occur if the entire French mother tongue population is bilingual, but all native English speakers remain monoglots. The latter would occur if all those with French-mother-tongue are monoglots, but the entire English-mother-tongue group learn French.

The communication advantage index within an ethnic group reflects the combined effects of mother-tongue composition and the rate of bilingualism among each mother-tongue component. At the initial stages of linguistic contact, when French is the mother tongue of the entire French ethnic group, the proposed index has a particularly decided explanatory advantage over measures of mother-tongue composition per se. The high association between French-mother-tongue composition and the index of communication advantage, as well as the logical difficulties in applying the mother-tongue variable to all phases of contact, suggest that the mother-tongue composition of the French ethnic group by itself need not be considered in this model.

"Ethnic drawing power" is based on a comparison between the French ethnic group and the remainder of the city's population in the acquisition of French as a second language. It is derived from the French bilingualism rates among those with a different mother tongue. In all 29 "lesser" cities the French ethnic group has a greater propensity to learn French than other residents if their mother tongue was English or some other language. The differences between the French ethnic group and the remainder of the community are not great, however, ranging from 2.8 percent in Peterborough to 10 percent in Toronto.

The tau between the retention ratios and the measure of ethnic drawing power is .34, suggesting that cities where the French ethnic group are drawn back into the linguistic fold are also more likely to have higher French-mother-tongue retention among the children of bilinguals. As one might suspect, ethnic drawing power is correlated with the measure of communication advantage (tau is —.44), such that relatively low communication advantage for English tends to occur in cities with high drawing power. The partial tau between retention and drawing power is .15 after taking communication advantage into account. This suggests that ethnic cohesion has some small influence on mother-tongue shifting independent of communication advantage.

Summary

Before attempting a longitudinal analysis, a review of the results based on the model's application to a cross section of lesser cities in 1961 is in order. The rate of retention (based on the number of bilingual French parents whose children are raised in French) is the dependent variable under consideration. The linguistic skills of the French ethnic group influences the language transferred by bilinguals: namely, French retention is most likely in those cities where English has the least advantage over French as a medium of communication. The positions of these two languages within the remainder of the city's population are less closely linked to French retention. This suggests that the pool of language skills within the ethnic group is a more important determinant of language shift. To be sure, the language skills of the ethnic group reflect the language pressures generated by the entire city. But it remains the case that the index of communication advantage within the French ethnic group operates as an independent force.

Ethnic composition has an influence on retention that is partially independent of the influence of communication advantage. Intergenerational shift among French bilinguals tends to vary inversely with the French ethnic group's proportion of the total city population. Ethnic cohesion, as measured in this study, also has a small influence on retention after the index of communication advantage is taken into account.

It is noteworthy that the mother-tongue composition of the French ethnic group has little or no influence on retention after communication advantage within the group is considered. To be sure, mother-tongue composition places certain limits on the possible range of the communication advantage index, but by no means does mother-tongue completely determine the index. More significantly, however, the index of communication advantage allows for a more meaningful consideration of linguistic skills as an influence on retention, particularly in the initial stages of language contact when each ethnic group has a distinctive and homogeneous mother tongue.

Changes Between 1951 and 1961

Retention ratios can be measured for 19 cities in both 1951 and 1961. This permits some analysis of the changes over time and an opportunity to see whether the associations found on the cross-sectional level for 29 cities still hold on a more dynamic basis. Many of the cities under consideration here have small concentrations of the French ethnic group and would rank as "lesser" centers in this regard. The 19 cities, however, including such major French centers as Montreal-Verdun, Trois-Rivières,

Quebec, and Ottawa, are far more varied in ethnic and linguistic composition than the previous group.

There is no clear-cut trend between 1951 and 1961 in the communication advantage index. In eight of the cities the position of French improved, but the communication index changed in favor of English in the remaining 11 cities. In all but one of the cities, Ottawa, there was no reversal in the direction of the advantage within the French ethnic group, but some of the cities with a strong English advantage were among those in which French made gains and vice versa.

Changes in the retention ratio during this period are correlated with changes in the index of communication advantage in the direction expected on the basis of the earlier findings. Cities with relatively sizable increases in English as a communication medium within the French ethnic group also experience the sharpest decline in French retention during this period (tau is .43).

Shifts in ethnic composition have essentially no influence on shifts in retention, although it was an important influence in the earlier cross-sectional analysis. Changes in French ethnic composition are not related to changes in either retention or the index of communication advantage; tau is only .05 and .01, respectively. There is little reason to view absolute shifts in French ethnic composition as having any influence on changes in the retention ratio either before or after the index of communication advantage is taken into account. This finding also suggests that earlier cross-sectional analysis of the influence of ethnic composition may have been spurious, although clearly further research is necessary before this can be resolved.

Ethnic cohesion, as measured by the drawing power index, also fails to show any influence on retention when these variables are examined longitudinally. Although there was some association on a cross-sectional basis in 1961, the tau between changes in these two variables over the decade is only —.04. Changes in the index of communication advantage are also unrelated to drawing power, tau is —.01. As before, these longitudinal findings suggest the possibility of a spurious association on a cross-sectional basis. It is also possible that counterbalancing forces operated between 1951 and 1961 to offset the influence of these factors. Moreover it should be kept in mind that the longitudinal and cross-sectional analyses are based on somewhat different sets of cities.

In review, the index of communication advantage is the only factor in the demographic model found to influence retention on both a longitudinal and cross-sectional basis. This measure does provide a more satisfactory way of viewing linguistic influences on later retention than the more commonly employed feature of mother-tongue composition. A number of other variables that appeared to influence retention, when the model was restricted to one point in time, fail to show any association with changes in retention between 1951 and 1961. The absence of similar rates of change suggests that some of these factors may have been only spuriously associated with retention in the cross-sectional analysis. No definitive answer can be offered at this point, however. Ideally, an analysis based on path coefficients would have been most appropriate for this problem, but the small number of cities makes this type of analysis unfeasible. The findings do suggest that many "reasonable" hypotheses and theories about the causes of intergenerational switching may be doomed to rejection, even if they hold empirically for cross-sectional analyses.

SUMMARY

This chapter is an extension of the preceding one in that both deal with factors influencing mother-tongue maintenance among the children of bilingual parents. Three aspects of the problem were examined in this chapter: the influence of segregation, trends in retention and bilingualism, and a model of demographic influences.

The residential patterns of the bilingual population, along with population composition, was found to influence retention in each city. An important difference was observed between bilinguals with English and French mother tongue. The former are less segregated from English monoglots than are the latter from French monoglots. This means that the retention of English is helped more than French by the residential patterns among the bilingual components of each mother-tongue group. What causes these different patterns of residential location? Bilingualism among the French-mother-tongue group has different consequences than English bilingualism. Because of the economic dominance of English, the bilingual and monolingual components of the English-mother-tongue population are less sharply differentiated socioeconomically than are the bilingual and monolingual segments of the French-mother-tongue group. The advantages for bilingualism among native French speakers means much greater occupational differences between the French monolingual and bilingual components. The net effect is for French bilinguals to be more isolated from their compatriots than are British bilinguals from those speaking only English.

In both 1951 and 1961 there tends to be a correlation between the frequency of bilingualism and the degree of French-mother-tongue retention. Cities with low French retention ratios tend to have relatively high rates of bilingualism among the French-mother-tongue group and a low rate of bilingualism among the English-mother-tongue residents. Much of this association, however, may be spurious. First, the frequency of intergenerational mother-tongue shifting increased among the French bilinguals between 1951 and 1961; yet bilingualism among the French decreased while bilingualism among the English-mother-tongue residents rose. Second, there is virtually no association between *changes* in bilingualism during the decade and *changes* in the retention ratios. This provides further evidence suggesting that there need be no simple correlation between the frequency of bilingualism and the occurrence of mother-tongue shift among those who are bilingual.

Finally, a demographic view of French-mother-tongue retention was employed, involving five different variables. Although some appeared to influence retention on a cross-sectional basis in 1961, only the index of "communication advantage" within the French ethnic group was found to affect the dependent variable both longitudinally and cross sectionally. This index reflects the communication within the ethnic group that is potentially available to a child about to learn one of the official languages. Although influenced by the mother tongue composition of the group, the index gives the current advantage or disadvantage of English and French as a medium for communication among a city's French Canadian residents. The findings suggest that cross-sectional associations between retention and several other variables, however, are spurious because similar correlations are not found when changes in retention are measured.

8

Implications for the Study
of Linguistic Pluralism and Ethnic Relations

This volume is devoted to two main issues. These are the causes of bilingualism and the causes of mother-tongue shift among children of bilingual parents. The factors generating bilingualism are distinguished from those influencing the behavior of bilinguals. In a multilingual setting obviously the first step toward linguistic shift is the acquisition of a second language. Bilingualism is a necessary, but not sufficient, prerequisite to mother-tongue shift between the generations. It is also necessary that bilingual parents choose to raise their children in the acquired language.

There is little to be gained at this point in rehashing the findings and models reported in earlier chapters. Two matters do merit further consideration. One is to examine the contention that the causes of bilingualism have either no effect or very different consequences for mother-tongue shifts. A second is about the role of language in maintaining an ethnic group. If the appropriate data were available, it would be possible to test these propositions directly by the use of path coefficients or other multivariate techniques for causal chains.

CAUSES OF BILINGUALISM AND
MOTHER TONGUE MAINTENANCE

A strong relationship exists among Canadian communities between population composition and the retention of French among the children of bilingual parents. However, among the cities where French is the mother tongue of less than 10 percent of the residents, the "lesser cities," there is very great variation in the rates of intergenerational shifting. The question now is whether the factors influencing intergenerational maintenance also influence the occurrence of bilingualism in these communities?

236

Although retention varies considerably between the 29 lesser cities, there is a rather high and consistent pattern of bilingualism for the French. The standard deviation for the latter is 2.7, compared with 21.4 for the retention ratios. The standard deviation of French-mother-tongue bilingualism in the lesser cities is only 3 percent of the mean for these places, whereas the standard deviation for the retention ratios is nearly two-thirds of the mean retention ratio. Lesser cities differ radically in their intergenerational maintenance of French, but the same cities are very uniform in the frequency of bilingualism among French residents. Accordingly, it is rather unlikely that factors which influence the great variation between cities in retention ratios could account for the very slight differences in bilingualism among the same cities.

School Systems and Manufacturing

An opportunity to examine the implications of this thesis is presented by the data on school systems and the degree of manufacturing activity in these lesser cities. Earlier, a mildly positive association was observed between the French retention ratio and manufacturing employment in the lesser cities (tau is .22). Dividing the lesser cities into those with high and low retention ratios, the former are much more likely to offer French medium instruction in either their public, parochial, or private schools. The question now is whether these two factors also influence the degree of bilingualism in the very same communities?

In both instances, there is no connection between bilingualism and either schooling or manufacturing employment. As Table 1 below indicates, if anything there is likely to be more bilingualism in cities where French-medium instruction is available for the children. This difference is minor and not too much should be made of it. However, the point remains that school instruction in these lesser cities does influence the intergenerational maintenance of French, but has no influence on the acquisition of English among the French-mother-tongue residents. The absence of an association between bilingualism and this institutional factor is readily understood for these cities. Other forces generating bilingualism in these communities are sufficiently strong that the availability of French-medium instruction cannot overcome the pressure to acquire English.

The influence on bilingualism of the percent employed in manufacturing is nil (tau is .04), despite the fact that manufacturing has some effect on the retention ratios in the same communities. Regardless of the kind of employment opportunities, again one suspects that the pressure to become bilingual is very strong in communities where French is the mother tongue of less than 10 percent of the residents. Although the kind of employment influences the retention of French insofar as it affects the breadth and

TABLE 1

French-Mother-Tongue Bilingualism in Lesser Cities by Educational System

French-Medium	French-Mother-Tongue Bilingualism	
School Support	High	Low
Present	5	4
Absent	7	9

scope of the English mastered by bilinguals, the industrial composition of these communities has no bearing on existence of bilingualism. In this regard more sensitive linguistic data would allow for some determination of the influence of industrial employment on the quality of second-language skills acquired.

The fact that manufacturing employment does not influence bilingualism in cities may seem somewhat surprising in view of the positive correlation in Quebec's counties between manufacturing employment and bilingualism reported in chapter 4. The reader should keep in mind that these earlier associations dealt largely with manufacturing as opposed to agricultural employment, whereas this analysis compares manufacturing employment with other *urban* industrial pursuits. At any rate, the point remains that manufacturing employment in these lesser cities has more influence on French intergenerational retention than it does on whether or not the French become bilingual.

Different Causes

Aside from the data reported above, evidence has been amassed along the way to suggest that mother-tongue shift among the children of bilinguals is partially independent of the causes influencing the occurrence of bilingualism. The reader is reminded of the finding that bilingualism among the French has, if anything, declined in recent decades whereas English is an increasingly important mother tongue of the French ethnic group in many parts of Canada.

There are several reasons to expect that the causes of bilingualism will not be automatically translated by parents into causes of mother-tongue shift. One very simple feature is the timing of bilingualism. Bilingualism ending before parenthood or occurring after parenthood will fail to undermine the mother-tongue maintenance in the next generation.

There are more complicated processes that may also generate bilingualism, but not an intergenerational shift; for example, a gap between adult male and female bilingualism is found in a number of cities and is attributed to the occupational pressures operating on men. If we make the assumption that bilingualism is necessary for both French-mother-tongue parents before an intergenerational shift will occur, the added bilingualism among adult men will not directly generate any increment in the rate of shifting among their children. To be sure, native fluency in English may offer employment advantages that lead some bilingual parents to pass on English as their child's mother tongue. Still, it is easy to see how occupational pressures will not create the same rate of intergenerational shift as some other factors leading to bilingualism.

On a more abstract plane there are four distinctive ways for factors to influence bilingualism and intergenerational mother-tongue shift. The simplest case is when a variable affects both phenomena in a consistent direction. Population composition might be visualized in this fashion. All other factors held constant, a community with a small percentage of X will tend to create bilingualism among the X group and to also raise their intergenerational rate of mother-tongue shift.

A second type of relationship occurs when a variable influences both bilingualism and retention, but in an opposite direction from expectation; for example, if a variable causes higher bilingualism but also a higher retention ratio. This is not an altogether unlikely possibility if viewed within the context of multple causation. If a factor has a greater influence on bilingualism than retention, it may very well increase the numbers exposed to the risk of passing on a different mother tongue but lower the proportion of bilinguals whose children shift. Suppose there are 1000 bilingual members of mother tongue X in a community and that 80 percent (800) transfer X to their offspring. Suppose, further, that some additional variable is introduced into the situation which leads a thousand more members of X to become bilingual but that 900 of these pass on their mother tongue. In effect, the total retention ratio is raised from 80 to 85 percent, $(800 + 900)/(1000 + 1000)$, even though the rate of bilingualism has doubled.

A third type of situation occurs when a variable influences bilingualism, but has no effect on the retention ratio. In predominantly English-speaking cities a small segment of the English-mother-tongue girls learn French as a second language, but by the time the childbearing ages are reached many are no longer able to speak French. Accordingly, this cause of bilingualism in the particular setting has little or no effect on mother-tongue shift among the children.

A fourth type of situation is a variable that influences retention but not bilingualism. This was illustrated in the case of manufacturing and the medium of school instruction, both of which influence retention but have no effect on bilingualism in the lesser cities.

To draw an analogy visualize bilingualism as the equivalent of becoming alcoholic and visualize mother-tongue shift as the equivalent of losing one's job because of alcoholism. Suppose, like bilingualism, there are many causes of alcoholism. One cause would be "unhappiness" and another cause might be the alcoholism that results from a sales occupation in which a considerable amount of business drinking is necessary. We can visualize these two different forces operating to cause alcoholism just as we have seen more than one cause of bilingualism. Further, compared with business alcoholics, probably a larger proportion of employees who have become alcoholics because of unhappiness will be fired from their jobs. Those required to drink a moderate amount because of business reasons can probably get away with being alcoholics more than those whose source of alcoholism is unrelated to their work. Likewise, one can visualize how the different causes of bilingualism will differ in their consequences for language maintenance in the next generation.

Because very likely there is statistical interaction rather than mere additivity among these causal factors, the operation of the four types of bilingualism are complicated; for example, the influence of some variables on bilingualism and retention may be different in the lesser cities than in communities in which French is a more important mother tongue. Earlier a number of instances of "overdetermination" of bilingualism were encountered in lesser cities; that is, when a given cause of bilingualism is superfluous since virtually everyone would have been bilingual anyway. To put the point in a somewhat different manner a factor influencing retention may have different consequences for bilingualism, depending on the operation of other forces in the community.

With better data and a more rigorous statistical approach it should be possible in the future to examine further the proposition that the factors influencing bilingualism and retention not only may differ but can have a contradictory influence on each of the two major dependent variables.

LINKAGE BETWEEN ETHNIC MAINTENANCE AND LANGUAGE

Ethnic groups may be maintained without a unique mother tongue. There are many other forms of delineation, ranging from physical features to religion, yet it is readily apparent that a distinctive language is one of the most common ethnic markers. The conditions of physical isolation and restricted communication that yield a new language or an identifiable dialect are the same forces that normally lead to the evolution of a new ethnic group. All over the globe, when ethnic populations are drawn into contact, there is a disruption of the isolating features normally responsible for the creation of both ethnic and mother-tongue groups. In contact settings how does the undermining of an ethnic group's linguistic bond affect the group's continuity and cohesion?

The answer varies along several dimensions. For some groups arrival in the new world is their first form of basic and extensive contact with other ethnic populations. The institutional and cultural forms brought into the setting are not particularly suited to pluralistic existence since these groups come from a setting of either homogeneity or at least overwhelming numerical, social, and political dominance. Such would be the case for the Italian, French, and Scandinavian groups. Under these circumstances, the consequences of mother-tongue loss for ethnic disintegration are greater.

Other ethnic groups in Canada have a background that required the development of many more forms of ethnic maintenance. For these groups mother-tongue continuity is less crucial for retarding assimilation. One is reminded of two classical illustrations, Jews and Gypsies. Both have more than a distinctive mother tongue to support ethnic maintenance in contact settings. Before arrival in the new world these groups possess institutional and cultural forms that permit them to disintegrate at a slower pace than other ethnic populations. In short, among groups formerly living in an isolated setting that did not require special institutional and cultural forms to insure survival, linguistic shift should have a more profound impact on ethnic continuity after contact. It must be kept in mind, however, that these propositions apply under the assumption of similar positions among groups as subordinate-migrant populations. The French, although they come from a homogeneous background in Europe where their language and culture were not under challenge, had become an indigenous group in Canada at the time of their conquest and subordination by the British. (For a more extensive discussion of subordination and superordination as factors in ethnic relations between indigenous and migrant peoples see Lieberson, 1961.)

Taking into account both mother tongues and bilingualism, what is the actual role of language in setting off ethnic groups from one another through the maintenance of distinctive ties within a group? There are two parts to the problem: first, the role of language as a bond between and within ethnic groups; second, the relative importance of the linguistic bond compared to other forces which may distinguish ethnic groups.

Mother Tongue, Bilingualism, and Ethnic Communication

The linguistic bonds among the British and French ethnic groups in Canada's 17 metropolitan areas are examined for 1961. In order to ease comparison with the H indexes reported below, I will use 1-A, rather than the A index to describe the mother-tongue bond within and between the British and French ethnic populations. The index 1-A gives the degree of mother-tongue homogeneity, whereas A gives the probability of a mother tongue *not* being commonly shared. For within-group analysis 1-A may be described as the probability of a common mother tongue existing among randomly paired members of the same ethnic group. For between-group analysis 1-A gives the probability of a commonly held mother tongue among randomly paired members of the two ethnic groups.

In 12 of the 17 metropolitan areas the mother-tongue bond between the British and French groups is actually greater than that within the French ethnic population (Table 2). The probability of a commonly shared mother tongue among randomly paired members of the French ethnic group in Calgary, for example, is .58. This is lower than the probability of a common mother tongue between randomly paired representatives from the British and French ethnic groups, .71. In the majority of these metropolitan areas, in effect, the probability of a common mother-tongue bond between the British and French ethnic groups is greater than the probability of a common mother tongue within the latter population.

With the exceptions of Montreal and Quebec, the probability of a commonly held mother tongue is highest of all within the British ethnic group. Typically, 1-A runs in the high 90's. In Calgary, for example, it is .99.

It is not too difficult to account for the typical pattern of high British mother-tongue unity, relatively low French unity, and an intermediate level of mother-tongue bond between the two ethnic groups. The British are very homogeneous in nearly every city, with almost everyone reporting English as their mother tongue. Accordingly, the mother-tongue bond within this group is extremely high. In most of the cities, on the other hand, the French ethnic population is divided into sizable French- and English-mother-tongue segments. Outside French Canada the ethnic group is in a state of incomplete mother-tongue shift to English. In Calgary slightly more than 70 percent of the French ethnic group report English is their mother tongue. The consequences for this split are twofold. First, compared to the homogeneity among the British, the division between English and French mother tongues within the French ethnic group leads to higher mother-tongue diversity. Second, in cities where English is the numerically most important mother tongue within the French ethnic group, there is less diversity between the French and British ethnic groups than within the former. Mother tongue in these cities no longer serves as a unifying and distinctive bond within the French ethnic population. To be sure, in places in which intergenerational shift within the French group has been minimal mother tongue remains a significant factor in separating the ethnic groups. In metropolitan Ottawa, for example, the

TABLE 2

Mother Tongue and Official Language Communication Potential Between and Within the British and French Ethnic Groups, Metropolitan Areas: 1961

Metropolitan Area	Mother-Tongue Diversity (1-A)			Mutual Intelligibility (H)			Percent of French In-Group Communication Requiring		
	British	French	Between British and French	British	French	Between British and French	English	French	Either
Calgary	0.99	0.58	0.71	0.99+	0.97	0.98	89	1	10
Edmonton	0.99	0.49	0.53	0.99+	0.96	0.97	74	3	22
Halifax	0.99	0.58	0.70	0.99+	0.98	0.98	87	1	12
Hamilton	0.99	0.54	0.65	0.99+	0.95	0.96	84	2	13
Kitchener	0.99	0.56	0.70	0.99+	0.95	0.97	92	2	7
London	0.99	0.62	0.75	0.99+	0.97	0.98	90	1	9
Montreal	0.89	0.94	0.08	0.97	0.98	0.59	1	82	17
Ottawa	0.95	0.78	0.14	0.99	0.94	0.72	12	50	38
Quebec	0.54	0.98	0.35	0.91	0.99	0.81	0	95	5
Saint John	0.99	0.50	0.54	0.99+	0.95	0.95	73	5	22
St. John's	0.99+	0.79	0.88	0.99+	0.98	0.99	97	0	2
Sudbury	0.94	0.69	0.19	0.99	0.94	0.86	24	22	53
Toronto	0.99	0.53	0.64	0.99+	0.95	0.96	82	2	16
Vancouver	0.99	0.52	0.62	0.99+	0.96	0.97	81	2	16
Victoria	0.99	0.56	0.69	0.99+	0.96	0.97	86	2	12
Windsor	0.98	0.50	0.54	0.99+	0.96	0.97	74	3	22
Winnipeg	0.98	0.53	0.35	0.99+	0.96	0.94	52	8	41

probability of a commonly shared mother tongue within the French ethnic group is .78 compared to a between-group probability of .14.

Bilingualism, in cities where the mother-tongue bond within the French ethnic group is weak, tends to raise ethnic unity much more than it builds up the linguistic bond between the British and French ethnic groups. The H indexes shown in Table 2 give the probability of randomly paired persons having a common official language, whether it be English or French, mother tongue or second language. The potential for communication within the French ethnic group jumps enormously after bilingualism is taken into account. In Calgary, for example, the probability of a commonly understood language is .97, compared with the probability of a commonly shared mother tongue of only .58. Indeed the lowest probability of in-group communication among the French ethnic residents in 17 cities is about .94.

In most instances bilingualism does not raise British in-group communication very much since it is already so high just on the basis of mother tongue. Bilingualism, however, does raise between-group communication in many of the cities since the French mother-tongue residents largely acquire English as a second language. In a few notable exceptions such as Montreal, Ottawa, and Quebec, potential communication between the ethnic groups remains lower than in-group communication after bilingualism is taken into account. Most typically, however, bilingualism makes communication potential very high and very similar both within and between the groups.

For the French ethnic group in most of Canada's major metropolitan areas the fact is that communication is highly probable between randomly drawn members. This linguistic bond however, is not based on their distinctive mother tongue. Indeed, the communication bond based on mother tongue is not high in an absolute sense nor is it as high as the potential for mother-tongue communication across ethnic lines. Moreover English is the main language bond for communication within the French ethnic group in most of these cities. In most mutually intelligible random pairings of French Canadians, English is the language which must be used. In Calgary, for example, where H is .97, nearly 90 percent of the mutual intelligibility occurring between randomly drawn pairs of French Canadians would *require* the use of English for communication; in only 1 percent of such pairs would French be required, and in about 10 percent of the cases there would be an option of either English or French (last 3 columns of Table 2). In other words, the vast majority of mutually intelligible meetings between randomly drawn French Canadians in this city would involve either two English-speaking monoglots or an English monoglot and a bilingual. In either case English would be the mandatory language of communication.

There are several notable exceptions to this pattern. In Quebec virtually no part of the very high H within the French ethnic group is based on the *requirement* that English be the medium of communication, and in only about 5 percent of the time is English even an alternative to French. In fully 95 percent of the cases of mutually intelligible contact French is the required language of communication. In this city, in other words, pairs with a common official language involve either two French monoglots, or one bilingual and a French monolglot. Quebec provides an excellent contrast to Calgary. In the latter city the potential for communication within the French ethnic group is also very high after bilingualism is taken into account, but it is largely based on the English medium.

In the majority of the Canadian cities examined English is the mandatory medium of communication for the great bulk of mutually intelligible contacts. There are some notable exceptions, such as Montreal, Ottawa, and Quebec, in which French is a major medium. There are also some intermediary cases such as Sudbury, in which a language option exists for more than half the in-group contacts, and Winnipeg, in which about 40 percent of the contacts involve a choice (however, most of the remainder in Winnipeg require English). The majority of cities examined illustrate how an ethnic group's mother tongue may no longer function to provide a distinctive barrier to contact with other groups. Ironically, it is through bilingualism that in-group communication potential is raised, but this high in-group communication potential is based largely on the English language.

The Importance of Language for Ethnic Maintenance

Having observed variation in the role of mother tongue as a source of division between ethnic groups, the empirical question remains of how important a distinctive mother tongue is for ethnic group maintenance? Two facets of this problem are investigated: first, the influence of mother tongue on variations in assimilation between ethnic groups of the same city; second, the influence of mother tongue on intercity variations in the assimilation of the same ethnic group.

The methodology and variables employed are identical in each case. Assimilation of the ethnic groups is measured on the basis of the overall pattern of ethnic residential segregation from the remainder of the city's residents. The index of dissimilarity measures this pattern of segegration, with potential values ranging from 0 (no segregation) to 100 (maximum segregation). In view of the use of residential segregation in a somewhat different form and for different theoretical purposes in earlier chapters, the reader may be surprised to find this measure employed here as a general indicator of assimilation. There is reasonably good evidence, at least for United States cities, that the general pattern of spatial isolation in a city is a good overall summary measure of various dimensions of ethnic assimilation (see Duncan and Lieberson, 1959; Lieberson, 1963).

Two characteristics of each ethnic group, mother-tongue and religious composition, are examined as possible influences on the pattern of assimilation. This allows for comparison between the relative importance of mother tongue and religion for assimilation. In each case the index of dissimilarity is used to compare the ethnic group's distribution with that of the remainder of the population in the city. On this basis it is possible to determine how similar or dissimilar the ethnic group's mother tongue distribution is to that of other residents in the city. Likewise the index permits quantitative comparison between the religious distribution of an ethnic group and the remainder of the population. The hypotheses are that dissimilarity in religion or mother tongue tends to retard assimilation. In this case segregation should vary directly with dissimilarity in religion and mother tongue. The reader must recognize that the computations shown in Tables 3 and 4 below are based on small numbers of ethnic groups and cities.

In each of four metropolitan areas in 1961 variation in ethnic segregation correlates in the hypothesized direction with ethnic differences in either religion or mother tongue. The coefficients of correlation are strikingly high in Winnipeg on the zero-order level when segregation is viewed as a function of either mother tongue or religious dissimilarity from the remainder of the residents (in both cases, r is .87). They are lowest in Montreal, where the correlation between ethnic residential segregation and, respectively, mother tongue and religious dissimilarity are .31 and .44 (see Table 3). Ottawa and Toronto differ in the relative closeness of the association between the two independent variables and the general indicator of assimilation, but in all cases correlations are in the hypothesized direction.

Given the presence of zero-order correlations between residential segregation and both mother-tongue and religious dissimilarity from other residents, the question remains of the importance each causal factor has for segregation after the other is taken into account. Beta coefficients are partial or net regression coefficients expressed in standard form that take into account differences between the variables in scale and dispersion. They permit us to determine the relative impact on segregation of standard unit changes in either religion or mother-tongue distribution after the other independent variable is taken into account. The beta weights in Table 3, indicated by the symbols $b^*_{12.3}$ and $b^*_{13.2}$, indicate that both religion and mother tongue influence the magnitude of residential segregation in the four metropolises; for example, after taking into account the influence of religion on segregation in Winnipeg, the beta coefficient for mother tongue indicates that an increase of one standard deviation in

mother-tongue diversity yields a corresponding increase in segregation of
.47 of one standard deviation.

The relative influence of mother tongue and religion on segregation
varies considerably from city to city. In Winnipeg both mother-tongue
and religious differences from the remainder of the population are equally
potent forces for retarding assimilation. In Ottawa an ethnic group's
mother-tongue composition has a far more significant influence on assimilation than does religious composition. The exact opposite holds for
Toronto, where religious differences have far greater consequences for
ethnic assimilation. In Montreal religion also tends to exert more influence
than does mother tongue. In all four cities, although there is variation in
the relative importance of the two independent variables, the assimilation
of the various European ethnic groups reflects the influence of mother-
tongue differences from the remainder of the residents.

Another approach is to consider the influence of religion and mother
tongue on segregation of the same ethnic group in different cities. The dependent and the two independent variables are measured as before, except they are computed for the same ethnic group in 13 cities (12 only
for the Italians and 10 for the Ukrainians because of their small number
in certain cities). The reader should keep in mind that intercity comparisons of segregation indexes based on the index of dissimilarity can be

TABLE 3

*Influence of Religious and Mother-Tongue Dissimilarity on Ethnic Segregation
Within Four Metropolitan Areas: 1961*[a]

Measure of Association	Metropolitan Area			
	Montreal	Ottawa	Toronto	Winnipeg
r_{12}	.31	.91	.47	.87
r_{13}	.44	.58	.85	.87
$b^*_{12.3}$	.29	.80	.15	.47
$b^*_{13.2}$	.43	.29	.79	.50

[a]Variables:
1. Ethnic residential segregation.
2. Ethnic dissimilarity in mother tongue.
3. Ethnic dissimilarity in religion.

Ethnic Groups:
British   Italian
French   Polish
Dutch   Russian
German   Scandinavian
        Ukrainian

affected by the spatial grid patterns in each city. This factor is not readily adjusted.

On the zero-order level again there are positive correlations between segregation and either religious or mother-tongue differences from the remainder of the residents (Table 4). The only exception is a very mild negative association between Italian segregation and religious differences from the remainder of the population.

Mother-tongue differences, after religion is taken into account, are a far more significant influence on assimilation than is religion. Among the French ethnic group variation between cities in their residential segregation is not influenced very much by religious differences after the effect of mother tongue is taken into account (the beta weight is only .04). On the other hand, mother-tongue differences play a very important role in explaining the magnitude of the French group's pattern of residential isolation even after religious differences are considered (the beta weight is .86). In similar fashion the beta weights disclose that mother-tongue differences have more importance than religious differences for determining German, Italian, and Ukrainian ethnic segregation.

TABLE 4

Influence of Religious and Mother-Tongue Dissimilarity on Intercity Variations in Segregation of the French, German, Italian, and Ukrainian Ethnic Groups: 1961[a]

Measure of Association	Ethnic Group			
	French	German	Italian	Ukrainian
r_{12}	.88	.63	.64	.83
r_{13}	.46	.25	−.14	.74
$b^*_{12.3}$	.86	.74	.79	.69
$b^*_{13.2}$	.04	−.19	−.43	.16

[a]Variables:
1. Ethnic residential segregation.
2. Ethnic dissimilarity in mother tongue.
3. Ethnic dissimilarity in religion.

Metropolitan Areas:
Calgary   Regina
Hamilton   Sherbrooke
London   Sudbury
Montreal   Toronto
Ottawa   Trois Rivières
Quebec   Windsor
          Winnipeg

A CONCLUDING NOTE

As indicated in the preface, this volume is the product of an interest in contact between racial or ethnic groups with different mother tongues. The substantive elements of the study are concerned with an ecological analysis of French and English bilingualism in Canada. In the long run, however, the merit of the approach taken will be determined by its utility to other investigators working on linguistic pluralism in one or more of its many settings around the world.

The study represents a potential way of approaching linguistic diversity and bilingualism. It would be foolhardy to pretend that the application of this approach has received an adequate test in this volume. The cruel truth is that the available data in many instances were not altogether adequate. However, the application of some of the models earlier in this chapter for measuring in-group and between-group communication, based on both mother tongue and official language, does seem to suggest that the data and measures employed can provide an extremely useful way of gauging the degree that language binds a group together and keeps it apart from others.

In this regard the empirical findings about the role of mother-tongue in various Canadian cities has great potential for application elsewhere; that is, in most Canadian metropolitan areas the French ethnic group is only weakly held together by their mother-tongue distribution. Indeed, most often, the mother-tongue bonds with the British are greater than among the French ethnic group. Ironically, it is through bilingualism—which largely means the learning of English by the French mother-tongue segment—that mutual intelligibility is raised to a high level. From the point of view of its implication for the study of linguistic pluralism these findings demonstrate how an ethnic group that has partly disintegrated along mother-tongue lines may reach the point at which its ancestral mother tongue can fail to provide any basis for ethnic cohesion.

Another theme in this last chapter—one that probably needs no reiteration at this point—is based on the empirical evidence offered to show that the causes of bilingualism and the causes of language shift among the children of bilinguals can be separate and distinct. The evidence offered for this proposition is admittedly based on data that are far from definitive, but the key proposition can still be restated; namely, in virtually any contact setting involving people with different native languages it is necessary for at least one segment to learn to communicate with the other. Given this assumption about the nature of society, it follows that one form or another of bilingualism will result from linguistic contact. It may take the form of learning the other group's language or it may evolve into the development of some pidgin, but, at any rate bilingualism will occur. The causes of this bilingualism are to be seen in the context of the societal conditions under which the groups interact. Such matters as the occupational pressures, compositional factors, institutional factors, and the like were shown to operate in the Canadian scene. There is no reason at this time, however, to think that they are unique to Canada.

The causes of bilingualism are distinct from the causes of language shift in the next generation. Assuming that parents are free to raise their children in any tongue they know and choose, the determinants of the language of socialization are not fully or necessarily the same as the determinants of the parents' bilingualism. The inconveniences or disadvantages suffered by the parents' failure to have complete fluency in some acquired language may lead them to try to avoid this disadvantage for their children. In many contact settings a high level of fluency may be acquired fairly early in the child's life. Also, nativelike fluency in a tongue is not always all that crucial in some domains. Mother-tongue retention by the children of a bilingual couple may also be rewarded by the communication potential within the ethnic group to which they belong. Accordingly, the pressures for and against acquisition of a second language are at least partly different from the pressures operating on the parents in the tongue they use to raise their children.

Finally, this chapter also provides evidence directly relevant to another central theme of this volume, namely, that language is a significant influence on the assimilation of ethnic groups in contact. The effect of mother-tongue and religious composition on segregation in Canadian cities does indicate that language is not the only basis on which ethnic groups retain their boundaries. From the evidence reported above, however, maintenance of a distinct mother tongue is probably more closely linked to ethnic maintenance than is religion. There are yet other factors not included such as those ethnic delineations based on physical features, commonly referred to as "race." Even the relative importance of a distinctive religion as opposed to a distinctive mother tongue may vary greatly between contact settings, but, tossing all these necessary qualifications aside, the fact remains that mother-tongue maintenance is a central feature in the continuity of an ethnic group in contact.

References

Arès, Richard. 1964a. "Comportement linguistique des minorités françaises au Canada— I," *Relations*. April: 108–110.

_____. 1964b. "Comportement linguistique des minorités françaises au Canada— II," *Relations*. May: 141–144.

Bachi, Roberto. 1956. "A Statistical Analysis of the Revival of Hebrew in Israel," *Scripta Hierosolymitana*. Jerusalem: Hebrew University. Vol. 3.

Bell, Wendell. 1954. "A Probability Model for the Measurement of Ecological Segregation," *Social Forces*. 32: 357–364.

Berger, Earl. 1964. "A City of Immigrants," *The Globe and Mail*. Sept. 9, 10, 11.

Bloomfield, Leonard. 1933. *Language*. New York: Henry Holt.

Boeke, Julius H. 1955. "Colonialism and Dualism," in Andrew W. Lind, Ed. *Race Relations in World Perspective*. Honolulu: University of Hawaii Press.

Bram, Joseph. 1955. *Language and Society*. New York: Random House.

Brazeau, Jacques. 1958. "Language Difference and Occupational Experience," *Canadian Journal of Economics and Political Science*. 49: 536.

Breton, Albert. 1964. "The Economics of Nationalism," *Journal of Political Economy*. 72: 376–386.

Charles, Enid. 1948. *The Changing Size of the Family in Canada*. Ottawa: Dominion Bureau of Statistics.

Citizenship and Immigration, Department of. 1963a. *Annual Report*. Ottawa: Queen's Printer.

_____. 1963b. *Immigration, 1962*. Ottawa: Statistics Section.

Delgado de Carvalho, Carlos M. 1962. "The Geography of Languages," in Philip L. Wagner and Marvin W. Mikesell, Eds. *Readings in Cultural Geography*. Chicago: University of Chicago Press. pp. 75–93.

de Jocas, Yves and Guy Rocher. 1961. "Inter-Generational Occupational Mobility in the Province of Quebec," in Bernard R. Blishen, Frank E. Jones, Kaspar D. Naegele, and John Porter, Eds. *Canadian Society*. New York: The Free Press. pp. 466–477.

Deutsch, Karl W. 1953. *Nationalism and Social Communication*. Cambridge: Technology Press of the Massachusetts Institute of Technology.

Diebold, A. Richard, Jr. 1961. "Incipient Bilingualism," *Language*. 37: 97–112.

Dominion Bureau of Statistics. 1962. *Canada Yearbook, 1962*. Ottawa: Queen's Printer.

Dufresne, Bernard. 1965. "A Problem in Semantics: Define Nation," *The Globe Magazine*. March 20: 3.

Duncan, Otis Dudley and Beverly Duncan. 1955. "A Methodological Analysis of Segregation Indexes," *American Sociological Review.* 20: 210–217.

———— and Stanley Lieberson. 1959. "Ethnic Segregation and Assimilation," *American Journal of Sociology.* 64: 364–374.

Elkin, Frederick. 1961. "A Study of Advertisements in Montreal Newspapers," *Canadian Communications.* 1: 15–22, 30.

Engelmann, Frederick C. and Mildred A. Schwartz. 1967. *Political Parties and the Canadian Social Structure.* Scarborough, Ontario: Prentice-Hall of Canada.

Epstein, Leon D. 1964. "A Comparative Study of Canadian Parties," *American Political Science Review.* 58: 46–59.

Ervin, Susan M. 1964. "Language and TAT Content in Bilinguals," *Journal of Abnormal and Social Psychology.* 68: 500–507.

External Affairs, Department of. 1963. *Bilingualism in Canada.* Ottawa: Information Division.

Farley, Reynolds, and Karl E. Taeuber. 1968. "Population Trends and Residential Segregation since 1960," *Science.* 159: 953–956.

Fellegi, Ivan P. no date. "Population Quality Check: Content," unpublished memorandum.

————. 1964. "Response Variance and Its Estimation," *Journal of the American Statistical Association.* 59: 1016–1041.

Ferguson, Charles A. 1962. "The Language Factor in National Development," in Frank A. Rice, Ed. *Study of the Role of Second Languages.* Washington, D.C.: Center for Applied Linguistics. pp. 8–14.

Fishberg, Maurice. 1911. *The Jews: A Study of Race and Environment.* New York: Charles Scribner's Sons.

Fishman, Joshua A., Vladimir C. Nahirny, John E. Hofman, and Robert G. Hayden. 1966. *Language Loyalty in the United States.* The Hague: Mouton.

Gagnon, Onésime. 1952. "Cultural Developments in the Province of Quebec," Toronto: University of Toronto Pamphlet Series.

Garigue, Philippe. 1962. *La vie Familiale des Canadiens Français.* Montreal and Paris: Presses Universitaires.

Goodman, Leo A. and William H. Kruskal. 1959. "Measures of Association for Cross Classifications. II: Further Discussion and References," *Journal of the American Statistical Association.* 54: 123–163.

Greenberg, Joseph H. 1956. "The Measurement of Linguistic Diversity," *Language.* 32: 109–115.

Hall, Oswald. 1940. "Types of Medical Careers," *American Journal of Sociology.* 45: 243–253.

————. 1948. "The Stages of a Medical Career," *American Journal of Sociology.* 53: 327–336.

Haugen, Einar. 1953. *The Norwegian Language in America.* Philadelphia: University of Pennsylvania Press. Vol. 1.

Heer, David M. 1966. "Negro–White Marriage in the United States," *Journal of Marriage and the Family.* 28: 262–273.

Henripin, Jacques. 1960. "Aspects démographiques," in Mason Wade, Ed. *Canadian Dualism.* Toronto: University of Toronto Press. pp. 149–180.

Hertzler, Joyce O. 1965. *A Sociology of Language.* New York: Random House.

Hughes, Everett C. 1943. *French Canada in Transition.* Chicago: University of Chicago Press.

Irving, John A., Ed. 1962. *Mass Media in Canada.* Toronto: Ryerson Press.

Kelley, Gerald. 1966. "The Status of Hindi as a Lingua Franca," in William Bright, Ed. *Sociolinguistics*. The Hague: Mouton.

Keyfitz, Nathan. 1950. "The Growth of Canadian Population," *Population Studies*. 4: 47–63.

―――――. 1960. "Some Demographic Aspects of French–English Relations in Canada," in Mason Wade, Ed. *Canadian Dualism*. Toronto: University of Toronto Press. pp. 129–148.

―――――. 1963. "Canadians and Canadiens," *Queen's Quarterly*. 70: 163–182.

Kirkconnell, Watson. 1960. "Religion and Philosophy: An English-Canadian Point of View," in Mason Wade, Ed. *Canadian Dualism*. Toronto: University of Toronto Press. pp. 129–148.

Kloss, Heinz. 1966a. "Types of Multilingual Communities: A Discussion of Ten Variables," *Sociological Inquiry*. 36: 135–145.

―――――. 1966b. "German-American Language Maintenance Efforts," in Joshua A. Fishman, Vladimir C. Nahirny, John E. Hofman, and Robert G. Hayden, *Language Loyalty in the United States*. The Hague: Mouton. pp. 206–252.

Kohn, Hans. 1960. *Pan-Slavism: Its History and Ideology*. 2nd ed. revised. New York: Random House.

Kuper, Leo, Hilstan Watts, and Ronald Davies. 1958. *Durban: A Study in Racial Ecology*. London: Jonathan Cape.

Lamontagne, Léopold. 1960. "Ontario: The Two Races," in Mason Wade, Ed. *Canadian Dualism*. Toronto: University of Toronto Press. pp. 351–373.

Lennon, John. 1964. Book review of Stanley Lieberson. *Ethnic Patterns in American Cities* in *Sociological Quarterly*. 5: 168–170.

Lieberson, Stanley. 1958. "Ethnic Groups and the Practice of Medicine," *American Sociological Review*. 23: 542–549.

―――――. 1961. "A Societal Theory of Race and Ethnic Relations," *American Sociological Review*. 26: 902–910.

―――――. 1963. *Ethnic Patterns in American Cities*. New York: The Free Press.

―――――. 1964. "An Extension of Greenberg's Linguistic Diversity Measures," *Language*. 40: 526–531.

―――――. 1965a. "Bilingualism in Montreal: A Demographic Analysis," *American Journal of Sociology*. 71: 10–25.

―――――. 1965b. "Linguistic and Ethnic Segregation in Montreal," unpublished report submitted to Royal Commission on Bilingualism and Biculturalism.

―――――. 1966. "Language Questions in Censuses," *Sociological Inquiry*. 36: 262–279.

―――――. 1969. "Measuring Population Diversity," *American Sociological Review*. 34: 850–862.

Mackey, William F. 1962. "The Description of Bilingualism," *Canadian Journal of Linguistics*. 7: 51–85.

―――――. 1965. "Bilingual Interference: Its Analysis and Measurement," *Journal of Communication*. 15: 239–249.

Malherbe, Ernest G. 1943. *The Bilingual School*. Johannesburg: Central News Agency.

Mayer, Kurt. 1956. "Cultural Pluralism and Linguistic Equilibrium in Switzerland," in Joseph J. Spengler and Otis D. Duncan, Eds. *Demographic Analysis*. Glencoe, Ill.: The Free Press. pp. 478–483.

McRae, Kenneth D. 1964. *Switzerland: Example of Cultural Coexistence*. Toronto: Canadian Institute of International Affairs.

O'Brien, Denis. 1964. "The Restoration of the Irish Language," *Montreal Star.* August 1: 4.

Ontario Department of Education. 1956. *Report of the Minister.*

Park, Robert E. 1922. *The Immigrant Press and Its Control.* New York: Century.

Price, Charles A. 1965. "Some Problems of International Migration Statistics: An Australian Case Study," *Population Studies.* 19: 17–27.

Polsky, Ned. 1964. "The Hustler," *Social Problems.* 12: 3–15.

Porter, John. 1958. "Higher Public Servants in the Bureaucratic Elite in Canada," *Canadian Journal of Economics and Political Science.* 24: 483–501.

————. 1961. "The Economic Elite and the Social Structure in Canada," in Bernard R. Blishen, Frank E. Jones, Kaspar D. Naegele, and John Porter, Eds. *Canadian Society.* New York: The Free Press. pp. 486–500.

Public Instruction of the Northwest Territories, Council of. 1901. *Report, 1900.* Regina: John A. Reid.

Ross, Aileen D. 1943. "Cultural Effects of Population Changes in the Eastern Townships," *Canadian Journal of Economics and Political Science.* 9: 447–462.

————. 1954. "French and English Canadian Contacts and Institutional Change," *Canadian Journal of Economics and Political Science.* 20: 281–295.

Royal Commission on Bilingualism and Biculturalism. 1965. *Preliminary Report.* Ottawa: Queen's Printer.

————. 1967. *Report, Volume One.* Ottawa: Queen's Printer.

Royal Commission of Inquiry on Education in the Province of Quebec. 1963. *Report, Part One.* Quebec: Pierre Des Marais.

————. 1965. *Report, Part Two.* Quebec: Pierre Des Marais.

Royal Institute of International Affairs. 1939. *Nationalism.* London: Oxford University Press.

Ryder, Norman B. 1955. "The Interpretation of Origin Statistics," *Canadian Journal of Economics and Political Science.* 21: 466–479.

Saskatchewan Department of Education. 1913. *Annual Report, 1911.* Regina: J. W. Reid.

Scott, Francis R. 1960. "Areas of Conflict in the Field of Public Law and Policy," in Mason Wade, Ed. *Canadian Dualism.* Toronto: University of Toronto Press. pp. 81–105.

Siekman, Philip. 1965. "Le Canada Français en Révolte: The Revolt of French Canada," *Fortune.* 71: 156–163, 192, 194, 196, 198.

Solomon, David N. 1961. "Ethnic and Class Differences among Hospitals as Contingencies in Medical Careers," *American Journal of Sociology.* 66: 463–471.

Stanley, George F.G. 1960. "French and English in Western Canada," in Mason Wade, Ed. *Canadian Dualism.* Toronto: University of Toronto Press. pp. 311–350.

Statistics, Dominion Bureau of. 1960. *Survey of Elementary and Secondary Education, 1956–58.* Ottawa: Queen's Printer.

————. 1962. *1961 Census of Canada, Population.* Bulletin 1.2-11. Ottawa: Queen's Printer.

————. 1964. *1961 Census of Canada, Labour Force.* Bulletin 3.2-5. Ottawa: Queen's Printer.

Taeuber, Karl E. and Alma F. Taeuber. 1965. *Negroes in Cities.* Chicago: Aldine.

Thomas, Brinley. 1954. *Migration and Economic Growth.* Cambridge: Cambridge University Press.

Thompson, Edgar T. 1961. "Language and Race Relations," in Jitsuichi Masuoka and Preston Valien, Eds. *Race Relations: Problems and Theory.* Chapel Hill: University of North Carolina Press. pp. 228–251.

Truesdell, Leon E. 1943. *The Canadian Born in the United States.* New Haven: Yale University Press.

Tylor, Sir Edward B. 1881. *Anthropology.* Reprinted by Ann Arbor: University of Michigan Press.

United Nations Commission on Human Rights. 1950. *Definition and Classification of Minorities.* Lake Success, New York: United Nations.

Useem, John and Ruth Useem. 1945. "Minority-Group Pattern in Prairie Society. *American Journal of Sociology.* 50: 377–385.

Wade, Mason. 1955. *The French Canadians, 1760–1945.* New York: Macmillan.

Weinreich, Uriel. 1953. *Languages in Contact.* New York: Linguistic Circle of New York.

————. 1957. "Functional Aspects of Indian Bilingualism," *Word.* 13: 203–233.

Younge, Eva R. 1944. "Population Movements and the Assimilation of Alien Groups in Canada," *Canadian Journal of Economics and Political Science.* 10: 372–380.

Znaniecki, Florian. 1952. *Modern Nationalities.* Urbana: University of Illinois Press.

Author Index

257

Places Index

Subject Index

Acadian French, 77
Age, differences in bilingualism, 22–24,
    99–116
  influence on mother-tongue shift, 192–
    197
Agriculture, 128–129
A index, 241–245
Apartment houses, 154, 161
Asiatics, 16

Bakers, 157, 161
Beauty Salons, 156–157, 161
Bilingualism, age differences, 22–24,
    99–116, 192–197
  causes, variety of, 91
  cohort analysis, 23, 99–100, 102–116,
    193–197
  by counties, 43
  definitions of, 18
  by education, 26, 29, 103, 111, 140, 237
  employment pressures and, 22, 25–26,
    83–84, 102–106, 111–114, 116–
    120, 124, 127–128, 138–175, 239
  income and, 25–26, 167–175
  intermediate step to monolingualism,
    12–15
  and manufacturing industries, 237–238
  migrants to Canada, 59, 63
  and mother-tongue shift, 26–27
  necessary product of contact, 12
  and occupation, 127–129, 138–175
  "overdetermination" of, 23, 240
  population composition and, 23–24,
    46–50, 193, 195, 237
  residential segregation and, 24, 28, 98,
    129–137, 213–221, 234
  sex differences and, 22–24, 99–120, 143
  stable end product, 13–15
  trends in, 106, 109, 221–224
  in yellow page listings, 122
Billiard halls, 154–155, 161
Blue-collar workers, 141–142, 152
Bookkeepers, 149
Bowling alleys, 25, 154–155, 161
British North America Act of 1867, 21,
    72, 75

Cashiers, 149
Census Data, 17–20
Central business district, 159, 163–167,
    175
Churches, 154
Cleaners and dyers, 157, 161
Clerks, 149
Cohort analysis, bilingualism, 23, 99–100,
    102–116, 193–197
  mother-tongue shift, 193–197
Commercial travelers, 150
Communication Advantage, Index of,
    see Index of Communication
    Advantage
"Compensating" bilingualism, 109
Competition between languages, 9–12
Composition, see Population Composition
Consumer vs. non-consumer services, 24,
    122, 124–127, 198
Cooks, 150
Customers, 11, 25, 154–158

Diversity, see A Index; Language
    diversity; Mother-tongue diversity
Downtown, see Central business district
Draftsmen, 152
Driver-salesmen, 150
Dutch ethnic group, 16, 21, 37, 247

Ecological approach, vii-viii
Economic power and language, 22, 84–
    85, 127, 220–221, 234
Education, 4
  and bilingualism, 26, 29, 103, 111, 140,
    237
  contemporary, 21–23, 75–79, 81–83
  early, 79–81
  and mother-tongue shift, 27, 29, 197,
    199, 204, 237
Employment pressures and bilingualism,
    22, 25–26, 83–84, 102–106, 111–
    114, 116–120, 124, 127–128,
    138–175, 239
  see also Yellow pages
Engineers, 149
Equilibrium, 11–13

261